THE WALKED *with* God

INTIMATE BIOGRAPHIES OF PATRIARCHS FROM THE BOOK OF GENESIS

ADAM • SETH • ENOCH • NOAH • MELCHIZEDEK
ABRAHAM • ISAAC • JACOB • JOSEPH

DUANE S. CROWTHER

HORIZON PUBLISHERS

ISBN 13: 978-0-88290-968-4

Published by Horizon Publishers, an imprint of Cedar Fort, Inc., 2373 W. 700 S., Springville, UT 84663
Distributed by Cedar Fort, Inc., www.cedarfort.com

LIBRARY OF CONGRESS CATALOGING-IN-PUBLICATION DATA

Crowther, Duane S.
  They walked with God : intimate biographies of patriarchs from the Book of
Genesis / Duane S. Crowther.
    p. cm.
  Includes index.
  ISBN 978-0-88290-968-4
  1. Patriarchs (Bible) 2. Bible. O.T. Genesis--Biography. 3. Church of
Jesus Christ of Latter-day Saints--Doctrines. 4. Mormon Church--Doctrines.
I. Title.
  BS573.C76 2010
  222'.110922--dc22
                      2009032141

Cover design by Angela D. Olsen
Cover design © 2009 by Lyle Mortimer

Printed in the United States of America

10 9 8 7 6 5 4 3 2 1

Printed on acid-free paper

OTHER BOOKS BY DUANE S. CROWTHER

America: God's Chosen Land of Liberty

Amonestaciones Proféticas Inspiradas: Profecías Modernas y del Libro de Mormón Sobre el Futuro de América

Atlas and Outline of the Acts of the Apostles

Atlas and Outline of the Life of Christ

Come Unto Christ

A Comprehensive Harmony of the Gospels

Conceptos Corales: Enseñando Técnicas y Herramientas que Ayudarán a Su Coro Lucir Maravillosamente

Doctrinal Dimensions: Major Missionary Messages of the Restored Gospel

Gifts of the Spirit

God and His Church

The Godhead: New Scriptural Insights on the Father, the Son, and the Holy Ghost

The Gospel Rolls Forth: 352 New Testament Events from Acts Through Revelation

A Guide to Effective Scripture Study

How to Understand the Book of Daniel

How to Understand the Book of Ezekiel

How to Understand the Book of Isaiah

How to Understand the Book of Jeremiah

How to Understand the Book of Mormon

How to Write Your Personal History

Inspired Prophetic Warnings: Book of Mormon and Modern Prophecies About America's Future

Jesus of Nazareth, Savior and King: 414 Events in the Life of Christ

José Smith: Un Verdadero Profeta de Dios

The Joy of Being a Woman: Guidance for Meaningful Living by Outstanding LDS Women

Key Choral Concepts: Teaching Techniques & Tools to Help Your Choir Sound Great

Life Everlasting: A Definitive Study of Life after Death

The Life of Joseph Smith: An Atlas, Chronological Outline and Documentation Harmony

Music Reading: Quick and Easy—a Singer's Guide

CASSETTE TAPES AND CDS BY DUANE S. CROWTHER

Anarchy in America: Prophecies of Events Preceding the Establishment of the New Jerusalem

Are You Saved? A Mormon's View of Faith, Works, Grace, and Salvation

Armageddon

Biblical Proofs of the Book of Mormon

Biblical Proofs of the Restored Church

Doctrinal Evidences that Mormons are Christians: A Refutation of Misleading Statements Circulated by Anti-Mormon Critics

Exaltation and the Kingdoms of Glory

Forty Keys to Family Emergency Readiness

From First Draft to First Edition: A Step-by-Step Guide to Self-Publishing

God Speaks Through Prophets Today

God's Eternal Plan of Salvation

The Great and Abominable Church in Prophecy

He Comes in Glory: The Second Coming of Jesus Christ and Events Prophesied to Precede It

How to Recognize Spiritual Promptings

How to Seek the Gifts of the Spirit

Interpreting the Book of Revelation

Israel: Past, Present and Future

Joseph Smith: A True Prophet of God

A Latter-day Saint View of Christ and the Trinity

Missionary and Temple Work for the Dead

Nephi's Panoramic Preview: 2,500 Years in Prophecy

The New Jerusalem and Council at Adam-ondi-Ahman

Paradise: The Spirit-world Home of the Righteous

Recognizing Techniques of Deception in Anti-Mormon Literature

The Resurrection: Doctrine, History and Prophecy

Through Death Unto Life Everlasting

Understanding Isaiah in the Book of Mormon

Why Join the Mormons?

World War III: God's Judgments Upon the Nations

Ye Must Be Born Again

CONTENTS

Chapter Two
SETH
pages 33–40

Chapter Three
ENOCH
pages 41–61

Chapter Four
NOAH
pages 63–87

Chapter Five
MELCHIZEDEK
pages 89–98

Chapter Six
ABRAHAM
pages 99–137

Chapter Seven
ISAAC
pages 139–66

Chapter Eight
JACOB
pages 167–91

Chapter Nine
JOSEPH
pages 193–225

INDEX
pages 227–35

ABOUT THE AUTHOR
pages 237–38

PREFACE

About the Book of Genesis

The book of Genesis is a remarkable book! It spans a third of this earth's six-thousand-year history since its Creation as a physical entity: more than a two-thousand-year period! As the first canonical book of both Jewish and Christian scriptures, it is held in high esteem as a valued historical source as well as a major theological document.

The word *genesis* is a Greek word that means "origin" or "beginning." Indeed, the book of Genesis truly is a record of many beginnings:

+ the spiritual and physical Creation of this planet, earth
+ the placing of man and woman upon it
+ the creation and placing of animals upon it
+ the introduction of evil upon it
+ the Fall of Adam and Eve, hence the beginning of "fallen man"
+ the beginning of personal accountability for sin
+ the beginning of God-sent revelations to earth's inhabitants
+ the beginning of knowledge concerning the mission and atoning sacrifice of Jesus Christ
+ the beginning of knowledge of the glorious plan of probation, salvation, and exaltation
+ the beginning of priesthood ordinations and lines of authority
+ the beginning of the Abrahamic Covenant
+ the beginning of God's chosen covenant people: the House of Israel
+ the beginning of tribes, races, and nations
+ the beginnings of literacy: reading and writing
+ the beginning of genealogical records
+ the beginning of commerce and trade
+ and many other sacred and secular events of major significance!

Latter-day Saints are truly fortunate because they have received revealed additions to the book of Genesis—records which greatly corroborate, illuminate, and add to the profound understandings recorded in that book. These revealed additions include:

+ historical and doctrinal insights found in the Book of Mormon
+ historical and doctrinal insights found in revelations contained in the Doctrine and Covenants

+ the book of Moses in the Pearl of Great Price
+ the book of Abraham in the Pearl of Great Price
+ additions and corrections recorded in the Joseph Smith inspired translation of the Bible

The book of Genesis is organized and based on life stories and genealogies of key individuals. The words "These are the generations," followed by a genealogical list of family members, typically begins each major section.

ABOUT *THEY WALKED WITH GOD*

This book, *They Walked with God*, is based on nine key individuals who are highlighted in the "generations" sections of the book of Genesis. The nine individuals are Adam, Seth, Enoch, Noah, Melchizedek, Abraham, Isaac, Jacob, and Joseph. Their life stories are amplified beyond the Genesis accounts by adding many dozens of insights from other scriptural sources. Sometimes more information about those key individuals is found in the supplementary revelations than in the Genesis record.

For instance, more is known about many aspects of Abraham's life from the book of Abraham than from Genesis. The Book of Mormon tells more about Melchizedek than Genesis does. The book of Moses tells more about Enoch than is recorded in Genesis. Some passages from Joseph Smith's inspired translation add historical asides and doctrinal gems not available from any other source. This book ties all those sources together to relate as much information about each of the nine as can be found in the scriptures.

They Walked with God, however, does more than piece together various clues about places, ages, activities, and relationships. Though it uses those clues to form far more detailed biographical accounts than would otherwise be available, its greatest contribution lies in the area of doctrinal analysis. There are profound scriptural passages which give detailed explanations concerning such essential doctrines as the Creation, the Fall of man, the gospel and atoning mission of Jesus Christ, the nature of the first principles of the gospel (faith, repentance, baptism, and the reception and mission of the Holy Ghost), the nature of God, the nature of revelation, the nature of salvation, the Abrahamic covenant, the house of Israel, and other doctrinal principles and themes.

When those types of passages occur in the midst of biographical narratives, the book switches from story-telling mode to phrase-by-phrase listings of doctrinal elements. Often, these complex passages contain so many profound concepts, piled one on top of another, that the tendency is to skim right past them, picking up only a concept or two while overlooking a dozen others. This book slows the pace by labeling each key concept so it won't be bypassed and forgotten. I hope this will be a valuable technique that will serve to amplify the doctrinal understanding and comprehension of many readers.

With that same objective in mind, please be aware that I have frequently italicized portions of scriptural passages so their messages will be more readily apparent. The italics in these scriptures are obviously this author's insertions and are not italicized in the actual scriptures. The same applies to the few passages where I have sought for extra emphasis by displaying various words in bold type. Obviously, the bold type face didn't appear in the original typeset passages.

While reading this book, the astute reader will look for little pieces of minutia that will amplify his understanding of historical events. He'll focus on age relationships as they pertain to family situations, look for moves caused by climate changes and geographical situations, consider how much and what kinds of work had to be performed to accomplish specific tasks, and he'll be conscious of who is prospering and why. He'll be alert for priesthood and birthright blessings and connections, and he'll watch for marriage relations and family conflicts that change the course of history. This book is full of those kinds of details!

So biographically, historically, and doctrinally—*They Walked with God* will give you, the reader, an increased understanding of the "beginnings" doctrines of the Bible and of this planet, earth.

May the Lord, through that knowledge, bless you and keep you fit for His kingdom!

CHAPTER 1
ADAM

THE FATHER OF ALL, THE PRINCE OF ALL, THE ANCIENT OF DAYS, THE ARCHANGEL MICHAEL

To contemplate the tremendous blessings that have come from Father Adam to all mankind is inspiring beyond measure. To list and organize his vast accomplishments and the rich doctrines that were first revealed to him is a monumental challenge. The scriptural sources are scattered and varied: they come from all four of the standard works, with each scriptural volume adding profound insights concerning his life, his mission, and his great contributions.

So, where should this chapter begin? No place could be more appropriate than "In the beginning . . ." (Genesis 1:1)[1], meaning the beginning of the Creation of this earth.

THE CREATION OF THIS EARTH AND ITS INHABITANTS

The first chapter of Genesis speaks of the Creation taking place in seven creative periods. Since the focus of this chapter is on Adam and Eve, rather than on the entire process by which this earth came into being, we will begin with the "sixth day," when man was created. Concerning that day, the Creation record in the book of Genesis says:

And God said, Let us make man in our image, after our likeness: and let them have dominion over the fish of the sea, and over the fowl of the air, and over the cattle, and over all the earth, and over every creeping thing that creepeth upon the earth.

So God created man in his own image, in the image of God created he him; male and female created he them. (1:26–27)

---

1. Since this entire book is based on the scriptural record found in the Old Testament book of Genesis, the word *Genesis* will be omitted in many scriptural references where items are being shown in lists. Thus, Genesis 1:26–27 may be referenced only as 1:26–27. References cited from other scriptural sources will contain the name of the book, unless there is a list format utilized where numerous references are obviously being cited from that book.

The record continues, telling how God gave Adam and Eve four specific commandments concerning the missions they were to accomplish as mortal life on the earth began. They were (1) to have children—lots of them (be fruitful); (2) to replenish the earth; (3) to subdue the earth; and (4) to exercise dominion over every living thing:

> And God blessed them, and God said unto them, *Be fruitful*, and multiply, and *replenish the earth*, and *subdue it:* and *have dominion* over the fish of the sea, and over the fowl of the air, and *over every living thing that moveth* upon the earth.
>
> And God said, Behold, I have given you every herb bearing seed, which is upon the face of all the earth, and every tree, in the which is the fruit of a tree yielding seed; to you it shall be for meat. (1:28–29)

And the record shows that God was pleased with his work: "God saw every thing that he had made, and, behold, it was very good. And the evening and the morning were the sixth day" (1:31).

The Spiritual and Physical Creations. But the Creation record goes on to show that there were two types of creation: a "spiritual creation" prototype, which was produced during Creation days one through six, as recorded in Genesis chapter 1, and then a physical creation (meaning a temporal, or mortal creation), as recorded in Genesis chapter 2, on the seventh day of Creation:

> These are the generations of the heavens and of the earth when they were created, in the day that the LORD God made the earth and the heavens,
>
> And *every plant of the field before it was in the earth, and every herb of the field before it grew:* for the LORD God had not caused it to rain upon the earth, and there was not a man to till the ground.
>
> But there went up a mist from the earth, and watered the whole face of the ground.
>
> And *the LORD God formed man of the dust of the ground, and breathed into his nostrils the breath of life; and man became a living soul.* (2:4–7)

According to the record in Genesis, the Garden of Eden wasn't created until after the first man had become a living being:

> And *the LORD God planted a garden eastward in Eden;* and *there he put the man whom he had formed.*
>
> And out of the ground made the LORD God to grow every tree that is pleasant to the sight, and good for food; *the tree of life* also in the midst of the garden, and *the tree of knowledge of good and evil.* (Genesis 2:8–9)

As the first man was introduced into the newly created garden, he was given a responsibility: to dress and maintain the garden. Then he was given a profound commandment that would shape the destiny of all mankind: to not eat the fruit of a particular tree—the tree of the knowledge of good and evil:

And the LORD God took the man, and put him into the garden of Eden to dress it and to keep it.

And the LORD God commanded the man, saying, *Of every tree of the garden thou mayest freely eat:*

But of the tree of the knowledge of good and evil, thou shalt not eat of it: for in the day that thou eatest thereof thou shalt surely die. (2:15–17)

As the creation process continued, the animals were created, and God brought them to the first man to give them names. At this point the Old Testament scriptural record begins to call the first man "Adam."

And out of the ground *the LORD God formed every beast of the field, and every fowl of the air; and brought them unto Adam* to see what he would call them: and whatsoever Adam called every living creature, that was the name thereof.

And *Adam* gave names to all cattle, and to the fowl of the air, and to every beast of the field; but for *Adam* there was not found an help meet for him. (2:19–20)

As this work proceeded, the record indicates that "the LORD God said, *It is not good that the man should be alone;* I will make him an help meet for him" (2:18). And so,

the LORD God caused a deep sleep to fall upon Adam, and he slept: and he took one of his ribs, and closed up the flesh instead thereof;

And *the rib, which the LORD God had taken from man, made he a woman,* and brought her unto the man. (2:21–22)

Adam, using his naming prerogative, proceeded to name his newly created helpmeet who began the feminine gender of humankind on this earth "woman." And it's obvious that his premortal understanding of marriage and familial relationships remained with him in mortality:

And Adam said, This is now bone of my bones, and flesh of my flesh: she shall be called Woman, because she was taken out of Man.

Therefore shall a man leave his father and his mother, and shall cleave unto his wife: and they shall be one flesh. (2:23–24)

Before moving on to the numerous other insights found in the Pearl of Great Price concerning the Creation, it is appropriate to recall that Luke, in his genealogy of the Christ child, records that Adam is a "son of God":

Sem, which was the son of Noe, which was the son of Lamech,

Which was the son of Mathusala, which was the son of Enoch, which was the son of Jared, which was the son of Maleleel, which was the son of Cainan,

Which was the son of Enos, which was the son of Seth, which was the son of *Adam, which was the son of God.* (Luke 3:36–38)

Latter-day Saints recognize that Adam was a premortal spirit child of God the Father, as well as a created mortal son, as set forth in the Genesis account above. (See also Genesis 5:1–3.)

Creation Insights from the Pearl of Great Price

Additional insights concerning the Creation of this earth and of man are found in the books of Moses and Abraham in the Pearl of Great Price. Together, they serve to enlarge Latter-day Saint understandings of the creation process significantly. Key doctrinal concepts are identified in this list so they won't be overlooked. Obviously, the passages should be read along with this listing to glean further insights and understandings. The book of Moses (chapters 1–3) indicates that

1. Many earths have been created and inhabited (Moses 1:33).
2. There are many heavens (Moses 1:37).
3. Earths and heavens pass away (Moses 1:38).
4. There are many Adams (Moses 1:34).
5. Only knowledge of this earth is given (Moses 1:35).
6. Creation is a part of God's work (Moses 1:39).
7. All three members of the Godhead participated in the creation process (Moses 2:1–2).
8. Man is created in the image of the spirit and physical body of Jesus Christ (who, in turn, is in the image of the physical and spiritual body of his father, God the Father) (Moses 2:27; see also Ether 3:6–16).
9. This earth and all its inhabitants were created in heaven prior to this earth's physical creation (Moses 3:5, 7, 9).
10. The earth, itself, is a living soul (Moses 3:9).

Further valuable Creation insights come from the book of Abraham (chapters 3–5):

1. Kolob governs the planets of this earth's order (Abraham 3:9, 16; Facsimile 2, Fig. 2).
2. The Lord's creations are many (Abraham 3:11–12).
3. The Lord will create what he decides to (Abraham 3:17).
4. Spirits are eternal (Abraham 3:18).
5. God rules over all the intelligences (Abraham 3:21).
6. Intelligences were organized before this earth was created (Abraham 3:22).
7. God chose rulers for this earth prior to its Creation (Abraham 3:23).
8. This earth was created from materials available where it was created (Abraham 3:24).

9. This earth was created to be a place of probation for its inhabitants (Abraham 3:24–25).

10. The decision to create this earth was made before the council was held in which Christ was chosen over Lucifer (Abraham 3:24, 27).

11. This earth was created by "the Gods." (Abraham 4:1–5:16).

12. In the Creation, earth's heaven divided the waters which were over it from other waters which were under it (Abraham 4:6–8).

13. In the Creation, the gods organized the lights in heaven to provide seasons and years (Abraham 4:14).

14. The Gods formed earth's males and females in their image and likeness (Abraham 4:26–27).

15. The Gods expected those they created to be very obedient (Abraham 4:31).

16. In forming man, the gods took his spirit and placed it within his mortal body (Abraham 5:7).

17. When God created man and commanded him to refrain from eating from the tree of knowledge of good and evil, the earth was still under Kolob's time reckoning (Abraham 5:12–13).

18. A day of time on Kolob equals a thousand years of earth's time (Abraham, Facsimile 2, Fig. 1; see also 2 Peter 3:8).

WHERE AND WHEN WAS THIS EARTH CREATED?

Let's indulge in a little speculation in this section—examining some theories that are not yet substantiated as doctrine in the scriptures, but that are worthy of consideration and pondering.

It is the prophet Abraham whose writings tell where this earth was created. They also indicate time relationships—relationships that perhaps answer some intriguing questions about the age of the earth and why its earliest inhabitants lived close to a thousand years.

Abraham was privileged to possess a Urim and Thummim, a revelatory instrument that the Lord had furnished to him. Through that instrument he gained a broad understanding of astronomy, not just of this universe but also of realms far beyond and above. He reported the existence of *Kolob*, the governing planet nigh unto where God dwells:

> And I, Abraham, had the Urim and Thummim, which the Lord my God had given unto me, in Ur of the Chaldees;
>
> And I saw the stars, that they were very great, and that one of them was nearest unto the throne of God; and there were many great ones which were near unto it;
>
> And the Lord said unto me: These are the governing ones; and *the name*

of the great one is Kolob, because it is near unto me, for I am the Lord thy God: I have set this one to govern all those which belong to the same order as that upon which thou standest. (Abraham 3:1–3)

In his writings, Abraham indicated that Kolob (or perhaps its rotations) governs all the planets among which this earth is located: "Kolob is after the reckoning of the Lord's time; which Kolob is set nigh unto the throne of God, to govern all those planets which belong to the same order as that upon which thou standest" (Abraham 3:9). His writings also indicate that "the name Kolob, signifies 'the first creation,' the one "nearest to the celestial, or the residence of God." His writings concerning that great sphere indicate that it is "first in government, the last pertaining to the measurement of time" and that its "measurement according to celestial time" equals a relative rotation of "one day to a cubit" and that "one day in Kolob is equal to a thousand years according to the measurement of this earth" (Abraham Facsimile 2, Figure 1).

Then his writings indicate that the Creation of this planet, earth, took place on or near Kolob, or at least someplace within the area of Kolob's time reckoning:

And the Gods took the man and put him in the Garden of Eden, to dress it and to keep it.

And the Gods commanded the man, saying: Of every tree of the garden thou mayest freely eat,

But of the tree of knowledge of good and evil, thou shalt not eat of it; for in the time that thou eatest thereof, thou shalt surely die. Now *I, Abraham, saw that it was after the Lord's time, which was after the time of Kolob; for as yet the Gods had not appointed unto Adam his reckoning.* (Abraham 5:11–13)

Why is it that the Old Testament patriarchs who lived before the flood lived such extraordinarily long lives? Adam, Seth, Enos, Jared, Methusaleh and Noah all lived more than nine hundred years, according to mortal reckoning. And how was it that they and their mates had the strength and ability to sire such large families that they were able to populate this earth so rapidly? Perhaps their geographical location holds the key to that query.

While Adam was still a spirit being, prior to the seventh "day" of this earth's Creation, he was given an understanding of the nature and timing of physical death. He was told that the trigger event that would begin his cycle of physical life and death would be to partake of the fruit of the tree of knowledge of good and evil. Also, he was told, in effect, that when he entered that cycle which would bring his mortal death he would still be within Kolob's time span, for the instruction was that "in the *day* that thou eatest thereof thou shalt surely die" (Genesis 2:17). And, apparently, that is what happened: he died in the twilight of that Kolob-reckoned day, but when his mortal reckoning was granted to him, the Kolob "day" was recalculated into earth years: "all the days that Adam lived were nine hundred and thirty years" (Genesis 5:5).

It is known that this earth was created nigh unto Kolob, and that it no longer is situated in that proximity. It somehow had to be moved to its present location. How did that repositioning take place?

Apostle (later President) John Taylor wrote of "this earth, which had fled and fallen from where it was first created, near the Planet Kolob."[2] That understanding is presumed to be the general understanding of the early brethren on the subject. But how did that falling take place?

Did God (or the gods) command it to move, so it moved? Was someone or something sent to guide it through space? Was it part of the "big bang" process, which many modern scientists believe took place? And was it still moving when the long-lived Old Testament patriarchs were functioning, and did mortal life-spans eventually shorten as the earth arrived in its present position? Answers to these questions as yet have not been revealed. Again, the Lord's indication to Moses was, "only an account of this earth, and the inhabitants thereof, give I unto you" (Moses 1:35).

Did that falling and moving through space process play a part in the dividing of the earth in the days of Shem's great-great grandson, Peleg? (Genesis 10:25: "Peleg; for in his days was the earth divided.") And more important, did earth's moving through space in some way trigger the great flood in Noah's day? (See Genesis 7:11–12: "In the six hundredth year of Noah's life, in the second month, the seventeenth day of the month, the same day *were all the fountains of the great deep broken up, and the windows of heaven were opened.* And the rain was upon the earth forty days and forty nights.")

In the last days, when the "stars shall fall" in the heavens, will that be an indication that this earth will be moving upward as part of the Savior's Second Coming cleansing processes, rather than multitudes of stars suddenly changing their positions and orbits? (See Matthew 24:29; Mark 13:25; Revelation 6:13; D&C 29:14; 34:9; 45:42; and 88:87.)

Since this earth was created from materials already existing and located in the vicinity of Kolob (see Abraham 3:24), perhaps from earths that had

---

2. Taylor, John. *The Mormon* (New York City: August 29, 1857), as cited in Crowther, Duane S. *Life Everlasting* (Springville, Utah: Horizon Publishers, an imprint of Cedar Fort, Inc., 2007), p. 106.

"passed away" (see Moses 1:35, 38), could the use of those recycled materials have any effect on modern-day scientists' calculations concerning the age of this earth? Could the remains of prehistoric animals and beings have been embedded in those materials before those materials became part of this planet?

Another possible explanation for the centuries-long life-spans of the early patriarchs and their families may lie in the words of the Prophet Lehi as he was instructing his son, Jacob. He spoke of God's extending the length of their lives so they might have adequate time to repent:

> And the days of the children of men were prolonged, according to the will of God, that they might repent while in the flesh; wherefore, their state became a state of probation, and *their time was lengthened*, according to the commandments which the Lord God gave unto the children of men. (2 Nephi 2:21)

Is that the reason for their lengthy life-spans, or does their longevity have to do with the moving-of-the-earth process, or both? It certainly is easier to ask profound questions than to answer them, but these queries are posted here because pondering is good for the soul. Right?

What Is Known about "Our Glorious Mother Eve"?

Before plunging into the challenging accounts of their mortal escapades, it is appropriate to contemplate what is known about Adam's helpmeet: Eve.

How many people are spoken of in every one of the standard works of the Church? Very few! But references to Eve are made in every one of them. What a wonderful, blessed, and unique woman she was and is! What do the scriptures reveal about her?

1. "Adam and Eve, our first parents" (1 Nephi 5:11).
2. "Adam was first formed, then Eve" (1 Timothy 2:13).
3. "Eve . . . was the mother of all living" (Genesis 3:20).
4. "Eve . . . for thus have I, the Lord God, called the first of all women, which are many" (Moses 4:26).
5. Eve wanted to be able to discern between good and evil (2 Nephi 2:18).
6. Satan sought to beguile Eve (Moses 4:6).
7. Eve was deceived but saved in childbearing (1 Timothy 2:14–15).
8. Driven out after partaking of forbidden fruit (2 Nephi 2:19).
9. Adam and Eve are parents of the family of all the earth (2 Nephi 2:20).
10. The Lord made coats for Adam and Eve (Moses 4:27).
11. Eve worked alongside Adam (Moses 5:1).

12. Adam and Eve prayed together (Moses 5:4).
13. Adam and Eve were shut out from God's presence (Moses 5:4).
14. Eve rejoiced at the beneficial results of their Fall (Moses 5:11).
15. Adam and Eve taught their family (Moses 5:12).
16. Eve recognized her newborn son as coming from the Lord (Moses 5:16).
17. Eve and her daughters are known in the spirit world (D&C 138:39).

So really, quite a lot is known about Eve. This author looks forward to meeting her (or remeeting her) beyond the veil!

THE FALL OF ADAM AND EVE, AND OTHER GARDEN OF EDEN EVENTS

No indication is given in the scriptures of how long Adam and his helpmeet, Eve, lingered in the beautiful Garden of Eden which had been provided for their growth and enjoyment. Presumably, they continued in their assignments to dress and keep the garden (2:15) and to continue naming and interacting with all the cattle, fowls, and beasts of the field (2:19–20). This probably was a pleasant time for them, but as yet they neither were capable of experiencing real joy nor profound sorrow (see 2 Nephi 2:23).

It is assumed that Adam and Eve were married, though no details of such a event or ceremony are provided in the scriptures. However, from the beginning, the Genesis account speaks of Eve as being Adam's wife (2:24–25).

Satan tempted Eve through a serpent. The account in Genesis says:

> Now the serpent was more subtil than any beast of the field which the LORD God had made. And he said unto the woman, Yea, hath God said, Ye shall not eat of every tree of the garden?
> And the woman said unto the serpent, We may eat of the fruit of the trees of the garden:
> But *of the fruit of the tree which is in the midst of the garden, God hath said, Ye shall not eat of it, neither shall ye touch it, lest ye die.*
> And the serpent said unto the woman, Ye shall not surely die:
> For *God doth know that in the day ye eat thereof, then your eyes shall be opened, and ye shall be as gods, knowing good and evil.* (3:1–5)

The account in Moses, however, indicates that the serpent was not Satan, himself, but rather that Satan "spake by the mouth of the serpent":

> Satan put it into the heart of the serpent, (for he had drawn away many after him,) and he sought also to beguile Eve, for he knew not the mind of God, wherefore *he sought to destroy the world.*
> And he said unto the woman: Yea, hath God said—Ye shall not eat of every tree of the garden? (*And he spake by the mouth of the serpent.*) (Moses 4:6–7)

The Fall of Eve and Adam. The scripture below lists three reasons for Eve choosing to partake of the forbidden fruit: (1) it was good for food, (2) it had a pleasant appearance, and (3) it would made one wise:

> And when the woman saw that the tree was good for food, and that it was pleasant to the eyes, and a tree to be desired to make one wise, she took of the fruit thereof, and did eat, and gave also unto her husband with her; and he did eat. (3:6)

What was the immediate result? "The eyes of them both were opened, and they knew that they were naked; and they sewed fig leaves together, and made themselves aprons (3:6–7).

Jehovah[3] (or the Godhead) explained to Adam and Eve the changes that would result from their partaking of the forbidden fruit. The Genesis account is presented below, in verse by verse analysis form:

1. Jehovah, or He and God the Father, came to see Adam and Eve in the Garden of Eden (3:8).
2. Adam and Eve hid because they recognized their nakedness (3:8–10).
3. God knew of their transgression (3:11).
4. Adam and Eve both passed the blame (3:12–13).
5. God cursed the serpent (3:14–15).
6. Result 1: pain and sorrow in childbearing (3:16).
7. Result 2: the husband is to preside over the wife (3:16).
8. Result 3: the ground is cursed, requiring more work in food production (3:17–18).
9. Result 4: a lifetime of hard work is required (3:18–19).

---

3.   In the Torah, the Hebrew scriptures, "the name of the four letters" occurs about seven thousand times. The exact pronunciation of the name is unknown, but mainline Hebrew translators have agreed it probably is "Yahveh," "Yahweh," or "Yahve." They also agree that "Jehovah" may not be an altogether correct rendering of the name, but they have declined to substitute a different form because the name "Jehovah" has become familiar and has widespread usage. It is called "the name of four letters" because the translation of the Hebrew letters is YHVH in English. The Jewish rabbis had so much reverence for this name that they refrained from pronouncing it, or even writing it, as much as possible (Why? See Leviticus 24:16.)

The name "Jehovah" is generally printed as Lord (with a larger first-letter capital and the other three letters in smaller capitals) in the King James version. When imported into other books, such as this one, it comes over in all-capital letters: LORD.

The word "Elohim" means "God." It appears about three thousand times

10. Result 5: physical death would be required (3:19).

11. Result 6: Adam and Eve gained knowledge of good and evil and, therefore, agency (3:22).

12. Result 7: Adam and Eve were sent out of the Garden of Eden (3:23).

13. Result 8: Adam and Eve began having children (3:20).

Commentary: Were all these results *cursings*? To this author, they appear more like the kind of "facts of life" speech parents give to their children when the kids decide they're ready to leave home and go out on their own. In such situations, parents talk to their children about how they'll need to support themselves, to make wise choices, to pay their bills, to choose the right and avoid temptations, and so forth.

Adam and Eve now were going to have to leave the Garden of Eden and adapt to life in the "cruel world"—where weeds grow; where if you don't plant, water, and sow your seeds you won't eat; where if you don't weed and fertilize your garden, the tomatoes will be scrawny; and where if you get pregnant, you're going to have morning sickness and lots of backaches.

Behind the scenes, I can imagine God rejoicing that his children now were ready to strike out on their own. He clothed them and got them ready: "Unto Adam also and to his wife did the LORD God make coats of skins, and clothed them" (3:21) and then rejoiced that "the man is become as one of us, to know good and evil" (3:22). And so they wouldn't try to come back into the Garden of Eden, "he placed at the east of the garden of Eden Cherubims, and a flaming sword which turned every way, to keep the way of the tree of life." (3:24)

A modern revelation lends more insight concerning the expulsion of

---

in the Hebrew Bible. In the King James version, it is always translated as the generic term "God," though it doesn't refer, consistently, to any one member of the Godhead. In most cases it has reference to Jehovah, the premortal name of Jesus Christ.

When the words "Jehovah" and "Elohim" are combined in the Bible, as in "LORD God" or "Lord GOD," the entire Godhead may sometimes (but not always) be implied. It should be remembered, however, that in the Old Testament, a clear concept of two members of the three members of the Godhead (God the Father and God the Holy Spirit) had not yet been revealed to the people at large.

For a comprehensive discussion of the names of Godhead members in the Bible and other scriptures, see Crowther, Duane S. *The Godhead: New Scriptural Insights on the Father, the Son, and the Holy Ghost* (Springville, Utah: Horizon Publishers, an Imprint of Cedar Fort, Inc., 2007), pp. 373–86.

Adam and Eve from the Garden and what happened to Adam in the Fall. It is found in Doctrine and Covenants section 29:

1. All things are spiritual to the Lord (D&C 29:1, 34).
2. Jesus Christ created Adam (29:1, 34).
3. Jesus Christ gave Adam his agency (29:35).
4. Jesus Christ gave Adam spiritual commandments (29:35).
5. Lucifer, the devil who was thrust down, was before Adam (29:36–38).
6. If there were no temptation, men couldn't be agents unto themselves (29:39).
7. One must know bitter to be able to recognize sweet (29:39).
8. The devil tempted Adam, who partook of the forbidden fruit and transgressed the commandment (29:36, 40).
9. Adam became subject to the devil by yielding unto temptation (29:40).
10. Being cast out from God's presence resulted in "spiritual death." (29:41).
11. Spiritual death, the "first death," is the same as the "last death," when the wicked will be permanently expelled from God's presence (29:41).
12. The Lord prolonged the lives of Adam and his descendants until angels could declare repentance to them (29:42).
13. The angels' messages: repentance, redemption, faith in Christ (29:42).
14. The Lord determines the length of man's mortal life (29:43).
15. Believers in Christ can be raised in immortality unto eternal life (29:43).
16. Unrepentant non-believers are cast into damnation because they won't repent (29:44).
17. Unrepentant non-believers love darkness and follow Satan by doing evil deeds (29:44–45).
18. Little children are redeemed by Christ (29:46).
19. Satan isn't allowed to tempt little children until they begin to become accountable (29:47).

SCRIPTURAL EXPLANATIONS OF THE FALL

It grieves this author's heart not to have sufficient space allotted in this book to present in detail some of the rich explanations of Adam's Fall. They need to be coupled with teachings concerning the Savior's atoning sacrifice, His Resurrection, and the eternal benefits of both the Fall and the redemption. At least, there is sufficient space allotted here to be able to recommend some key passages, identifying each of them with a memorable phrase:

FROM THE BOOK OF MORMON

1. 2 Nephi 2:2–29: "Adam fell that men might be; and men are, that they might have joy."
2. 2 Nephi 9:1–26: "It must needs be an infinite atonement."
3. Mosiah 3:5–20: "The natural man is an enemy to God."
4. Alma 22:5–18: "The plan of redemption, . . . through Christ, . . . for all who believe."
5. Alma 42:1–31: "Do ye suppose that mercy can rob justice? Nay, not one whit."

FROM THE NEW TESTAMENT

6. Romans 5:8–21: "While we were sinners, Christ died for us, being justified by his blood."
7. 1 Corinthians 15:12–29: "If there be no resurrection, then Christ is not risen."
8. 1 Corinthians 15:38–49: "There are also celestial bodies, and bodies terrestrial."

FROM THE PEARL OF GREAT PRICE

9. Moses 6:48–66: "All men must repent, or they can in nowise inherit the kingdom of God."

THREE OTHER SIGNIFICANT EVENTS IN THE GARDEN OF EDEN

At least three other highly significant events took place in the Garden of Eden, apparently sometime prior to Adam and Eve's departure from that lovely environment. First, they were forgiven for their transgression—their Fall—that generally misunderstood act that brought about man's mortality. Second, an angel explained the reason for which sacrifices were to be offered. And third, important priesthood keys were granted to Adam there in the Garden. Each of these events will be considered in this section.

Adam and Eve are forgiven for their fall. One of the most significant of all the revelations granted to mankind is found in two short verses in the book of Moses—part of the rich store of historical information granted for the well-being of the Saints in these latter days:

> And the Lord said unto Adam: *Behold I have forgiven thee thy transgression in the Garden of Eden.*
>
> Hence came the saying abroad among the people, that *the Son of God hath atoned for original guilt, wherein the sins of the parents cannot be answered upon the heads of the children, for they are whole from the foundation of the world.* (Moses 6:53–54)

This glorious revelation recorded in Latter-day Saint scripture is not known nor understood by the world at large. Other Christian churches still believe that mortals are born into sin and will be held responsible, in part, for "Adam's sin" unless they are "saved."

Not so among the Latter-day Saints. Knowledge of forgiveness for the Fall having been granted unto Adam (and Eve) forms the basis for the second and third of the Church's Articles of Faith:

> We believe that men will be punished for their own sins, and not for Adam's transgression.
>
> We believe that through the Atonement of Christ, all mankind may be saved, by obedience to the laws and ordinances of the Gospel (Articles of Faith 1:2–3)

Moses 6:53–54 and the second and third Articles of Faith are all short verses of scripture, but their power greatly surpasses their length. The profound knowledge they convey to the Saints constitutes one of the most important differences between The Church of Jesus Christ of Latter-day Saints and every other church, faith, sect, and religious belief!

An angel explains the purpose of sacrifices. Many days after the Lord first commanded Adam and Eve to worship him and offer sacrifices, an angel appeared to Adam and gave him a significant explanation concerning the purpose of sacrifices:

> After many days an angel of the Lord appeared unto Adam, saying: Why dost thou offer sacrifices unto the Lord? And Adam said unto him: I know not, save the Lord commanded me.
>
> And then the angel spake, saying: *This thing is a similitude of the sacrifice of the Only Begotten of the Father, which is full of grace and truth.*
>
> Wherefore, thou shalt do all that thou doest in the name of the Son, and *thou shalt repent and call upon God in the name of the Son forevermore.* (Moses 5:6–8)

And in that same day, "the Holy Ghost fell upon Adam," and Adam "began to prophesy concerning all the families of the earth" (Moses 5:9–10).

The revealing to Adam of priesthood keys in the Garden of Eden. Another event of significance must have taken place during their sojourn in the Garden of Eden. It is recorded in a comparatively unread place: in the book of Abraham, in the explanation of one of the drawings recorded in that book, which reads as follows: "[This drawing] Is made to represent *God,* sitting upon his throne, clothed with power and authority; with a crown of eternal light upon his head; representing also *the grand Key-words of the Holy Priesthood, as revealed to Adam in the Garden of Eden*" (Abraham, Facsimile 2, item 3; see also item 7).

That's about the only scriptural clue available concerning this momen-tous event, yet it deals with a subject of such profound importance that speculation on the exact meaning of this scriptural fragment seems inap-propriate. Suffice it to say that something of everlasting value was bestowed on or restored to Adam.

As will be discussed later in this chapter, Latter-day Saints know that the mortal Adam was the embodiment of the premortal Michael, one of the seven archangels who stand in the highest rank of God's angelic hosts. Surely he was not left to wander without knowledge and authority here on the earth for almost a millennium. He had work to do—a world to populate and start off on God's appointed course of action as mankind began its chal-lenging walk through God's eternal plan of probation!

After Their Expulsion from the Garden

It's interesting that though the book of Genesis reports an overview of the lives of Adam and Eve, considerably more information about them can be learned from the Pearl of Great Price book of Moses.

What happened to Adam and Eve after Jehovah sent them out of the Garden of Eden? The Lord, himself, answered that query more than two mil-lennia later, in a revelation granted to Moses. He related that "It came to pass that after I, the Lord God, had driven them out, that Adam began to till the earth, and to have dominion over all the beasts of the field, and to eat his bread by the sweat of his brow, as I the Lord had commanded him. And Eve, also, his wife, did labor with him" (Moses 5:1). So there's the picture: In today's terminology, Adam became a farmer and an animal-keeper, and Eve worked right along with him.

What about their family? Moses was given more details than those found in Genesis. The Lord told Moses:

Adam knew his wife, and *she bare unto him sons and daughters,* and they began to multiply and to replenish the earth.

And from that time forth, *the sons and daughters of Adam began to divide two and two in the land, and to till the land, and to tend flocks, and they also begat sons and daughters.* (Moses 5:2–3)

No numbers are provided, but it appears that Adam and Eve took the commandment to "be fruitful, and multiply, and replenish the earth" quite seriously—this obviously is speaking of more children than is common in a twenty-first-century family! Note too that these verses encompass two gen-erations: not only their children, but their grandchildren also.

Where did Adam and Eve dwell? At first, they must have lived very close to the Garden of Eden. The first-recorded post-expulsion revelation they received indicates that they "called upon the name of the Lord, and they *heard the voice of the Lord from the way toward the Garden of Eden, speaking unto them,* and they saw him not; for they were shut out from his presence" (Moses 5:4).

This revelation began a long series of instructions which were given to the two of them from on high: "He gave unto them commandments, that *they should worship the Lord their God, and should offer the firstlings of their flocks, for an offering unto the Lord.* And Adam was obedient unto the commandments of the Lord" (Moses 5:5).

How faithful and obedient were the father and mother of all mankind? The scriptures give repeated indications of their spirituality and diligence:

1. "Adam and Eve, his wife, called upon the name of the Lord" (Moses 5:4).
2. "Adam was obedient unto the commandments of the Lord" (Moses 5:5).
3. "In that day the Holy Ghost fell upon Adam" (Moses 5:9).
4. "In that day Adam blessed God and was filled, and began to prophesy concerning all the families of the earth" (Moses 5:10).
5. "Adam and Eve blessed the name of God" (Moses 5:12).
6. "Adam and Eve, his wife, ceased not to call upon God" (Moses 5:16).
7. "Adam hearkened unto the voice of God, and called upon his sons to repent" (Moses 6:1).
8. "This prophecy Adam spake, as he was moved upon by the Holy Ghost, and a genealogy was kept of the children of God" (Moses 6:8).
9. "Our father Adam spake unto the Lord, and said: Why?" (Moses 6:53).
10. "Adam cried unto the Lord, and he was caught away by the Spirit of the Lord" (Moses 6:64).
11. "The Spirit of God descended upon him, and thus he was born of the Spirit, and became quickened in the inner man" (Moses 6:65).

THE KNOWN CHILDREN OF ADAM AND EVE

It has been noted that Adam and Eve gave birth to numerous sons and daughters, who in turn became parents of children of their own (Moses 5:2–3). After those children had come into their family, the scriptures only speak of three other sons who were born to Adam and Eve: Cain, Abel, and Seth. Their births are recorded in these verses: "Adam knew Eve his wife; and she conceived, and bare *Cain,* and said, I have gotten a man from the LORD. And she again bare his brother *Abel*" (Genesis 4:1–2). Years later, after Cain had married and moved away, Seth was born: "And Adam knew his wife again; and she bare a son, and called his name *Seth:* For God, said she, hath appointed me another seed instead of Abel, whom Cain slew" (Genesis 4:25).

THE ONSLAUGHT OF WICKEDNESS

When Jehovah put enmity between Lucifer's seed (his followers) and the descendants of Adam and Eve (Genesis 3:14–15), it certainly didn't deter Satan from continuing to pursue his devilish goals. The book of Moses indicates that even before the birth of Cain and Abel, the devil had begun to lead some of Adam's children into wickedness. It states that when Adam and Eve attempted to teach key gospel principles to their children, "Satan came among them, saying: I am also a son of God; and he commanded them, saying: Believe it not; and they believed it not, and they loved Satan more than God. And men began from that time forth to be carnal, sensual, and devilish" (Moses 5:13). And even in that era, prior to Cain's birth, it was recognized that "as many as believed not and repented not, should be damned" (Moses 5:15).

The Genesis 4:1–15 account of Abel being slain by his brother is known worldwide, as is Cain's defensive question: "Am I my brother's keeper?" Equally significant is the Lord's response to Cain: "If thou doest well, shalt thou not be accepted? and if thou doest not well, sin lieth at the door." Less well-known is the Pearl of Great Price account of the wicked deed and its outcomes. The book of Moses provides intriguing background to the events leading up to Cain's heinous murder of his brother:

Cain loved Satan more than God. And Satan commanded him, saying: Make an offering unto the Lord.

And in process of time it came to pass that Cain brought of the fruit of the ground an offering unto the Lord.

And Abel he also brought of the firstlings of his flock, and of the fat thereof. And the Lord had respect unto Abel, and to his offering;

But unto Cain, and to his offering, he had not respect. Now Satan knew this, and it pleased him. And Cain was very wroth, and his countenance fell.

And the Lord said unto Cain: Why art thou wroth? Why is thy countenance fallen?

If thou doest well, thou shalt be accepted. And if thou doest not well, sin lieth at the door, and Satan desireth to have thee; and except thou shalt hearken unto my commandments, I will deliver thee up, and it shall be unto thee according to his desire. And thou shalt rule over him;

For from this time forth thou shalt be the father of his lies; thou shalt be called Perdition; for thou wast also before the world.

And it shall be said in time to come—That these abominations were had from Cain; for he rejected the greater counsel which was had from God; and this is a cursing which I will put upon thee, except thou repent.

And Cain was wroth, and listened not any more to the voice of the Lord, neither to Abel, his brother, who walked in holiness before the Lord.

And Adam and his wife mourned before the Lord, because of Cain and his brethren.

And it came to pass that *Cain took one of his brothers' daughters to wife, and they loved Satan more than God.*

And *Satan said unto Cain:* Swear unto me by thy throat, and if thou tell it thou shalt die; and swear thy brethren by their heads, and by the living God, that they tell it not; for if they tell it, they shall surely die; and this that thy father may not know it; and *this day I will deliver thy brother Abel into thine hands.*

And *Satan sware unto Cain that he would do according to his commands.* And all these things were done in secret.

And Cain said: *Truly I am Mahan, the master of this great secret, that I may murder and get gain. Wherefore Cain was called Master Mahan, and he gloried in his wickedness.*

And Cain went into the field, and Cain talked with Abel, his brother. And it came to pass that while they were in the field, *Cain rose up against Abel, his brother, and slew him.* (Moses 5:18–32)

The scriptures give no indication of murder having been committed upon this earth prior to Abel's untimely death, so it is generally assumed that Cain's tragic deed introduced murder to this sphere. If so, it constitutes an important, though tragic, milestone in the course of this planet's history.

It is significant that more details concerning the motivations for the sordid event have been revealed in these latter days. Since the above-cited episode is not recorded in the Bible, only the Latter-day Saints know that Cain was given ascendancy over Lucifer and became the "father of his lies," and also that he (Cain) became Master Mahan—the master of the secret that one may murder to get gain. Surely the murder of Abel, "who walked in holiness before the Lord," is of far more significance than millions of the murders which have followed down through the ages.

ADAM AND EVE'S EFFORTS TO
TEACH THEIR CHILDREN

It is interesting to note the repeated emphasis the book of Moses places on Adam and Eve's efforts to instruct their children and their efforts to maintain proper genealogical records. Those passages include the following:

1. "And Adam and Eve blessed the name of God, and *they made all things known unto their sons and their daughters*" (Moses 5:12).

2. "And then began these men to call upon the name of the Lord, and the Lord blessed them; And a book of remembrance was kept, in the which was recorded, in the language of Adam, for it was given unto as many as

called upon God to write by the spirit of inspiration; And *by them their children were taught to read and write, having a language which was pure and undefiled*" (Moses 6:4–6).

3. "Now this prophecy Adam spake, as he was moved upon by the Holy Ghost, and *a genealogy was kept of the children of God*" (Moses 6:8).

4. "And this is the genealogy of the sons of Adam, who was the son of God, with whom God, himself, conversed. *And they were preachers of righteousness, and spake and prophesied, and called upon all men, everywhere, to repent; and faith was taught unto the children of men*" (Moses 6:22–23).

5. "Even the first of all we know, even Adam. *For a book of remembrance we have written among us, according to the pattern given by the finger of God;* and it is given in our own language" (Moses 6:45–46).

6. "And the Lord spake unto Adam, saying: Inasmuch as thy children are conceived in sin, even so when they begin to grow up, sin conceiveth in their hearts, and they taste the bitter, that they may know to prize the good. And it is given unto them to know good from evil; wherefore they are agents unto themselves, and I have given unto you another law and commandment. *Wherefore teach it unto your children, that all men, everywhere, must repent, or they can in nowise inherit the kingdom of God, for no unclean thing can dwell there,* or dwell in his presence" (Moses 6:55–57).

7. "Therefore *I give unto you a commandment, to teach these things freely unto your children,* saying: That by reason of transgression cometh the fall, which fall bringeth death, and inasmuch as ye were born into the world by water, and blood, and the spirit, which I have made, and so became of dust a living soul, even so ye must be born again into the kingdom of heaven, of water, and of the Spirit, and be cleansed by blood, even the blood of mine Only Begotten; that ye might be sanctified from all sin, and enjoy the words of eternal life in this world, and eternal life in the world to come, even immortal glory; For by the water ye keep the commandment; by the Spirit ye are justified, and by the blood ye are sanctified; . . . And now, behold, I say unto you: This is the plan of salvation unto all men, through the blood of mine Only Begotten, who shall come in the meridian of time" (Moses 6:58–62).

THE LINEAL DESCENDANTS OF ADAM AND EVE

Chapter 5 of Genesis begins with the designation: "This is the book of the generations of Adam." (Genesis 5:1) It then proceeds to provide a list of ten additional generations of lineal descendants of earth's first parents.

That list is presented here in summary form:

Generation	Name	Adam's Age when Born	Father's Age when Born	Age at Death
1	Adam			930
2	Seth	130	130	912
3	Enos	235	105	905
4	Cainan	325	90	910
5	Mahalaleel	395	70	895
6	Jared	460	65	962
7	Enoch	622	162	365 (taken up)
8	Methusaleh	687	65	969
9	Lamech	874	187	777
10	Noah		182	950
11	Shem		500	600

It's obvious that those listed above aren't necessarily their parents' first-born sons. It appears, also, that each of the above individuals came from large families and then, in turn, parented large families. By the tenth generation, in Noah's day, it is probable that millions of inhabitants had been born on this earth, and there probably were millions who died in the great flood in that generation.

Revelations and Spiritual Experiences Granted to Adam and Eve

It seems beneficial to list the revelations granted to Adam and Eve, and to summarize the glorious gospel teachings which were granted unto them throughout their lives. A summary list of these revelatory events is first provided, and then a brief but detailed listing of many of the doctrines received in those revelatory events will be made.

1. Adam was a participant in the planning and Creation of this earth (Genesis 1:1–2:14; Moses 2:1–3:14; Abraham 4:1–5:10).

2. Adam, placed in the Garden of Eden, was instructed concerning the Tree of the Knowledge of Good and Evil (Genesis 2:16–17; Moses 3:15–17: Abraham 5:11–13).

3. Adam received Eve to be his helpmeet (Genesis 2:18–24; Moses 3:18–24; Abraham 5:14–18).

4. Eve was visited and tempted by the serpent (Genesis 3:1–6; Moses 4:5–12).

5. Adam, Eve, and the serpent were confronted and cursed by God the Father and Jehovah and then expelled from the Garden of Eden (Genesis 3:7–24; Moses 4:13–32).

6. Adam was given the priesthood while still in the Garden of Eden— order of events uncertain (Abraham, Facsimile 2, Items 2, 3, 7).

7. Adam and Eve heard the voice of the Lord and were given commandments—near the Garden of Eden (Moses 5:4–5).

8. An angel appeared unto Adam and instructed him—after many days (Moses 5:6–8).

9. Adam was filled with the Holy Ghost and prophesied—the same day, after the angel appeared (Moses 5:9–11).

10. Satan came among them, and led some astray (Moses 5:13).

11. The Lord God called upon men by the Holy Ghost—everywhere (Moses 5:14–15).

12. God spoke to Adam by his own voice, and answered Adam's questions— sometime after the birth of Seth (Moses 6:50–63).

13. Adam was caught away by the Spirit of the Lord and was baptized and born of the Spirit—apparently immediately following his conversation with God (Moses 6:64–65).

14. A voice spoke to Adam from heaven—immediately following his baptism (Moses 6:66–68).

15. The Lord appeared unto Adam and his righteous posterity in the valley of Adam-ondi-Ahman—three years before Adam's death (D&C 107:53–57).

16. The Lord gave Adam his agency—in the Garden of Eden (D&C 29:34–41).

17. The Lord promised Adam that he and his seed would not die before angels would be sent to preach the gospel unto them—this may have occurred in the Garden of Eden (D&C 29:42–45).

The following is a listing of the messages received and the spiritual experiences found in the scriptural accounts of the above events:

1. Adam was a participant in the planning and Creation of this earth (Genesis 1:1–2:14; Moses 2:1–3:14; Abraham 4:1–5:10).

2. God revealed to Moses concerning this heaven and earth (Moses 2:1).

3. Jehovah is the principle creator of this earth (Moses 2:1).

4. Plants are to reproduce their own kind (Moses 2:11).

5. Earth's sun and moon are to govern earth's rotations (Moses 2:16).

6. Commandments to water, animals, and birds (Genesis 1:22; Moses 2:22).

7. Commandments to the earth (Genesis 1:24; Moses 2:24).

8. Mortal males and females created in the image of God (Genesis 1:26–27, Moses 2:26–27).

9. Commandments to mankind (Genesis 1:28; Moses 2:28).

10. Herbs and fruits given as food for man and beasts (Genesis 1:29–30; Moses 2:29–30).

11. God (the gods) blessed and sanctified the Sabbath (Genesis 2:3; Moses 3:3).

12. Heaven and earth went through generations during their Creation (Genesis 2:4, Moses 3:4).

13. The spiritual creation took place in heaven (Moses 3:5).

14. Man became a living soul (Moses 3:7; Genesis 2:7).

15. All things were previously created spiritually (Moses 3:7).

16. The Garden of Eden also became a living soul (Moses 3:8–9).

17. The Garden of Eden remained where God created it (Moses 3:9).

18. Trees to be pleasant to the sight, good for food (Genesis 2:9).

19. Two special trees placed in the Garden of Eden (Genesis 2:9; Moses 3:9).

20. Precious metals and stones were found (Genesis 2:11–12; Moses 3:11–12).

21. Adam assigned to tend the Garden of Eden (Genesis 2:15).

22. Adam informed that eating forbidden fruit would begin mortal life and death (Genesis 2:17).

23. All things are spiritual to God (D&C 29:34).

24. Jesus Christ (Jehovah) created Adam (D&C 29:1, 34).

25. Jesus Christ commanded Adam to use his agency and be responsible for his decisions (D&C 29:35).

26. Christ's commandments are not temporal, carnal, or sensual (D&C 29:35).

27. The devil rebelled against Jesus Christ (D&C 29:36).

28. Hell is the place prepared for the followers of Satan (D&C 29:37–38).

29. The devil must tempt mankind or they can't exercise agency (D&C 29:39).

30. Adam's yielding to temptation made him subject to the devil's will (D&C 29:40).

31. Spiritual death is to be cut off from God's presence (D&C 29:41).

32. The Lord prolonged the lives of Adam's seed until angels declared gospel principles to them (D&C 29:42).

33. The Lord appointed unto man the days of his probation (D&C 29:43).

34. Men receive eternal wages from whom they obey on earth (D&C 29:45).

ADAM AS PATRIARCH AND PRIESTHOOD
LEADER OF HIS POSTERITY

Section 107 of the Doctrine and Covenants provides information concerning Adam, and concerning the priesthood, that is not found elsewhere in the scriptures. First of all, it indicates that the patriarchal order was established in Adam's day, that the priesthood was to be passed down from father to son, and that the right to the priesthood belonged to Adam's literal descendants:

> The order of this priesthood was confirmed to be handed down from father to son, and rightly belongs to the literal descendants of the chosen seed, to whom the promises were made.
> This order was instituted in the days of Adam. (D&C 107:40–41)

Then the ordination order of the priesthood lineage is enumerated for ten generations:

> This order was instituted in the days of Adam and came down by lineage in the following manner:
> From *Adam* to *Seth, who was ordained by Adam* at the age of sixty–nine years, and was *blessed by him three years previous to his (Adam's) death*, and received the promise of God by his father, that his posterity should be the chosen of the Lord, and that they should be preserved unto the end of the earth;
> Because he (Seth) was a perfect man, and his likeness was the express likeness of his father, insomuch that he seemed to be like unto his father in all things, and could be distinguished from him only by his age.
> *Enos* was ordained at the age of one hundred and thirty–four years and four months, *by the hand of Adam*.
> God called upon *Cainan* in the wilderness in the fortieth year of his age; and he met Adam in journeying to the place Shedolamak. He was eighty–seven years old when he received his ordination.
> *Mahalaleel* was four hundred and ninety–six years and seven days old when he was *ordained by the hand of Adam*, who also blessed him.
> *Jared* was two hundred years old when he was *ordained under the hand of Adam*, who also blessed him.
> *Enoch* was twenty–five years old when he was *ordained under the hand of Adam*; and he was sixty–five and Adam blessed him.
> And he saw the Lord, and he walked with him, and was before his face continually; and he walked with God three hundred and sixty–five years, making him four hundred and thirty years old when he was translated.
> *Methuselah* was one hundred years old when he was *ordained under the hand of Adam*.
> *Lamech* was thirty–two years old when he was *ordained under the hand of Seth*.

Noah was ten years old when he was *ordained under the hand of Methuselah.* (D&C 107:41–52)

One of the most significant events in Adam's life was the family reunion which he hosted in the valley of Adam-ondi-Ahman. There he assembled his descendants who were all high priests, with the rest of his righteous posterity, and pronounced upon them his last blessing. He also prophesied events which would take place "unto the latest generation." One of the most important aspects of the gathering is that the Lord appeared unto them and administered comfort unto Adam, telling him that he would be a prince over all the nations that came from his loins forever.

> *Three years previous to the death of Adam, he called Seth, Enos, Cainan, Mahalaleel, Jared, Enoch, and Methuselah, who were all high priests,* with the residue of his posterity who were righteous, into the *valley of Adam-ondi-Ahman,* and there bestowed upon them his last blessing.
>
> And *the Lord appeared unto them,* and they rose up and blessed Adam, and called him Michael, the prince, the archangel.
>
> And *the Lord administered comfort unto Adam, and said unto him: I have set thee to be at the head; a multitude of nations shall come of thee, and thou art a prince over them forever.*
>
> And Adam stood up in the midst of the congregation; and, notwithstanding he was bowed down with age, being full of the Holy Ghost, *predicted whatsoever should befall his posterity unto the latest generation.*
>
> These things were *all written in the book of Enoch,* and are to be testified of in due time. (D&C 107:53–57)

ADAM IN THE SPIRIT WORLD

LDS Church President Joseph F. Smith received a glorious view of events in the spirit world following the Savior's crucifixion. He saw the Lord enter the spirit world and organize the faithful leaders who had served him in Old Testament times to serve as missionaries to teach the gospel "to them that were in darkness."

> And as I wondered, my eyes were opened, and my understanding quickened, and I perceived that *the Lord went not in person among the wicked and the disobedient* who had rejected the truth, to teach them;
>
> But behold, *from among the righteous, he organized his forces and appointed messengers,* clothed with power and authority, and commissioned them to go forth and carry the light of the gospel to them that were in darkness, even to all the spirits of men; and thus was the gospel preached to the dead.
>
> And the chosen messengers went forth to declare the acceptable day of the Lord and proclaim liberty to the captives who were bound, even unto all who would repent of their sins and receive the gospel. . . .

And so it was made known among the dead, both small and great, the unrighteous as well as the faithful, that *redemption had been wrought through the sacrifice of the Son of God upon the cross.*

Thus was it made known that our Redeemer spent his time during his sojourn in the world of spirits, *instructing and preparing the faithful spirits of the prophets who had testified of him* in the flesh;

That they might carry the message of redemption unto all the dead, unto whom he could not go personally, because of their rebellion and transgression, that they through the ministration of his servants might also hear his words. (D&C 138:29–31, 35–37)

Who were these righteous leaders whom the Savior enlisted to preach His gospel in the world of spirits? The name Adam leads the list:

Among the great and mighty ones who were assembled in this vast congregation of the righteous were *Father Adam, the Ancient of Days and father of all,*

And our glorious Mother Eve, with *many of her faithful daughters* who had lived through the ages and worshiped the true and living God. . . .

All these and *many more,* even *the prophets who dwelt among the Nephites* and testified of the coming of the Son of God, mingled in the vast assembly and waited for their deliverance. (D&C 138:38–39, 49)

Concerning the Old Testament and Book of Mormon prophets whom the Savior enlisted—those who had passed away before the Savior's ministry in the meridian of times—President Smith was shown that the Savior gave them power to come forth as resurrected beings at the time of His resurrection, back in the first century AD:

These the Lord taught, and gave them power to come forth, after his resurrection from the dead, to enter into his Father's kingdom, there to be crowned with immortality and eternal life,

And continue thenceforth their labor as had been promised by the Lord, and be partakers of all blessings which were held in reserve for them that love him. (D&C 138:51–52)

Pertaining to those resurrections in the meridian of time, the scriptures say:

+ "Jesus, when he had cried again with a loud voice, yielded up the ghost. And, behold, the veil of the temple was rent in twain from the top to the bottom; and the earth did quake, and the rocks rent; *And the graves were opened; and many bodies of the saints which slept arose, And came out of the graves after his resurrection, and went into the holy city, and appeared unto many*" (Matthew 27:50–53).

+ "Yea, at the time that he shall yield up the ghost there shall be thunderings and lightnings for the space of many hours, and the earth shall shake and tremble; . . . And many highways shall be broken up, and many cities shall become desolate. *And many graves shall be opened, and shall yield up many of their dead; and many saints shall appear unto many*" (Helaman 14:21, 24–25).

- "Verily I say unto you, I commanded my servant Samuel, the Lamanite, that he should testify unto this people, that *at the day that the Father should glorify his name in me that there were many saints who should arise from the dead, and should appear unto many, and should minister unto them.* And he said unto them: Was it not so? And his disciples answered him and said: Yea, Lord, Samuel did prophesy according to thy words, and *they were all fulfilled.* And Jesus said unto them: How be it that ye have not written this thing, that *many saints did arise and appear unto many and did minister unto them?*" (3 Nephi 23:9–11)

Thus, it can safely be assumed that Adam, and many or all the other great Old Testament and Book of Mormon prophets, have been resurrected and taken their places in the eternal realms of celestial beings!

ADAM IN THE FUTURE AS THE ANCIENT OF DAYS

Section 116 of the Doctrine and Covenants is a unique scripture—a section that's only one verse long. In that one verse, however, four important understandings are conveyed: (1) Adam is the Ancient of Days spoken of by the Old Testament prophet Daniel, (2) Adam will come to visit his people, (3) that visit will happen in a place called Adam-ondi-Ahman, and (4) Spring Hill, Daviess County, Missouri is the location the Lord has revealed to be Adam-ondi-Ahman. This is what Section 116 says: "Spring Hill is named by the Lord Adam-ondi-Ahman, because, said he, it is the place where Adam shall come to visit his people, or the Ancient of Days shall sit, as spoken of by Daniel the prophet."

This is the vision the prophet Daniel recorded concerning the future coming of the Ancient of Days:

> I beheld till the thrones were cast down, and *the Ancient of days did sit,* whose garment was white as snow, and the hair of his head like the pure wool: his throne was like the fiery flame, and his wheels as burning fire.
>
> A fiery stream issued and came forth from before him: *thousand thousands ministered unto him, and ten thousand times ten thousand stood before him:* the judgment was set, and the books were opened. . . .
>
> I saw in the night visions, and, behold, *one like the Son of man came with the clouds of heaven, and came to the Ancient of days,* and they brought him near before him.

And *there was given him dominion, and glory, and a kingdom, that all people, nations, and languages, should serve him: his dominion is an everlasting dominion, which shall not pass away, and his kingdom that which shall not be destroyed....*

I beheld, and the same horn made war with the saints, and prevailed against them;

Until the Ancient of days came, and judgment was given to the saints of the most High; and the time came that the saints possessed the kingdom....

Thus he said, The fourth beast shall be the fourth kingdom upon earth, which shall be diverse from all kingdoms, and shall devour the whole earth, and shall tread it down, and break it in pieces....

And he shall speak great words against the most High, and shall wear out the saints of the most High, and think to change times and laws: and they shall be given into his hand until a time and times and the dividing of time.

But the judgment shall sit, and they shall take away his dominion, to consume and to destroy it unto the end.

And the kingdom and dominion, and the greatness of the kingdom under the whole heaven, shall be given to the people of the saints of the most High, whose kingdom is an everlasting kingdom, and all dominions shall serve and obey him. (Daniel 7:9–10, 21–22, 25–27)

Concerning the interpretation of this passage, the Prophet Joseph Smith said:

Daniel in his seventh chapter speaks of *the Ancient of days; he means the oldest man, our Father Adam, Michael, he will call his children together and hold a council with them to prepare them for the coming of the Son of Man.* He (Adam) is the father of the human family, and presides over the spirits of all men, and *all that have had the keys must stand before him in this grand council.* This may take place before some of us leave this stage of action. *The Son of Man stands before him, and there is given him glory and dominion. Adam delivers up his stewardship to Christ, that which was delivered to him as holding the keys of the universe, but retains his standing as head of the human family.*[4]

Joseph Smith added additional insights on another occasion:

Adam holds the keys of the dispensation of the fullness of times: i.e., the dispensation of all the times have been and will be revealed through him from the

---

4. *History of The Church of Jesus Christ of Latter-day Saints* (Salt Lake City: *Deseret News*, 1948), vol. 3, pp. 386–7; July 2, 1839. For a more in-depth discussion of the Council at Adam-ondi-Ahman, see: Crowther, Duane S. *Prophecy—Key To The Future* (Springville, Utah: Horizon Publishers, an Imprint of Cedar Fort, Inc., 2004), pp. 167–76 (emphasis added).

beginning to Christ, and from Christ to the end of all the dispensations that are to be revealed....

God purposed in Himself that there should not be an eternal fullness until every dispensation should be fulfilled and gathered together in one, and that all things whatsoever, that should be gathered together in one in those dispensations unto the same fullness and eternal glory, should be in Christ Jesus; therefore He set the ordinances to be the same forever and ever, and *set Adam to watch over them, to reveal them from heaven to man, or to send angels to reveal them....*

These angels are under the direction of Michael or Adam, who acts under the direction of the Lord....

This, then, is the nature of the Priesthood; every man holding the Presidency of his dispensation, and one man holding the Presidency of them all, even Adam; and Adam receiving his Presidency and authority from the Lord, but cannot receive a fullness until Christ shall present the Kingdom to the Father, which shall be at the end of the last dispensation.[5]

ADAM IS MICHAEL, THE ARCHANGEL

It is appropriate to recognize that Adam, from the days of his premortal existence, was and is one of the seven "highest angels," also known as the "archangels." These seven are sometimes referred to as "princes" in the heavenly realms.

The scriptures unequivocally assert that Adam is Michael. Doctrine and Covenants 27:11 refers to "Michael, or Adam, the father of all, the prince of all, the ancient of days," and Doctrine and Covenants 107:54 records that "the Lord appeared unto them, and they rose up and blessed Adam, and called him Michael, the prince, the archangel."

Passages from the Old Testament, the New Testament, and the Doctrine and Covenants make repeated references to Michael's great angelic stature. Those which speak of the archangel Michael's actions in premortal and Old Testament times will be considered first; then those which foretell his leadership and participation in last-days events will be considered.

Michael's ministrations in premortal and Old Testament times. In the final book of the New Testament, John the Revelator made a significant reference to Michael's premortal role: it was he who contended with Lucifer in the great premortal struggle when a third of the hosts of heaven were led astray by Satan:

---

5. History of The Church of Jesus Christ of Latter-day Saints (Salt Lake City: Deseret News, 1948), vol. 4, pp. 207–9; October 5, 1840 (emphasis added).

And there was war in heaven: *Michael and his angels fought against the dragon;* and the dragon fought and his angels,

And prevailed not; neither was their place found any more in heaven.

And the great dragon was cast out, that old serpent, called the Devil, and Satan, which deceiveth the whole world: he was cast out into the earth, and his angels were cast out with him. (Revelation 12:7–9)

In another New Testament passage, the author of the epistle of Jude alluded to Michael's efforts in an Old Testament situation. While warning against the evil-speaking men of his day, Jude commended the angel Michael's dignified speech when he contended against Satan for the body of Moses:

Likewise also these filthy dreamers defile the flesh, despise dominion, and speak evil of dignities.

Yet *Michael the archangel, when contending with the devil he disputed about the body of Moses,* durst not bring against him a railing accusation, but said, The Lord rebuke thee.

But these speak evil of those things which they know not: but what they know naturally, as brute beasts, in those things they corrupt themselves. (Jude 1:8–10)

The Old Testament prophet Daniel received communications and protective support from two of the seven archangels: Gabriel and Michael (Concerning Gabriel's appearances, see Daniel 9:21–27 and, probably, 10:13–12:4.) In one of these angelic visitations, Daniel was told that his angelic visitor, presumably Gabriel, had "to fight with the prince of Persia." The angelic visitor said that "Michael, one of the chief princes, came to help me." Then the angel indicated that he had to stand alone against the Persian hordes because "there is none that holdeth with me in these things, but Michael your prince" (Daniel 10:13, 21).

THE ARCHANGEL MICHAEL'S PARTICIPATION AND LEADERSHIP IN FUTURE EVENTS

The same angelic visitor that revealed numerous events to the Prophet Daniel concluded his lengthy revelation by speaking of important last-days events. He foretold a future time of terrible trouble in which the archangel Michael will apparently play a significant role as the Lord's second coming and the beginning of the first resurrection are drawing near:

And at that time shall Michael stand up, the great prince which standeth for the children of thy people: and there shall be a time of trouble, such as never was since there was a nation even to that same time: and at that time thy people shall be delivered, every one that shall be found written in the book. (Daniel 12:1)

A series of six prophecies found in the Doctrine and Covenants provides numerous insights on the responsibilities and activities of Michael, the archangel, in the last days.

First, a prophecy in section 29 speaks of two appearances of the archangel Michael—one in the past and the other in the future. The past appearance apparently took place on the banks of the Susquehanna River: "The voice of Michael on the banks of the Susquehanna, detecting the devil when he appeared as an angel of light!" (D&C 128:20).

Second, a future appearance will be when Michael joins Gabriel, Raphael, and other angels when they will appear to declare their dispensations and keys down to the present time. This appears to be a significant part of the great Council at Adam-ondi-Ahman where Adam, who will preside in the role of the Ancient of Days, will turn over all these keys to the Savior, who will join them in this much-anticipated meeting.

> And the voice of Michael, the archangel; the voice of Gabriel, and of Raphael, and of divers angels, from Michael or Adam down to the present time, all declaring their dispensation, their rights, their keys, their honors, their majesty and glory, and the power of their priesthood; giving line upon line, precept upon precept; here a little, and there a little; giving us consolation by holding forth that which is to come, confirming our hope! (D&C 128:21. See also Daniel 7:21–22, 25–27; D&C 116:1; D&C 107:53–57.)

Third, the Lord, through revelation has proclaimed that he has appointed Michael to hold the keys of salvation for the righteous saints of the kingdom in the last days, so they can be crowned with honor and made rulers over many kingdoms:

> That through my providence, notwithstanding the tribulation which shall descend upon you, that the church may stand independent above all other creatures beneath the celestial world;
> That you may come up unto the crown prepared for you, and be made rulers over many kingdoms, saith the Lord God, the Holy One of Zion, who hath established the foundations of Adam-ondi-Ahman;
> Who hath appointed Michael your prince, and established his feet, and set him upon high, and given unto him the keys of salvation under the counsel and direction of the Holy One, who is without beginning of days or end of life. (D&C 78:14–16)

Fourth, in another intriguing Doctrine and Covenants revelation, the Lord speaks of a time on earth when he will celebrate with Joseph Smith along with many of the heavenly beings who participated in establishing the restored gospel upon the earth once more. A long list of future participants is presented: Moroni, Elias, John the Baptist, Elijah, Abraham, Isaac, Jacob,

Joseph, Peter, James, John, "And also with Michael, or Adam, the father of all, the prince of all, the ancient of days." (D&C 27:5–13)

Fifth, in yet another end-of-times prophecy found in the Doctrine and Covenants, the Lord teaches that at the end of the millennium, it will be the archangel Michael who shall sound the trump that will call forth the dead from their graves in the second resurrection (see D&C 76:81–85):

> And again, verily, verily, I say unto you that *when the thousand years are ended, and men again begin to deny their God, then will I spare the earth but for a little season;*
>
> *And the end shall come, and the heaven and the earth shall be consumed and pass away, and there shall be a new heaven and a new earth. . . .*
>
> But, behold, verily I say unto you, *before the earth shall pass away, Michael, mine archangel, shall sound his trump, and then shall all the dead awake, for their graves shall be opened, and they shall come forth—yea, even all.* (D&C 29:22–23, 26)

Sixth, shortly after calling forth the remaining dead at the end of the millennium, another Doctrine and Covenants prophecy asserts that it will be Michael's lot to lead the hosts of heaven in the final "battle of the great God," when Satan will lead the hosts of hell in a final attempt to win eternal control of this earth:

> And so on, until *the seventh angel shall sound his trump; and he shall stand forth upon the land and upon the sea, and swear in the name of him who sitteth upon the throne, that there shall be time no longer; and Satan shall be bound, that old serpent, who is called the devil, and shall not be loosed for the space of a thousand years.*
>
> And then he shall be loosed for a little season, that he may gather together his armies.
>
> *And Michael, the seventh angel, even the archangel, shall gather together his armies, even the hosts of heaven.*
>
> And the devil shall gather together his armies; even the hosts of hell, and shall come up to battle *against Michael and his armies.*
>
> And then cometh the battle of the great God; and the devil and his armies shall be cast away into their own place, that they shall not have power over the saints any more at all.
>
> *For Michael shall fight their battles, and shall overcome him who seeketh the throne of him who sitteth upon the throne, even the Lamb.*
>
> This is the glory of God, and the sanctified; and they shall not any more see death. (D&C 88:110–116)

So end the scriptural accounts of Adam: the father of all mankind, the Prince of all, the Ancient of Days, and the archangel Michael! His service to mankind began prior to the Creation of this earth. It will continue through the Savior's second coming and millennial reign. He still will play major roles in protecting and blessing his ever-increasing posterity right up to the second resurrection and the final judgment. Clearly, he stands second only to our Creator, Savior, and King—Jesus Christ—as the most important player in this earth's mortal span. Truly, all mankind owes him a tremendous debt of love and gratitude!

CHAPTER 2
SETH

A PERFECT MAN, ONE OF THE MIGHTY ONES

What a remarkable person! Who else do the scriptures declare was "a perfect man"? Who else received a covenant from God "that his posterity should be the chosen of the Lord, and that they should be preserved unto the end of the earth"? (D&C 107:43).

Though relatively little is recorded in the scriptures concerning his life and ministry, enough is revealed about the patriarch Seth to show that he truly was among the greatest of the prophets sent to this earth.

HIS BIRTH

The historical setting concerning Seth's birth is known. After Adam and Eve were sent out of the Garden of Eden, they had numerous sons and daughters who paired off and began living together and raising families of their own:

> Adam knew his wife, and she bare unto him sons and daughters, and they began to multiply and to replenish the earth.
>
> And from that time forth, *the sons and daughters of Adam began to divide two and two in the land, and to till the land, and to tend flocks, and they also begat sons and daughters.* (Moses 5:2–3)

As these children were growing to adulthood and parenthood, their parents had spiritual experiences that caused them to draw close to the Lord. "Adam and Eve blessed the name of God, and they made all things known unto their sons and their daughters" (Moses 5:12).

But the evil one soon began to counter their efforts to raise their children in righteousness. "Satan came among them, saying: I am also a son of God; and he commanded them, saying: *Believe it not; and they believed it not, and they loved Satan more than God.*" The scripture records that "*men began from that time forth to be carnal, sensual, and devilish*" (Moses 5:13). However, "Adam and Eve, his wife, ceased not to call upon God" (Moses 5:16).

At that point, Adam again "knew Eve his wife, and she conceived and bare Cain" (Moses 5:16). Eve rejoiced in Cain's birth, and the scripture records her profound hope that this new child would be righteous. Eve said,

"I have gotten a man from the Lord; wherefore he may not reject his words" (Moses 5:16).

Yet another child was born: Eve "again conceived and bare his brother Abel" (Moses 5:17). But as the two young men grew and attained manhood, they chose different paths. "Abel hearkened unto the voice of the Lord," (Moses 5:17, 26), but "Cain hearkened not, saying: Who is the Lord that I should know him?" (Moses 5:16).

Their rivalry grew so intense that the older of the two brothers left home: "Cain took one of his brothers' daughters to wife, and they loved Satan more than God" (Moses 5:28). His falling away brought great grief to his parents: "Adam and his wife mourned before the Lord, because of Cain and his brethren" (Moses 5:27).

Sometime after that, Cain murdered his brother: "Cain went into the field, and Cain talked with Abel, his brother. And it came to pass that while they were in the field, Cain rose up against Abel, his brother, and slew him" (Moses 5:32). When the Lord chastised Cain, "*Cain was shut out from the presence of the Lord,* and with his wife and many of his brethren dwelt in the land of Nod, on the east of Eden," (Moses 5:41) and "from the days of Cain, there was a secret combination, and their works were in the dark, and they knew every man his brother" (Moses 5:51). Because of Cain's evil leadership, many of the descendants of Adam and Eve fell into great wickedness. The result:

> *God cursed the earth with a sore curse, and was angry with the wicked, with all the sons of men whom he had made;*
>
> *For they would not hearken unto his voice, nor believe on his Only Begotten Son, even him whom he declared should come in the meridian of time, who was prepared from before the foundation of the world.*
>
> *And thus the Gospel began to be preached, from the beginning, being declared by holy angels sent forth from the presence of God, and by his own voice, and by the gift of the Holy Ghost.* (Moses 5:56–58)

So it is in this setting, decades after the births of Cain and Abel, and long after Cain's becoming a murderer and falling away from God and from his parents, that Seth was born. "And Adam knew his wife again, and *she bare a son, and he called his name Seth*" (Moses 6:2).

It was a time of rejoicing for the new parents: "Adam glorified the name of God; for he said: God hath appointed me another seed, instead of Abel, whom Cain slew" (Moses 6:2).

IN HIS IMAGE

The Genesis account of the birth of Seth says: "Adam lived an hundred and thirty years, and *begat a son in his own likeness, after his image;* and called his name Seth" (Genesis 5:3).

Since the earliest days of the Church, Latter-day Saint missionaries have coupled this verse with two verses from the first chapter of Genesis as they have explained the physical nature of God:

> And God said, *Let us make man in our image, after our likeness:* and let them have dominion over the fish of the sea, and over the fowl of the air, and over the cattle, and over all the earth, and over every creeping thing that creepeth upon the earth.
>
> *So God created man in his own image, in the image of God created he him;* male and female created he them. (Genesis 1:26–27)

Protestant and Catholic apologists, who refuse to accept the scriptural doctrine that both God the Father and His Son Jesus Christ have physical bodies, have attempted to explain away this clear scriptural parallel, asserting that image reference concerning Seth, cited above, is referring to various character traits, rather than to his physical appearance. However, numerous scriptural passages rebuff this erroneous assertion. (In the Bible, see Genesis 9:6; 1 Corinthians 11:7; 2 Corinthians 4:4; Colossians 1:15; and Hebrews 1:1–3. In the Book of Mormon, see Mosiah 7:27; Alma 18:34; Alma 22:12; and Ether 3:8–16.)

However, another passage concerning Seth, in the book of Moses, makes the "image" comparison between Adam and Seth even clearer:

> A genealogy was kept of the children of God. And this was the book of the generations of Adam, saying: In the day that God created man, *in the likeness of God made he him;*
>
> *In the image of his own body, male and female, created he them,* and blessed them, and called their name Adam, in the day when they were created and became living souls in the land upon the footstool of God.
>
> And Adam lived one hundred and thirty years, and *begat a son in his own likeness, after his own image,* and called his name Seth. (Moses 6:8–9)

Seth's resemblance to his father must have been extremely close because comments are made about it in two Doctrine and Covenants sections. Doctrine and Covenants 107:43 says Seth "was a perfect man, and his likeness was the express likeness of his father, insomuch that he seemed to be like unto his father in all things, and could be distinguished from him only by his age." And their similar appearance was even remarked upon in President Joseph F. Smith's vision of the redemption of the dead, which speaks of "Seth, one of the mighty ones, who was in the express image of his father, Adam" (D&C 138:40).

But what of Seth's age and family relationships? Adam was 130 years old when he fathered Seth (Genesis 5:3). Then, "the days of Adam after he had begotten Seth were eight hundred years: and he begat sons and daughters: And all the days that Adam lived were nine hundred and thirty years: and he died" (Genesis 5:4–5). So it appears that in addition to the brothers and sisters born prior to his birth, Seth also had younger brothers and sisters. That must have been quite a family!

Adam lived 930 years. Seth lived 912 years. Since Adam was 130 when Seth was born, Seth and Adam were both on the earth for 800 years before Adam died; then Seth lingered on earth another 112 years before he passed through the veil of death (Genesis 5:3–7).

GOD APPEARS TO SETH

Moses 6:3 reports that "God revealed himself unto Seth." Few statements in the scriptures can surpass this one for being one of the greatest understatements of all time! The outcome of this heavenly visit, however, is reported, for the same verse records that Seth "rebelled not, but offered an acceptable sacrifice, like unto his brother Abel."

SETH'S FAMILY AND DESCENDANTS

That same verse, Moses 6:3, also records concerning Seth that "to him also was born a son, and he called his name Enos." Presumably, then, the birth of Enos followed shortly after the Lord's appearance to his father. It is not known if Enos was Seth's firstborn child—what is known is that the patriarchal priesthood line continued through Enos. The book of Genesis records that "Seth lived an hundred and five years, and begat Enos: And Seth lived after he begat Enos eight hundred and seven years, and begat sons and daughters: And all the days of Seth were nine hundred and twelve years: and he died" (Genesis 5:6–8).

Clearly, Seth was the father of several, perhaps many children, though their names are not recorded in the scriptures. The scriptures also fail to indicate what his wife was named. Perhaps, during the course of nine centuries, he had more than one wife.

Who were Seth's grandchildren? The Genesis 5 account lists eight generations of his descendants who were born during Seth's lifetime:

1. Seth was 105 when he begat his son, Enos.
2. He was 195 when his grandson, Cainan, was born.
3. He was 265 when his great-grandson, Mahalaleel, came into the world.
4. He was 330 when his great, great-grandson, Jared, arrived.
5. He was 492 when his great, great, great-grandson, Enoch was born

(but he died about ten years before Enoch and his city were taken to heaven).

6. His great, great, great, great-grandson, Methuselah, was born when he was 557 years old.

7. He was 664 when his great, great, great, great, great-grandson, Lamech, was born.

8. He was 846 when his great, great, great, great, great, great-grandson, Noah, was born. However, he died about 534 years before the great flood, which occurred during the 600th year of Noah's life (see Genesis 7:11).

READING AND WRITING IN THE LANGUAGE OF ADAM

The Lord's appearance to Seth apparently motivated him to raise up a righteous posterity, for the next verse in the book of Moses account, after telling of the Lord's appearance and then the birth of Enos, records that "then began these men to call upon the name of the Lord, and the Lord blessed them" (Moses 6:4).

The following verses then report and explain an event of great significance to the world: the advent of literacy—the ability to read and write. They state that

> A *book of remembrance* was kept, in the which was recorded, *in the language of Adam*, for it was given unto as many as called upon God *to write by the spirit of inspiration;*
>
> And *by them their children were taught to read and write*, having a language which was pure and undefiled. (Moses 6:5–6)

What a glorious blessing was granted to the righteous who were calling upon God! Ponder, if you will, how the ability to read and write and keep records and histories has blessed and altered the course of history. Few blessings upon mankind can be counted greater!

ORDINATIONS TO THE MELCHIZEDEK PRIESTHOOD

Much is explained about the higher priesthood—"the Holy Priesthood, after the Order of the Son of God" (D&C 107:3)—in section 107 of the Doctrine and Covenants. It is explained that "The order of this priesthood was confirmed to be handed down from father to son, and rightly belongs to the literal descendants of the chosen seed, to whom the promises were made. This order was instituted in the days of Adam, and came down by lineage" (D&C 107:40–41).

But before continuing the list of ordinations found in Doctrine and

Covenants section 107, a brief insert from Doctrine and Covenants section 84 is appropriate in this context. It says, "*Abel* . . . received the priesthood by the commandments of God, by the hand of his father Adam, who was the first man" (D&C 84:16). Abel was slain before Seth was born, so this ordination of necessity preceded the listing provided in Doctrine and Covenants 107. That section, however, gives many specific details about early ordinations. For instance, it explains that Seth "was ordained by Adam at the age of sixty-nine years" (D&C 107:42).

The same section indicates that Adam apparently reserved for himself the privilege of ordaining his descendants to the office of High Priest in the Melchizedek Priesthood. It relates that Adam not only ordained Seth, he also ordained his grandsons from the various descending generations to that same office. It shows that "Enos was ordained at the age of one hundred and thirty-four years and four months, by the hand of Adam" (D&C 107:44).

However, it appears that Adam did not ordain his great-grandson *Cainan*, for the record shows that "God called upon Cainan in the wilderness in the fortieth year of his age; and he met Adam in journeying to the place Shedolamak. He was eighty-seven years old when he received his ordination" (D&C 107:45). This may imply that God himself performed the ordination, or perhaps Seth could have ordained him.

But then, Adam was able to ordain his descendants in the next three generations:

> *Mahalaleel* was four hundred and ninety–six years and seven days old when he was ordained by the hand of Adam, who also blessed him.
>
> *Jared* was two hundred years old when he was ordained under the hand of Adam, who also blessed him.
>
> *Enoch* was twenty–five years old when he was ordained under the hand of Adam. . . .
>
> Methuselah was one hundred years old when he was ordained under the hand of Adam. (D&C 107:46–48, 50)

At that point the privilege of performing the ordinations passed from Adam to later generations. It was Seth who ordained Lamech when Lamech was only thirty-two years old (D&C 107:51). Then it was Methuselah who ordained Noah when Noah was only ten years old! (D&C 107:52).

It is presumed that it was Noah who ordained his son or sons, though the scriptures don't actually say so. It is known that Noah's son, Shem was "the great high priest" (D&C 138:41). The priesthood status of Japeth is unknown. It is also known that Noah blessed Ham, his son, "with the blessings of the earth, and with the blessings of wisdom, but *cursed him as pertaining to the Priesthood*" (Abraham 1:26; see verses 21–27).

One more word about Seth receiving the priesthood. Part of the explanation to Facsimile 2 in the book of Abraham contains these significant words:

> Fig. 3. Is made to represent God, sitting upon his throne, clothed with power and authority; with a crown of eternal light upon his head; representing also *the grand Key-words of the Holy Priesthood, as revealed to Adam in the Garden of Eden, as also to Seth, Noah, Melchizedek, Abraham, and all to whom the Priesthood was revealed.* (Abraham, Facsimile 2, Item 3)

SETH IN THE ADAM-ONDI-AHMAN
ADAM-AND-EVE FAMILY REUNION

Three years previous to his death, Adam called Seth, Enos, Cainan, Mahalaleel, Jared, Enoch, and Methuselah, who were all high priests, and also the residue of his posterity who were righteous, into the valley of Adam-ondi-Ahman and there bestowed upon them his last blessing (D&C 107:53–57). It's not known if Eve was still alive at this time, but those who gathered were her children and descendants.

It is presumed that at this reunion, Adam gave "patriarchal blessings" to his descendants who were gathered there. What blessings were spoken on the heads of the other attendees is not recorded in the present-day standard works of the Church, but Doctrine and Covenants section 107 contains a fragment of the blessing pronounced upon Seth. It reports that Seth "was blessed by him three years previous to his (Adam's) death, and received *the promise of God* by his father, that *his posterity should be the chosen of the Lord, and that they should be preserved unto the end of the earth; Because he [Seth] was a perfect man*" (D&C 107:42–43).

How choice it would be to receive a direct "promise of God" concerning one's posterity and one's own standing before God in this day and age! Truly Seth was, and remains, a remarkable and uniquely outstanding person among all of God's mortal children!

It is in this same locale that Adam, in his role as the Ancient of Days, will assemble the righteous from all generations in the glorious latter-day event foretold by the prophet Daniel (see Daniel 7:13–14, 21–22; D&C 78:15; 116:1; 117:8–11). Is it not probable that Seth will be the one to represent those of his generation?

SETH AMONG THE MIGHTY ONES
IN THE SPIRIT WORLD

On October 3, 1918—just a few weeks before the end of his long mortal ministry—the Prophet Joseph F. Smith was granted a glorious view of paradise and the spirit world between the time of the Savior's ignominious death on the cross and his glorious resurrection. In one portion of President Smith's vision, he reported that the prophets who had faithfully served their Lord Jehovah in the millennia prior to the meridian of time were together, awaiting their glorious resurrections. Among the great prophets seen there was "Seth, one of the mighty ones, who was in the express image of his father, Adam" (D&C 138:40). Seth's identification as "one of the mighty ones" is a fitting tribute to this great prophet who personally spoke with God.

Seth, Chosen Premortally, Is Now a Resurrected Being

As this chapter concludes, be sure to note two key concepts about these great men which President Smith reported in the vision mentioned above.

First, that they were among the noble and great ones chosen before the Creation of this earth and that they were trained and prepared to serve here on the earth (D&C 138:55–56). Clearly, Seth was one of these noble and great ones selected in premortality.

Second, note that the Lord gave them specific permission to partake of the resurrection immediately "after his resurrection," and "to enter into his Father's kingdom, there to be crowned with glory and eternal life, And continue thenceforth their labor as had been promised by the Lord, and be partakers of all blessings which were held in reserve for them that love him" (D&C 138:51–52; see also D&C 132:29).

It follows, then, that Seth has now been resurrected and crowned with glory, and that he is continuing his labors in a future phase of progression in the eternal kingdoms.

This author, and probably all of you readers, rejoices in his growth and glory! May we someday be found worthy to follow in his footsteps!

CHAPTER 3

ENOCH

BEFORE HIS TRANSLATION HE HAD THIS TESTIMONY, THAT HE PLEASED GOD

How interesting it is that so little is found in the Old Testament concerning this valiant Prophet of God! Of all the Prophets whose ministries are recorded or alluded to in the scriptures, he alone was caught up to heaven, with a city-full of righteous followers, to rule and reign in a heavenly Zion!

What a blessing it is to have 117 glorious verses in the Pearl of Great Price that reveal rich insights into his life and ministry! What a blessing it is to have some of his writings quoted in the New Testament, even though they aren't to be found today in the Old Testament writings of Moses. And what a blessing it is to have the words *"These things were all written in the book of Enoch, and are to be testified of in due time,"* which open additional avenues of knowledge concerning his labors (D&C 107:57).

ENOCH IN THE OLD TESTAMENT

Chapter 5, in the book of Genesis, begins with the words: "This is the book of the generations of Adam" (Genesis 5:1). That chapter lists a prophet from each of the first 11 generations of mankind: Adam, Seth, Enos, Cainan, Mahalaleel, Jared, Enoch, Methusaleh, Lamech, Noah, and Noah's three sons: Shem, Ham and Japheth. Enoch's was the seventh generation down from the Creation of this world.

The verses that span Enoch's relationships, from his birth through the birth of his son Methusaleh, are verses 18 through 24:

And Jared lived an hundred sixty and two years, and he begat *Enoch:*

And Jared lived after he begat Enoch eight hundred years, and begat sons and daughters:

And all the days of Jared were nine hundred sixty and two years: and he died.

And *Enoch lived sixty and five years, and begat Methuselah:*

And *Enoch walked with God after he begat Methuselah three hundred years, and begat sons and daughters:*

And all the days of Enoch were three hundred sixty and five years:

And Enoch walked with God: and he was not; for God took him. (Genesis 5:18–24. But see D&C 107:49.)

A little math indicates that Adam was 622 years old when Enoch was born, and he (Adam) died when Enoch was 308 years old.

ENOCH IN THE NEW TESTAMENT

There are three passages in the New Testament that make direct reference to Enoch.

1. Luke mentions him near the end in his genealogical listing of Christ's ancestry:

    Noe [Noah], which was the son of Lamech, Which was the son of Mathusala [Methusaleh], which was the son of *Enoch*, which was the son of Jared, which was the son of Maleleel [Mahalaleel], which was the son of Cainan, Which was the son of Enos, which was the son of Seth, which was the son of Adam, which was the son of God." (Luke 3:36–38)

2. The Apostle Paul, in the eleventh chapter of his Epistle to the Hebrews, records a great "roll call of faith," which begins with the Creation of this earth and moves forward through Old Testament history. He lists Enoch in proper chronological order, right between Abel and Noah:

    Through faith we understand that the worlds were framed by the word of God, so that things which are seen were not made of things which do appear.

    By faith *Abel* offered unto God a more excellent sacrifice than Cain, by which he obtained witness that he was righteous, God testifying of his gifts: and by it he being dead yet speaketh.

    By faith Enoch was translated that he should not see death; and was not found, because God had translated him: for before his translation he had this testimony, that he pleased God.

    But without faith it is impossible to please him: for he that cometh to God must believe that he is, and that he is a rewarder of them that diligently seek him.

    By faith *Noah*, being warned of God of things not seen as yet, moved with fear, prepared an ark to the saving of his house; by the which he condemned the world, and became heir of the righteousness which is by faith. (Hebrews 11:3–7)

3. A passage from Enoch's preaching is quoted in the book of Jude, even though those words are not included in the Old Testament. (They are, however, found in the non-canonical book of Enoch, about which more information will be provided later in this chapter.)

And *Enoch also, the seventh from Adam, prophesied of these, saying,* Behold, the Lord cometh with ten thousands of his saints,

To execute judgment upon all, and to convince all that are ungodly among them of all their ungodly deeds which they have ungodly committed, and of all their hard speeches which ungodly sinners have spoken against him. (Jude 1:14–15)

Though those who have studied the pseudepigraphal book of Enoch show dozens of New Testament passages that seem to have borrowed from or been influenced by that book, these are the only three direct allusions to the Prophet Enoch found in the New Testament.

ENOCH IN THE DOCTRINE AND COVENANTS

References are made to Enoch in six different sections of the Doctrine and Covenants. First, as the Savior begins section 38, he uses several verses to identify himself. In doing so, he alludes to the translation (taking to heaven) of Enoch and his Zion people:

Thus saith the Lord your God, even Jesus Christ, the Great I AM, Alpha and Omega, the beginning and the end, the same which looked upon the wide expanse of eternity, and all the seraphic hosts of heaven, before the world was made; . . .

I am the same which have taken the Zion of Enoch into mine own bosom; and verily, I say, even as many as have believed in my name, for I am Christ, and in mine own name, by the virtue of the blood which I have spilt, have *I pleaded before the Father for them.* (D&C 38:1, 4)

Second, another allusion to the city of Enoch being caught up into heaven is found in Section 45:

Wherefore, hearken ye together and let me show unto you even my wisdom—the wisdom of him whom ye say is *the God of Enoch, and his brethren,*

Who were separated from the earth, and were received unto myself—a city reserved until a day of righteousness shall come—a day which was sought for by all holy men. (D&C 45:11–12)

Third and fourth, there are three allusions to Enoch in Section 76, which speaks of the three degrees of glory. Two of them are mentioned when listing the rewards of those who will attain the celestial kingdom: they will be "priests of the Most High, *after the order of Melchizedek, which was after the order of Enoch,* which was after the order of the Only Begotten Son" (D&C 76:57). And also: "These are they who have come to an innumerable company of angels, *to the general assembly and church of Enoch,* and of the Firstborn" (D&C 76:67).

Fifth, the third reference in section 76 is in the context of those who will attain only the lowest, the telestial kingdom, indicating that some of those who won't receive the true gospel of Christ will assert they were followers of various earlier prophets:

> The glory of the telestial is one, even as the glory of the stars is one; for as one star differs from another star in glory, even so differs one from another in glory in the telestial world;
>
> For these are they who are of Paul, and of Apollos, and of Cephas.
>
> These are they who say they are some of one and some of another—some of Christ and some of John, and some of Moses, and some of Elias, and some of Esaias, and some of Isaiah, and *some of Enoch;*
>
> But received not the gospel, neither the testimony of Jesus, neither the prophets, neither the everlasting covenant. (D&C 76:98–101)

Sixth, the allusion to Enoch in section 84 is in a passage indicating the continuation of the priesthood in all the generations of this earth, showing the priesthood lineage of Abraham running back through Melchizedek and Noah:

> Abraham received the priesthood from Melchizedek, who received it through the lineage of his fathers, even till Noah;
>
> And *from Noah till Enoch,* through the lineage of their fathers;
>
> And *from Enoch to Abel,* who was slain by the conspiracy of his brother, who received the priesthood by the commandments of God, by the hand of his father Adam, who was the first man—
>
> Which priesthood continueth in the church of God in all generations, and is without beginning of days or end of years. (D&C 84:14–17)

Seventh, a more lengthy reference in section 107 adds significant insights about various aspects of Enoch's life: (1) his ordination by Adam to the priesthood while still in his youth (at a much younger age than Adam's other posterity); (2) Adam gave Enoch a special blessing when Enoch was sixty-five; (3) Enoch saw the Lord, then was "before his face continually" for 365 years, and (4) Enoch was 430 years old, (rather than 365 as reported in Genesis 5:23–24), when he was translated:

> *Enoch was twenty-five years old* when he was *ordained under the hand of Adam;* and he was sixty-five and Adam blessed him.
>
> And *he saw the Lord,* and he walked with him, and was before his face continually; and *he walked with God three hundred and sixty-five years,* making him *four hundred and thirty years old when he was translated.* (D&C 107:48–49)

Eighth, another section 107 allusion to Enoch is found in the account of the family reunion Adam hosted, at the age of 927, where he assembled his righteous posterity in the valley of Adam-ondi-Adam and granted them his final blessing: "Three years previous to the death of Adam, he called Seth, Enos, Cainan, Mahalaleel, Jared, *Enoch*, and Methuselah, who *were all high priests*, with the residue of his posterity who were righteous, into the valley of Adam-ondi-Ahman, and *there bestowed upon them his last blessing*" (D&C 107:53). More details were reported in the following verses, and they are cited elsewhere in this book.

Ninth, of special significance in this modern-day revelation is a unique allusion to a non-canonical book, suggesting that the writings of that book will come forth at a future date: "These things were all written in the book of Enoch, and are to be testified of in due time" (D&C 107:57).

Tenth, the last Doctrine and Covenants passage alluding to Enoch is included in the extensive list of valiant prophets who lived prior to the meridian of time, and who apparently were resurrected at the time of Christ's resurrection. This list is found in section 133 and says:

> Now the year of my redeemed is come; . . .
>
> In all their afflictions he was afflicted. And the angel of his presence saved them; and in his love, and in his pity, he redeemed them, and bore them, and carried them all the days of old;
>
> Yea, and *Enoch* also, and *they who were with him; the prophets who were before him*; and *Noah* also, and *they who were before him*; and *Moses also, and they who were before him*;
>
> And from *Moses to Elijah*, and from *Elijah to John, who were with Christ in his resurrection, and the holy apostles, with Abraham, Isaac, and Jacob, shall be in the presence of the Lamb.*
>
> And the graves of the saints shall be opened; and they shall come forth and stand on the right hand of the Lamb, when he shall stand upon Mount Zion, and upon the holy city, the New Jerusalem; and they shall sing the song of the Lamb, day and night forever and ever. (D&C 133:52–56. See also D&C 138:38–52.)

ENOCH IN THE PEARL OF GREAT PRICE

Chapters 6 and 7 of the book of Moses provide a wondrous supply of additional information about the life and ministry of the Prophet Enoch. The verses in these two chapters will be considered in sections. Since the doctrinal information in some of them is so extensive, so interwoven, and so complex, some of the verses in these two chapters will be provided in list form so that each doctrinal item can be highlighted.

Enoch's Family and Upbringing. Much is said in only a few words about the way Enoch was raised and nurtured. The scripture says that "Jared lived one hundred and sixty-two years, and *begat Enoch*; and Jared lived, after he begat Enoch, *eight hundred years*, and begat sons and daughters. And *Jared taught Enoch in all the ways of God"* (Moses 6:21). It isn't known if Enoch was Jared's first-born child—he probably wasn't, if his father was 162 years old when Enoch was born. Most likely Enoch had younger brothers and sisters. How many? The passage doesn't say.

The most important element of the verse is that "Jared taught Enoch in all the ways of God." And he apparently served as mentor to his son, for Jared's 800 remaining years on earth lasted far beyond the 430 years Enoch was on the earth before being caught up to heaven. (See again D&C 107:49.)

Additional information is learned from the next two verses of Moses chapter 6:

> This is the genealogy of *the sons of Adam, who was the son of God, with whom God, himself, conversed.*
>
> And *they were preachers of righteousness, and spake and prophesied,* and called upon all men, everywhere, to repent; and *faith was taught unto the children of men.* (Moses 6:22–23)

Enoch was the seventh generation down from Adam. By the time he came to earth, Adam had guided those of his children who would listen and follow him into the paths of righteous. They were actively preaching, trying to lead their brothers and sisters, aunts and uncles back to the presence of God. They were "preachers of righteousness," and "faith was taught unto the children of men." Indeed, the Lord himself called Enoch's grandfather and their righteous forefathers back to Adam "my servants, thy fathers" (Moses 6:30).

Enoch's Call to the Ministry: The Lord Spoke to Him from Heaven. Moses 6:26–30 tells of the revelation he received from the voice of God, calling him into active missionary service:

> And it came to pass that Enoch journeyed in the land, among the people; and as he journeyed, *the Spirit of God descended out of heaven, and abode upon him.*
>
> And he heard a voice from heaven, saying: *Enoch, my son, prophesy unto this people,* and say unto them—*Repent, for thus saith the Lord: I am angry with this people,* and my fierce anger is kindled against them; for their hearts have waxed hard, and their ears are dull of hearing, and their eyes cannot see afar off;
>
> And for these many generations, *ever since the day that I created them, have they gone astray, and have denied me,* and have sought their own counsels in the dark; and in their own abominations have they devised murder, and *have not kept the commandments, which I gave unto their father, Adam.*
>
> Wherefore, they have foresworn themselves, and, by their oaths, *they*

have brought upon themselves death; and a hell I have prepared for them, if they repent not. (Moses 6:26–29)

Enoch's Reverential but Timid Reply—I Am But a Lad. And how did Enoch respond to the Lord's call? "When Enoch had heard these words, *he bowed himself to the earth, before the Lord,* and spake before the Lord, saying: Why is it that I have found favor in thy sight, and am but a lad, and all the people hate me; for I am slow of speech; wherefore am I thy servant?" (Moses 6:31).

Enoch's reply was not unlike others who followed after him centuries later:

+ Moses: "Who am I, that I should go unto Pharaoh, and that I should bring forth the children of Israel out of Egypt?" (Exodus 3:11). "But, behold, they will not believe me, nor hearken unto my voice: for they will say, The LORD hath not appeared unto thee" (Exodus 4:1). "O my Lord, *I am not eloquent,* neither heretofore, nor since thou hast spoken unto thy servant: but *I am slow of speech, and of a slow tongue*" (Exodus 4:10).

+ Isaiah: "Woe is me! for I am undone; because *I am a man of unclean lips,* and I dwell in the midst of a people of unclean lips" (Isaiah 6:5).

+ Jeremiah: "Then said I, Ah, Lord GOD! behold, *I cannot speak: for I am a child*" (Jeremiah 1:6).

The Lord's Promises to Enoch if He Would Accept His Call. When calling Enoch to the ministry, numerous blessings were promised to him, including: (1) protection, (2) speaking ability and assistance, (3) the Spirit, (4) the justifying of his words, (5) control over mountains and rivers, and finally (6) that the Lord would abide in him and walk with him. Rich promises, indeed!

> the Lord said unto Enoch: Go forth and do as I have commanded thee, and *no man shall pierce thee.* Open thy mouth, and it shall be filled, and *I will give thee utterance,* for all flesh is in my hands, and I will do as seemeth me good.
>
> Say unto this people: Choose ye this day, to serve the Lord God who made you.
>
> Behold *my Spirit is upon you,* wherefore *all thy words will I justify;* and the *mountains shall flee before you, and the rivers shall turn from their course;* and *thou shalt abide in me, and I in you;* therefore *walk with me.* (Moses 6:32–34)

How Old Was Enoch When Called to the Ministry? This question can't be answered with certainty. Note, however, his response that he was "but a lad." Could he have been only twenty-five when the Lord called him, making that the reason Adam ordained him to the priesthood at so young an age? (See again D&C 107:48.)

Or was chronological order being followed when Moses 6:25 states that "Enoch lived sixty–five years, and begat Methuselah" before recording the Lord's call to Enoch (6:26–30) and Enoch's response and acceptance? (6:31–34). Could his call have come the same year Methuselah was born, which occasioned another blessing being pronounced by Adam upon Enoch's head? (See again D&C 107:48.)

Enoch's Vision of All Created Spirits and Other Unseen Things. It's not clear if this vision was granted to Enoch immediately after his acceptance of his mission call or sometime thereafter. However, the next verse after the Lord's promises to Enoch were listed says, "The Lord spake unto Enoch, and said unto him: Anoint thine eyes with clay, and wash them, and thou shalt see" (Moses 6:35).

Enoch did so and received a glorious vision or visions. The scripture reports that "*he beheld the spirits that God had created; and he beheld also things which were not visible to the natural eye*" (Moses 6:36). That choice vision undoubtedly gave Enoch great knowledge—a vast array of profound understandings.

Who knows how others learned of his experience, but they did, and the word soon circulated abroad in the land that "A seer hath the Lord raised up unto his people" (Moses 6:36).

Enoch's Preaching Upon the Hills and High Places. As he ranged across the land, preaching to the tent-keepers, their immediate response was that "There is a strange thing in the land; a wild man hath come among us," and though some "were offended" as he testified against their works, yet "fear came on all them that heard him; for *he walked with God.*"

> And it came to pass that Enoch went forth in the land, among the people, standing upon the hills and the high places, and cried with a loud voice, testifying against their works; and all men were offended because of him.
>
> And they came forth to hear him, upon the high places, saying unto the tent–keepers: Tarry ye here and keep the tents, while we go yonder to *behold the seer,* for *he prophesieth,* and there is a strange thing in the land; a wild man hath come among us.
>
> And it came to pass when they heard him, no man laid hands on him; for fear came on all them that heard him; for *he walked with God.* (Moses 6:37–39)

Enoch's Answer to Mahijah's Questions. When a man named Mahijah asked him to "Tell us plainly who thou art, and from whence thou comest," Enoch replied with words that told of his personal background and the vision in which he received his mission call. He indicated that (1) he came from a land of righteousness, (2) his father taught him in all the ways of God, (3) in his vision he saw the heavens, (4) the Lord gave him commandments, and (5) he was preaching in order to keep those commandments:

> And there came a man unto him, whose name was Mahijah, and said unto him: Tell us plainly who thou art, and from whence thou comest?
>
> And he said unto them: *I came out from the land of Cainan*, the land of my fathers, *a land of righteousness* unto this day. And *my father taught me in all the ways of God*.
>
> And it came to pass, as I journeyed from the land of Cainan, by the sea east, I beheld a vision; and lo, *the heavens I saw*, and *the Lord spake with me, and gave me commandment*; wherefore, for this cause, *to keep the commandment, I speak forth these words*. (Moses 6:40–42)

Was Enoch Preaching in the Land That Is Present-day Israel? It is important to remember that these events are all occurring hundreds of years before the days of Noah and the great flood. There's no realistic way of knowing what the contours of the lands on this earth were at that time. Nor is it known for sure whether the earth was still in the vicinity of Kolob, in transit to its present location, or situated here where it is now.

Cainan was Enoch's great-grandfather, and the land of Cainan may have been where his descendants were living.

Yes, modern Israel is superimposed over the ancient land of Canaan, but that land has no "sea east"—just the Mediterranean Sea to its west. The ancient "land of Cainan" is neither the same land nor location as the "land of Israel" is today.

ENOCH'S SERMON ABOUT ADAM, THE FALL, AND THE ATONEMENT

The query posed by Mahijah, above, apparently was posed as Enoch was beginning a profound sermon about the Creation and the effects of the Fall of Adam. Since almost every verse adds another valuable doctrinal insight, his discourse will be handled in a different manner, with verse-by-verse analysis, as follows:

1. Enoch's Lord is the God of Heaven (Moses 6:43).
2. Why Deny the God of Heaven? (Moses 6:43).
3. God made the heavens, the earth, and man (Moses 6:44).
4. Death came upon our fathers (Moses 6:45).
5. We know our fathers, and Adam (Moses 6:45).

6. A book of remembrance was written, in their own language (Moses 6:46).

7. God provided the pattern for the book of remembrance (Moses 6:46).

8. The people couldn't stand in Enoch's presence (Moses 6:47).

9. Man exists because of Adam's Fall (Moses 6:48).

10. The Fall brought death, misery, and woe (Moses 6:48).

11. Satan came among men and tempted them to worship him (Moses 6:49).

12. Men became carnal, devilish, and shut out from God (Moses 6:49).

13. All men must repent (Moses 6:50).

14. God spoke to Adam in his own voice (Moses 6:51).

15. God made the world and premortal man (Moses 6:51).

16. Believe, repent, be baptized, receive the Holy Ghost (Moses 6:52).

17. God's Only Begotten Son, full of grace and truth, is Jesus Christ (Moses 6:52).

18. Jesus Christ is the only name that brings salvation (Moses 6:52).

19. Ask in Christ's name and you will receive (Moses 6:52).

20. Adam's question: why must man repent? (Moses 6:53).

21. Adam was forgiven for the Fall while still in the Garden of Eden (Moses 6:53).

22. The Son of God atoned for original sin (Moses 6:54).

23. Children aren't responsible for their parents' sins ((Moses 6:54).

24. Children are whole from the foundation of the world (Moses 6:54).

25. As children grow up, sin comes into their hearts (Moses 6:55).

26. We must taste bitter to know good (Moses 6:55).

27. Knowing good from evil makes men free agents (Moses 6:56).

28. Another commandment: teach your children (Moses 6:56–57).

29. Men must repent or they can't inherit God's kingdom (Moses 6:57).

30. No unclean thing can dwell in God's presence (Moses 6:57).

31. God the Father's name is Man of Holiness (Moses 6:57).

32. Jesus Christ is the Son of Man (Moses 6:57).

33. Jesus will be a righteous judge in the meridian of time (Moses 6:57).

34. Teach gospel principles freely to your children (Moses 6:58).

35. Transgression brought the Fall and death (Moses 6:59).

36. Combining water, blood, spirit, and dust made man a living soul (Moses 6:59).

37. One must be born again into the kingdom of heaven (Moses 6:59).

38. We must be cleansed by the blood of Christ and sanctified from sin (Moses 6:59).

39. Enjoy words and eternal life (Moses 6:59).

40. Keep the commandments, be justified, sanctified (Moses 6:60).

41. The Comforter is to abide in you (Moses 6:61).
42. Many qualities of the Comforter (Moses 6:61).
43. The plan of salvation is through Christ (Moses 6:62).
44. All things bear witness of God (Moses 6:63).
45. Adam was baptized (Moses 6:64–65).
46. Adam was born of the spirit and quickened (Moses 6:65).
47. Baptism by the Holy Ghost is the record of the Father and Son (Moses 6:66).
48. Adam held the priesthood (Moses 6:67).
49. Becoming a son of Christ is to be one in Him (Moses 6:68).
50. Many believed and became sons of God (Moses 7:1).
51. Those who die in their sins fear the wrath of God (Moses 7:1).

Enoch Talked with the Lord
Face to Face and Viewed Future Events

Following his great discourse on Adam and the Fall, "Enoch began to prophesy" (Moses 7:2), and he also testified of a face-to-face interview with the Lord and a view of world events for many future generations:

> As I was journeying, and stood upon the place Mahujah, and cried unto the Lord, there came a voice out of heaven, saying—Turn ye, and get ye upon the mount Simeon.
>
> And it came to pass that I turned and went up on the mount; and as I stood upon the mount, *I beheld the heavens open, and I was clothed upon with glory;*
>
> And *I saw the Lord; and he stood before my face, and he talked with me, even as a man talketh one with another, face to face;* and he said unto me: Look, and I will show unto thee the world for the space of many generations. (Moses 7:2–4)

Note several key concepts found in these verses:

1. His vision came in response to his prayer (Moses 7:2).
2. When he beheld the heavens open, he was clothed upon with glory (Moses 7:3), perhaps to enable his physical body to stand in the presence of God.
3. Enoch was privileged to converse with the Lord face to face (Moses 7:4).
4. The Lord elected to show Enoch the events of coming generations, as a preparation for his responsibility to call the people to repentance and to baptize them (Moses 7:4, 10–11).

Enoch's vision of future events in the lands of Shum and Canaan. As his vision continued, Enoch was shown the people of Shum and then various events which would affect the people of Canaan: their destroying all the people of Shum, their splitting into divisions upon their own land, their land becoming barren because it would be cursed with much heat, and a blackness eventually coming upon the people of Canaan, which would make them despised among all people:

> And it came to pass that I beheld in the valley of Shum, and lo, a great people which dwelt in tents, which were the people of Shum.
>
> And again the Lord said unto me: Look; and I looked towards the north, and I beheld the people of Canaan, which dwelt in tents.
>
> And *the Lord said unto me: Prophesy; and I prophesied,* saying: Behold the people of Canaan, which are numerous, shall go forth in battle array against the people of Shum, and shall slay them that they shall utterly be destroyed; and the people of Canaan shall divide themselves in the land, and the land shall be barren and unfruitful, and none other people shall dwell there but the people of Canaan;
>
> For behold, *the Lord shall curse the land with much heat,* and the barrenness thereof shall go forth forever; and there was *a blackness came upon all the children of Canaan, that they were despised among all people.* (Moses 7:5–8)

Enoch was commanded to proselytize in seven lands. The next three verses were specific instructions as to where and how Enoch was to preach the gospel:

> And it came to pass that the Lord said unto me: Look; and I looked, and I beheld the *land of Sharon,* and the *land of Enoch,* and the *land of Omner,* and the *land of Heni,* and the *land of Shem,* and the *land of Haner,* and the *land of Hanannihah,* and all the inhabitants thereof;
>
> And the Lord said unto me: *Go to this people, and say unto them—Repent, lest I come out and smite them with a curse, and they die.*
>
> And he gave unto me a commandment that *I should baptize in the name of the Father, and of the Son, which is full of grace and truth, and of the Holy Ghost, which beareth record of the Father and the Son.* (Moses 7:9–11)

His call, at that time, was to preach in seven different communities, probably named after the individuals who originally settled them. His message was to deliver a severe warning: repent or God will smite you with a fatal curse. He was commanded to baptize in the name of the three members of the Godhead: God the Father, God the Son, and God the Holy Ghost.

Moses 7:11 is unique in that it is one of the earliest passages, after the Creation accounts, referring to all three members of the Godhead together.

And Enoch was obedient to the commandment. The following verse indicates "it came to pass that Enoch continued to call upon all the people, save it were the people of Canaan, to repent" (Moses 7:12).

ENOCH'S POWER OVER THE ELEMENTS IN DEFENSE OF THE PEOPLE OF GOD

Enoch's preaching caused a separation between his converts—the righteous people of God—and the wicked who rejected the gospel and became enemies of the people of God: "So great was the faith of Enoch that *he led the people of God, and their enemies came to battle against them.*" (Moses 7:13). Then, the following verses detail some of the tremendous powers that were exerted through Enoch to protect his followers:

1. Earthquakes in response to Enoch's commands (Moses 7:13).
2. Mountains were moved in obedience to Enoch's commands (Moses 7:13).
3. Rivers' courses were altered (Moses 7:13).
4. Wild beasts responded to his commands (Moses 7:13).
5. All nations feared the word of God manifested through Enoch (Moses 7:13).
6. Enemies of the people of God fled to a land thrust up in the sea (Moses 7:14).
7. Giants of the land avoided the people of God (Moses 7:15).
8. A curse upon the enemies of God; there was bloodshed among them (Moses 7:15–16).

ENOCH BUILT ZION, THE CITY OF HOLINESS

Now, back to the account of Enoch gathering out the people of God while their enemies fought against them. The following passage deserves verse-by-verse treatment:

1. Wars and bloodshed occured among the enemies of God (Moses 7:16).
2. The Lord came and dwelt with his people (Moses 7:16).
3. All nations feared the Lord because His glory was upon His people (Moses 7:17). Was this a visible shining, as the Israelites experienced in Moses' day? (See Exodus 10:23; 13:21–22; 14:20, 24; Numbers 14:14; Nehemiah 9:12, 19.)
4. The Lord blessed the people and they flourished (Moses 7:17). Does blessing the people upon the mountains indicate temple worship? The term "mountain of the Lord" has temple connotations: see Isaiah 2:2–3; Micah 4:1–2; Zechariah 8:3. If Enoch's followers were sufficiently righteous to be caught up to heaven, it would seem plausible that they partook of temple experiences while here on the earth.
5. The Lord called His people Zion (Moses 7:18).

6. Enoch built a city called the City of Holiness (Moses 7:19).
7. The Lord said Zion is blessed, others are cursed (Moses 7:20).

Enoch's Vision of All Earth's Inhabitants

Beginning with verse 21, this chapter changes from reporting historical conditions to detailing a glorious vision given by the Lord unto Enoch:

1. Enoch saw all earth's inhabitants (Moses 7:21).
2. Zion was taken into heaven (Moses 7:21).
3. Zion is to be the Lord's abode forever (Moses 7:21).
4. The seed of Cain were black, living apart (Moses 7:22).
5. Enoch was caught up to heaven (Moses 7:23–24).
6. Satan's power was upon all the earth (Moses 7:23–24).
7. Angels pronounced woes upon earth's inhabitants (Moses 7:25).
8. Satan veiled the whole earth with darkness, his angels rejoiced (Moses 7:26).
9. Angels bearing testimony descended from heaven (Moses 7:27).
10. Many were caught up into Zion (Moses 7:27).
11. The God of heaven wept over the wickedness of the people (Moses 7:28).
12. Enoch asked how God can weep (Moses 7:28–29).
13. Enoch commented on the millions of God's creations (Moses 7:30).
14. Enoch commented on God's qualities (Moses 7:30).
15. God has taken Zion to his bosom from all his creations, throughout eternity (Moses 7:31).
16. God's peace, justice, truth, and mercy (Moses 7:31).
17. God gave men knowledge as he created them (Moses 7:32).
18. God gave man [Adam] agency in the Garden of Eden (Moses 7:32).
19. God has commanded man to love one another and choose him (Moses 7:33).
20. Men are without affection; they hate their own relations (Moses 7:33).
21. God's indignation and anger is against them (Moses 7:34).
22. God will send in floods against them (Moses 7:34). Note that this statement from God to Enoch is made more than a thousand years before the flood in Noah's day.
23. God identifies Himself as Man of Holiness (Moses 7:35).
24. God can behold all His creations (Moses 7:36).
25. Earth's inhabitants are more wicked than any of God's other creations (Moses 7:36).
26. Their sins shall be upon their fathers (Moses 7:37).
27. Satan shall be their father and misery their doom (Moses 7:37).
28. All God's creations shall weep over them (Moses 7:37).

29. Shouldn't the heavens weep about what they will suffer? (Moses 7:37).
30. Those Enoch saw in vision will perish in the floods (Moses 7:38).
31. God will shut them up in a prison (Moses 7:38).
32. Christ has pled for mankind before God the Father (Moses 7:39).
33. Christ will suffer for men's sins if they will repent (Moses 7:39).
34. They shall be in torment until Christ returns to the Father (Moses 7:39). Concerning Christ's return to the Father, see Doctrine and Covenants 76:106–108.
35. The heavens and all God's workmanship weep for man's wickedness (Moses 7:40).
36. The Lord showed Enoch the wickedness of man, and he wept (Moses 7:41).
37. Enoch saw that Noah would build an ark to save his posterity (Moses 7:42–43).
38. Enoch saw the Lord would protect the ark (Moses 7:43).
39. Enoch saw the floods would swallow up the wicked (Moses 7:43).
40. Enoch wept for the wicked and refused to be comforted (Moses 7:44).
41. The Lord told Enoch to be glad and look (Moses 7:44).
42. Enoch, seeing all the families of the earth descended from Noah, asked when the Savior would come and his blood be shed (Moses 7:45).
43. Christ's shedding of His blood will enable those that mourn to be sanctified (Moses 7:45).
44. The Lord's meridian-of-time coming would be in days of wickedness (Moses 7:46).
45. Enoch rejoiced when he saw Christ's coming in vision (Moses 7:47).
46. Enoch recognized Christ's death was anticipated premortally (Moses 7:47).
47. Enoch recognized that through faith he would be with the Father and Zion (Moses 7:47).
48. Enoch heard the earth, a living entity, mourning (Moses 7:48).
49. Enoch plead with God to have compassion upon the earth (Moses 7:49).
50. Enoch asked God to never again cover the earth by floods (Moses 7:50).
51. God covenanted that He would stay (not repeat) the floods (Moses 7:51).
52. God decreed that a remnant of Noah's posterity would always be on the earth (Moses 7:52).
53. Blessed would be the forefathers of Jesus (Moses 7:53).
54. Those who come to Christ through the gate shall never fall (Moses 7:53).
55. Enoch asked if the earth will rest when Christ comes (Moses 7:54).
56. Enoch was shown Christ on the cross (Moses 7:55).
57. Enoch saw the first resurrection (Moses 7:56).

58. Some spirits will come forth (in the first resurrection): others are reserved (until the second resurrection) till the final judgment (Moses 7:57).
59. Enoch asked if Christ will return to the earth (Moses 7:58–59).
60. Enoch's right to a throne was not of himself, but through grace (Moses 7:59).
61. Christ will come to earth in the last days of wickedness to fulfill His oath (Moses 7:60).
62. Before the earth rests (in the millennium), there will be darkness and shaking (Moses 7:61).
63. God's people will be preserved in that day of tribulations (Moses 7:61).
64. Righteousness from heaven and truth from the earth will testify of the Savior (Moses 7:62).
65. Righteousness will sweep the earth to gather the Lord's elect (Moses 7:62).
66. The righteous will be gathered to an Holy City: a New Jerusalem (Moses 7:62).
67. Enoch and his city shall receive the righteous in the New Jerusalem (Moses 7:63).
68. People from all the creations will join the Lord in his abode: Zion (Moses 7:64).
69. The earth shall rest for a thousand years (Moses 7:64).
70. The Lord will dwell on the earth a thousand years (Moses 7:65).
71. There will be great tribulations before the Lord's coming (Moses 7:66).
72. The Lord showed Enoch all things until the end of the world (Moses 7:67).
73. The mortal days of Zion were 365 years before the city was translated (Moses 7:68–69).

INSIGHTS FROM THE JOSEPH SMITH TRANSLATION CONCERNING THE RETURN OF THE CITY OF ZION

A passage in the Joseph Smith Translation of the Bible adds insights on the city of Enoch in the last days. The passage is in the context of Genesis 9:16–17, in which the Lord is speaking to Noah following the abatement of the great flood. It comments on the covenant that the Lord had previously made with Enoch, and it speaks of the general assembly of the church of the first-born descending from heaven at a future time (In the passage cited below, the additions to the Bible passage are shown in italics.) It says,

> And the bow shall be in the cloud; and I will look upon it, that I may remember the everlasting covenant, *which I made unto thy father Enoch; that, when men should keep all my commandments, Zion should again come on the*

earth, the city of Enoch which I have caught up unto myself.

And this is mine everlasting covenant, that when thy posterity shall embrace the truth, and look upward, then shall Zion look downward, and all the heavens shall shake with gladness, and the earth shall tremble with joy;

And the general assembly of the church of the first-born shall come down out of heaven, and possess the earth, and shall have place until the end come. And this is mine everlasting covenant, which I made with thy father Enoch.

And the bow shall be in the cloud, and I will establish my covenant unto thee, which I have made between *me* and *thee*, for every living creature of all flesh that *shall be* upon the earth.

And God said unto Noah, This is the token of the covenant which I have established between me and *thee; for* all flesh that *shall be* upon the earth. (Joseph Smith Translation, Genesis 9:21–25. Compare Genesis 9:16–17)

ITEMS AND INSIGHTS FROM THE BOOK OF ENOCH

The Lord, speaking in section 107 of the Doctrine and Covenants, alluded to a great reunion held by Adam and his righteous posterity at Adam-ondi-Ahman. A partial description of the event was given, but the description ended with the postscript: "These things were all written in the book of Enoch, and are to be testified of in due time" (D&C 107:57).

So, exactly what is the book of Enoch? A Google search for "book of Enoch" brings up hundreds of commentaries on the book: its origins, its text, items of controversy, and so on.

A representative sample that provides some historical background is cited here in slightly edited form:

> We first learn of Enoch in Genesis 5, but it leaves us with questions. Hebrews 11 has the answers, and Jude quotes Enoch! How did Jude come to know the words of Enoch? They are not in the Bible. The answer of course, is The Book of Enoch—a book which is actually quoted by Jude in the New Testament. What is the Book of Enoch, and where did it come from?
>
> Enoch was the great-grandfather of Noah. The Book of Enoch chapter 68:1 states: "And after that my great-grandfather Enoch gave me all the secrets in the book and in the parables which had been given to him, and he put them together for me in the words of the book of the parables."
>
> The Book of Enoch was extant centuries before the birth of Christ and yet is considered by many to be more Christian in its theology than Jewish. It was considered scripture by many early Christians. The earliest literature of the so-called "Church Fathers" is filled with references to this mysterious book:
>
> + The early second century "Epistle of Barnabus" makes much use of the Book of Enoch.

- Second and Third Century "Church Fathers" like Justin Martyr, Irenaeus, Origin and Clement of Alexandria all make use of the Book of Enoch.
- Tertullian (160–230 C.E) called the Book of Enoch "Holy Scripture."
- The Ethiopic Church added the Book of Enoch to its official canon.
- It was widely known and read the first three centuries after Christ.
- This and many other books became discredited after the Roman Catholic Council of Laodecia in AD 363–64. Being rejected from the canon and under ban of the authorities, it afterwards gradually passed out of circulation.

At about the time of the Protestant Reformation, there came to be a renewed interest in the Book of Enoch which had long since been lost to the modern world. By the late 1400s rumors began to spread that somewhere a copy of the long lost Book of Enoch might still exist. During this time many books arose claiming to be the long lost book and were later found to be forgeries.

The return of the Book of Enoch to the modern western world is credited to the famous explorer James Bruce, who in 1773 returned from six years in Abyssinia with three Ethiopic copies of the lost book.

In 1821 Richard Laurence published the first English translation. The famous R.H. Charles edition was published in 1912.

In the following years several portions of the Greek text surfaced. Then, with the discovery of cave four of the Dead Sea Scrolls, seven fragmentary copies of the Aramaic text were discovered.

There are scholars who believe the Book of Enoch was published before the Christian era by some great unknown of Semitic race, who believing himself to be inspired in a post-prophetic age, borrowed the name of an antediluvian patriarch to authenticate his own enthusiastic forecast of the coming Messiah.

The Book of Enoch is divided into five basic parts, but it is The book of Parables (37–71) which gives scholars the most trouble for it is primarily concerned with a figure called "the messiah"; "the righteous one"; "the chosen one" and "the son of man."[1]

Various other sources written about the book of Enoch list over one hundred New Testament passages that seem to have been drawn from, or influenced by that book. It seems clear that the book of Enoch was in wide

---

1. "The book of Enoch," *The Reluctant Messenger.* http://reluctant-messenger.com/enoch.htm.

Further background information concerning The book of Enoch is provided in this website posting. This author has no link nor affiliation with this source.

circulation during New Testament times, that it was regarded as a sacred document, and that it influenced some of the authors of New Testament books and epistles in their concepts and phraseology.

Most scholars who write about the book of Enoch manuscripts which have been found during the past two centuries regard them as *pseudepigrapha*: a Greek word meaning "falsely superscribed," or "written under a pen name." Old Testament pseudepigrapha fall under the same general category as the Apocrypha: sacred books of the Jewish people that were not included in the Hebrew Bible. Section 91 of the Doctrine and Covenants deals with such books, as follows:

> Verily, thus saith the Lord unto you concerning the *Apocrypha*—There are many things contained therein that are true, and it is mostly translated correctly;
>
> There are many things contained therein that are not true, which are interpolations by the hands of men.
>
> Verily, I say unto you, that it is not needful that the Apocrypha should be translated.
>
> Therefore, whoso readeth it, let him understand, for the Spirit manifesteth truth;
>
> And whoso is enlightened by the Spirit shall obtain benefit therefrom;
>
> And whoso receiveth not by the Spirit, cannot be benefited. Therefore it is not needful that it should be translated. Amen. (D&C 91:1–6)

With those insights given by revelation to the Prophet Joseph Smith, only a few passages from the book of Enoch will be mentioned here. First, Enoch tells of being summoned to the throne of God and tries to describe God's glory, which he perceives as tongues of fire:

> In the vision *I saw clouds that invited and summoned me into a mist*, and the course of the stars and the flashes of lightning, and hurried me and drove me,
>
> And the winds in the vision caused me to fly and lifted me up, and bore me into heaven. And I went in until *I drew near to a wall which was built out of crystals and surrounded by tongues of fire*, and it began to frighten me.
>
> *I went into the tongues of fire and drew near a large house which was built of crystals: and the walls of the house were like a mosaic of hailstones and the floor was made of crystals like snow.*
>
> Its ceiling was like the path of the stars and lightning flashes, and between them were fiery cherubim,
>
> Their sky was clear as water. *A flaming fire surrounded the walls, and its doors blazed with fire.*
>
> I entered that house, and it was hot as fire and cold as ice; there were

no pleasures or life therein: fear covered me, and trembling got hold of me.

As I shook and trembled, I fell on my face.

And *I saw a vision,* And lo! there was a second house, greater than the first,

And then all the doors stood open before me, and it was built of flames of fire. And in every respect it was splendid and magnificent to the extent that I cannot describe it to you.

Its floor was of fire, and above it was lightning and the path of the stars, and its ceiling also was flaming fire.

And *I looked and saw a throne set on high,* its appearance was like crystal, and its wheels were like a shining sun, and there was the vision of cherubim.

And *from underneath the throne came rivers of fire* so that I could not look at it.

And *He who is Great in Glory sat on the throne, and His raiment shone more brightly than the sun and was whiter than any snow.*

None of the angels could enter or could behold his face because of the magnificence and glory, and no flesh could behold him.

The sea of fire surrounded Him, and a great fire stood in front of Him, and no one could draw close to Him: ten thousand times ten thousand stood before Him, but He needed no Holy council.

The most Holy Ones who were near to Him did not leave night or day.

And until then I had been prostrate on my face, trembling, and the Lord called me with His own mouth, and said to me:

"Come here, Enoch, and hear my word." And one of the Holy Ones came to me, picked me up and brought me to the door: and I bowed down my face.

And He answered and said to me, and I heard His voice: *"Do not be afraid, Enoch, you righteous man and scribe of righteousness.*

Approach and hear my voice. (book of Enoch 14:8–25; 15:1–2)

Second, another passage of interest from the book of Enoch gives the names of the seven archangels and supposedly describes their general areas of responsibility (Only three of their names are recorded in canonized scripture.)

These are the names of the holy angels who watch.

Uriel, . . . who is over the world, turmoil and terror.

Raphael, . . . who is over the spirits of men.

Raguel, . . . who takes vengeance on the world of the luminaries.

Michael, . . . set over the virtues of mankind and over chaos.

Saraqael, . . . who is set over the spirits, who sin in the spirit.

Gabriel, . . . who is over Paradise and the serpents and the Cherubim.

Remiel, . . . one of the holy angels, whom God set over those who rise (book of Enoch 20:1–8)[2]

A third passage of interest from the book of Enoch speaks of the Ancient of Days, whom Latter-day Saints know is Adam, and then describes the Lord as He appears to him. Compare this book of Enoch passage with Daniel 7:9, 13–14 and with Doctrine and Covenants 107:53–55:

> There I beheld the *Ancient of days* whose *head was like white wool, and with him another, whose countenance resembled that of a man.* His countenance was full of grace, like that of one of the holy angels. Then I inquired of one of the angels, who went with me, and who showed me every secret thing, concerning this *Son of man;* who he was; whence he was; and *why he accompanied the Ancient of days.*
>
> He answered and said to me, *This is the Son of man, to whom righteousness belongs; with whom righteousness has dwelt; and who will reveal all the treasures of that which is concealed:* for the Lord of spirits has chosen him; and his portion has surpassed all before the Lord of spirits in everlasting uprightness. (book of Enoch 46:1–2)

Those who wish to read more can easily obtain copies from online sources. Be aware that there are several different translations in circulation—they differ slightly in wording, as would be expected. What is not known is whether the actual book of Enoch, as spoken of in Doctrine and Covenants 107:57, is what has been found and is available.

Enoch is unique among the Old Testament prophets who walked with God. Only he was able to establish Zion on earth and adequately prepare his people to be translated into heaven. He was recognized as a seer by all who were around him and was respected by many—though feared by the rest. Satan mustered his demonic forces against him, but was unable to prevail.

He only merited a few verses in the Bible, but received extensive treatment in the book of Moses—a profound blessing to Latter-day Saints and to the rest of the world willing to receive that sacred volume of scripture.

---

2. It is interesting to compare these angelic names with other names found in the scriptures. *Michael* and *Gabriel* are found in the scriptures, and are treated herein in the chapters on Adam and Noah as they apply to the archangels. *Michael* was a popular name in Old Testament times, and appears in Numbers 13:13; 1 Chronicles 5:13, 14; 6:40; 7:3; 8:16; 12:20; 27:18; 2 Chronicles 21:2; and Ezra 8:8. *Gabriel* appears only in his archangel role. The name *Raphael* appears only once in the four standard works, in D&C 128:21. *Raguel* appears only once, in Numbers 10:29—a reference to Raguel the Midianite, Moses' father in law. *Uriel* appears four times, in 1 Chronicles 6:24; 15:5; 15:11, and 2 Chronicles 13:2. Neither *Saraqael* nor *Remiel* are found in the scriptures.

CHAPTER 4

NOAH

A Just Man, Perfect in His Generations, a Preacher of Righteousness

The accounts of Noah and the great flood he survived are found in the histories or mythologies of civilizations throughout the world today. Noah, like Adam before him, stands as a father of all mankind. And he, like Adam, was one of God's archangels, sent to earth to accomplish a task so gigantic in scope that he needed to be able to summon angelic assistance.

Noah's Birth and Heritage

Noah was the son of Lamech, who was 182 years old when Noah was born. Lamech was the father of other sons and daughters during his long life span. He lived 595 years after his son Noah's entrance into mortality, finally passing away at the age of 777, just a few years before the great flood that cleansed the earth (Genesis 5:28–31).

Noah was a grandson of Methusaleh and a great-grandson of Enoch who was taken up into heaven (Genesis 5:21–27). Noah's generation was the tenth generation after Adam.

It is clear that Noah was raised in a righteous family, though iniquity surrounded them on all sides. Several of his forefathers had been ordained to the holy priesthood by Adam. Most of them were well along in years before being ordained. However, beginning with Enoch, ordinations to the priesthood were given at a much earlier age, and Noah was the youngest of all of them—he was ordained when he was just ten years old:

> Enoch was twenty-five years old when he was ordained under the hand of Adam; ...
>
> Methuselah was one hundred years old when he was ordained under the hand of Adam.
>
> Lamech was thirty-two years old when he was ordained under the hand of Seth.
>
> Noah was ten years old when he was ordained under the hand of Methuselah. (D&C 107:48–52)

Of Noah's priesthood ordination, the book of Moses says: "The Lord ordained Noah after his own order, and *commanded him that he should go forth and declare his Gospel unto the children of men,* even as it was given unto Enoch" (Moses 8:19).

There is a huge time gap in the scriptural record of Noah's sojourn on earth. The accounts in both the books of Genesis and Moses jump ahead almost 450 years. Presumably, Noah raised a family during those four centuries, but the scriptural accounts tell only of his fathering three particular sons in his old age—Japheth, Shem, and Ham:

> Noah was four hundred and fifty years old, and begat *Japheth*; and forty-two years afterward he begat *Shem* of her who was the mother of Japheth, and when he was five hundred years old he begat *Ham....* *Noah and his sons hearkened unto the Lord, and gave heed,* and they were called the sons of God. (Moses 8:12–13)

GREAT WICKEDNESS: GIANTS, THE SONS OF GOD, AND THE DAUGHTERS OF MEN

From the days of Adam, when Satan came among his posterity and began leading them astray, wickedness grew, crescendoing as the generations passed. Enoch saw much of it in his day. By the tenth generation, wickedness was rampant. Genesis 6:1–8 describes the great wickedness that existed upon the earth during Noah's day:

> And it came to pass, when men began to multiply on the face of the earth, and daughters were born unto them,
>
> That the *sons of God* saw the daughters of men that they were fair; and they took them wives of all which they chose.
>
> And the LORD said, *My spirit shall not always strive with man, for that he also is flesh: yet his days shall be an hundred and twenty years.*
>
> There were giants in the earth in those days; and also after that, when the sons of God came in unto the daughters of men, and they bare children to them, the same became mighty men which were of old, men of renown.
>
> And GOD saw that *the wickedness of man was great in the earth, and that every imagination of the thoughts of his heart was only evil continually.*
>
> And it repented the LORD that he had made man on the earth, and it grieved him at his heart.
>
> And the LORD said, *I will destroy man whom I have created from the face of the earth;* both man, and beast, and the creeping thing, and the fowls of the air; for it repenteth me that I have made them.
>
> But *Noah found grace in the eyes of the LORD.* (Genesis 6:1–8)

A similar report is found in the Pearl of Great Price book of Moses. Fortunately, it includes considerably more detail. Among other things, it reveals that the daughters of Japheth, Shem, and Ham fell away and "sold themselves," involving themselves in ill-fated marriages. It also reveals that the "giants" who lived in that day attempted to slay Noah, and that God only allotted Noah and his sons 120 years to build the ark before He would send the floods upon the earth:

And Noah and his sons hearkened unto the Lord, and gave heed, and they were called the sons of God.

And *when these men began to multiply on the face of the earth, and daughters were born unto them, the sons of men saw that those daughters were fair, and they took them wives, even as they chose.*

And the Lord said unto Noah: *The daughters of thy sons have sold themselves; for behold mine anger is kindled against the sons of men, for they will not hearken to my voice.*

And it came to pass that *Noah prophesied, and taught the things of God, even as it was* in the beginning.

And *the Lord said unto Noah: My Spirit shall not always strive with man,* for he shall know that all flesh shall die; *yet his days shall be an hundred and twenty years;* and *if men do not repent, I will send in the floods upon them.*

And in those days *there were giants on the earth, and they sought Noah to take away his* life; but the Lord was with Noah, and the power of the Lord was upon him.

And *the Lord ordained Noah after his own order, and commanded him that he should go forth and declare his Gospel unto the children of men, even as it was given unto Enoch.*

And it came to pass that *Noah called upon the children of men that they should repent;* but they hearkened not unto his words;

And also, after that they had heard him, they came up before him, saying: *Behold, we are the sons of God; have we not taken unto ourselves the daughters of men? And are we not eating and drinking, and marrying and giving in marriage? And our wives bear unto us children, and the same are mighty men, which are like unto men of old, men of great renown. And they hearkened not unto the words of Noah.*

And *God saw that the wickedness of men had become great in the earth; and every man was lifted up in the imagination of the thoughts of his heart, being only evil continually.*

And it came to pass that Noah continued his preaching unto the people, saying: *Hearken, and give heed unto my words;*

Believe and repent of your sins and be baptized in the name of Jesus Christ, the Son of God, *even as our fathers, and ye shall receive the Holy Ghost,* that ye may have all things made manifest; and *if ye do not this, the floods will come in upon you; nevertheless they hearkened not.*

And *it repented Noah, and his heart was pained* that the Lord had made man on the earth, and it grieved him at the heart.

And *the Lord said: I will destroy man whom I have created, from the face of the earth, both man and beast, and the creeping things, and the fowls of the air; for it repenteth Noah that I have created them, and that I have made them; and he hath called upon me; for they have sought his life.*

And *thus Noah found grace in the eyes of the Lord; for Noah was a just man, and perfect in* his generation; and he walked with God, as did also his three sons, Shem, Ham, and Japheth.

The earth was corrupt before God, and it was filled with violence.

And God looked upon the earth, and, behold, it was corrupt, for all flesh had corrupted its way upon the earth.

And *God said unto Noah: The end of all flesh is come before me, for the earth is filled with violence, and behold I will destroy all flesh from off the earth.* (Moses 8:13–30)

ENOCH ALSO WAS OPPOSED BY THE GIANTS

Previously, Enoch, in his day, had to cope with enemies of righteousness, who fought against him and his converts, and he also reported that there were giants among them at that time:

So great was the faith of Enoch that he led the people of God, and their enemies came to battle against them; . . .

There also came up a land out of the depth of the sea, and so great was the fear of the enemies of the people of God, that they fled and stood afar off and went upon the land which came up out of the depth of the sea.

And *the giants of the land, also, stood afar off;* and there went forth *a curse upon all people that fought against God;*

And from that time forth there were wars and bloodshed among them. (Moses 7:13–16)

So Enoch, centuries before the days of Noah, learned from God that the great flood would come upon mankind. Why? Because the wickedness of those around him exceeded the level of wickedness in any of God's previous creations:

The Lord said unto Enoch: Behold these thy brethren; they are the workmanship of mine own hands, and *I gave unto them their knowledge, in the day I created them; and in the Garden of Eden, gave I unto man his agency;*

And unto thy brethren have I said, and also given commandment, that they should love one another, and that they should choose me, their Father; but behold, *they are without affection, and they hate their own blood;*

And the fire of mine indignation is kindled against them; and *in my hot displeasure will I send in the floods upon them, for my fierce anger is kindled against them.*

Behold, I am God; Man of Holiness is my name; Man of Counsel is my name; and Endless and Eternal is my name, also.

Wherefore, I can stretch forth mine hands and hold all the creations which I have made; and mine eye can pierce them also, and *among all the workmanship of mine hands there has not been so great wickedness as among thy brethren.*

But behold, *their sins shall be upon the heads of their fathers; Satan shall be their father, and misery shall be their doom;* and the whole heavens shall weep over them, even all the workmanship of mine hands; wherefore should not the heavens weep, seeing *these shall suffer?*

But behold, these which thine eyes are upon shall perish in the floods; and behold, *I will shut them up; a prison have I prepared for them.* (Moses 7:32–38)

WHO WERE THE GIANTS AND THE SONS OF GOD THAT MATED WITH THE DAUGHTERS OF MEN?

As seen above, both the Genesis passage and the book of Moses passages speak of "giants" and of "sons of God" mating with the "daughters of men." Exactly who were they?

It is obvious that the wickedness engendered by those "giants" and "sons of God" surpassed the magnitude of any wickedness in all of God's other creations. As cited above, the Lord told Enoch, concerning them, that "among all the workmanship of mine hands there has not been so great wickedness as among thy brethren" (Moses 7:36). They weren't ordinary "bad guys," by any definition.

The identifying of who the "giants" and "sons of God" were in the Genesis passage has been a matter of considerable speculation and religious contention within the ranks of Christendom for two millennia.

To see the widespread extent of the disagreement concerning the identity of those "giants" and "sons of God" reported in Genesis 6:1–8, one only has to do a web search on "the sons of God and the daughters of men." There are dozens of sites that comment on the various theories people have advanced and the doctrinal positions they have taken on the subject.

Their views are typically summed up as being one of three theories:

+ **Theory One: the descendants of Seth and Cain.** The "daughters of men" were descendants of Cain, who had been cursed by God (see Genesis 4:9–24; Moses 5:16–57). The "sons of God" were descendants of Seth—the righteous, priesthood-holding genealogical line descended down from Adam, through which the Messiah eventually would be born (see Genesis 4:25–5:32). The "giants" (called "Nephilim," from the Hebrew term translated "giants" in Genesis 6:4), were the ungodly, violent men who were products of the matings between "sons of God" and the "daughters of men." The pseudepigraphal work *Conflict of Adam and Eve with Satan* advocated this theory.[1]

+ **Theory Two: the "powers and rulers."** Advocates of this theory point out that the Hebrew term for God, *Elohim*, is a plural word that literally means "powers," so the interpretation is made that "sons of God" are ancient kings, nobles, and aristocrats. In ancient times, some pagan kings were referred to as sons of pagan gods. This theory has had little acceptance as the basis for interpreting Genesis 6:1–8.

+ **Theory Three: the "renegade angels."** According to this interpretation, the "sons of God" are fallen angels, who came down to earth and copulated with human women; their resulting offspring were giants—large people with great physical strength and superiority—warriors of old who achieved renown for their exploits. (See Numbers 13:33: "There we saw the giants, the sons of Anak, which come of the giants.") The term *Nephilim* is possibly related to the Hebrew root meaning "to fall." In this theory, they became a race descending from first-generation half-human creatures that engaged in much wickedness.

Those who embrace the "renegade angels" interpretation turn to various Biblical scriptures that mention "sons of God" to support their views, particularly passages which seem to indicate angels have or can assume physical forms since some Christian sects hold that angels are sexless beings (based on their interpretation of Matthew 22:29–30). These passages, which don't differentiate between good and evil "sons of God," are: (1) Job 1:6, (2) Job 2:1, (3) Job 38:7, (4) Psalm 89:6, (5) Daniel 3:25, (6), Hebrews 13:2, (7) Genesis 19:5, (8) 2 Peter 2:4–5, and (9) Jude 1:6.

Latter-day Saints are well aware that premortal spirits had their agency, and that a third of them elected to follow Satan and were cast out from the presence of God (D&C 29:36–38; 76:25–26; Isaiah 14:12–15; Revelation 12:7–9; 2 Nephi 2:16–18; 9:8; Moses 4:1–4; Abraham 3:27–28).

The "fallen angels" theory is, by far, the most widely accepted of the three theories of interpretation concerning Genesis 6:1–8 among many of the Christian churches today. It seems to fit correctly with both the Bible and with the additional insights revealed through Latter-day Saint scriptures. Assuming it is the correct understanding, (though it is beyond the realm of clearly defined LDS doctrine), then the question arises:

Are these fallen angels who mated with the daughters of men (1) among the spirits cast out with Satan, or (2) angels who were not cast out with Satan

---

1. For more information on this particular theory, you can google "Conflict of Adam and Eve with Satan."

but who were later tempted to come down and mingle with mortal women, and who later were cut off from the earth and cast into hell? It should be remembered that those who were cast out with Satan were bodiless spirits. Though they apparently take over and possess the bodies of human beings, that wouldn't explain how their progeny would be "giants."

This author is content to categorize these interpretations in his "I don't know" file and not embrace any position on them.

It should at least be noted that the book of Enoch dwells on the matter at considerable length. It reports that Enoch was summoned to heaven and given instructions as to how the influences of these fallen spirits and their mortal offspring were to be combated and overcome. While remembering that the book of Enoch is not canonized scripture (but falls within the purview of apocryphal writings, as per Doctrine and Covenants 91:1–6), some may find it interesting to scan the matter there. See book of Enoch 6:1–16:4.

NOAH IS THE ARCHANGEL GABRIEL

Before this account delves into the miraculous construction of the huge ark built by Noah and his helpers, it is appropriate to recognize a significant item known only by Latter-day Saints. As mentioned previously, Adam, the first man on this earth, was one of the Lord's most-trusted angelic assistants, the archangel Michael (D&C 107:54; 88:112; 78:16; 29:26; Jude 1:9). Latter-day Saints believe Noah also was an angel of archangel status.

The Prophet Joseph Smith gave an address to the Quorum of the Twelve on July 2, 1839. In it, he expounded on the priesthood and taught the Brethren as follows:

> *The priesthood was first given to Adam;* he obtained the First Presidency, and held the keys of it from generation to generation. *He obtained it in the Creation, before the world was formed, as in Genesis 26, 27, 28. He had dominion given him over every living creature. He is Michael the Archangel, spoken of in the Scriptures. Then to Noah, who is Gabriel; he stands next in authority to Adam in the Priesthood; he was called of God to this office, and was the father of all living in his day, and to him was given the dominion.* These men held keys first on earth, and then in heaven.[2]

---

2. Smith, Joseph. *History of The Church of Jesus Christ of Latter-day Saints* (Salt Lake City: *Deseret News*, 1948), vol. 3, pp. 385–6 (emphasis added). For scriptural passages concerning the archangel Gabriel, see: Daniel 8:15–27; 9:20–27; Luke 1:11–20; 1:26–38; D&C 128:21.

Building the Ark

The Lord finally gave the commandment: the flood would come, and through it the earth would be cleansed:

> The earth also was corrupt before God, and the earth was filled with violence.
>
> And God looked upon the earth, and, behold, it was corrupt; for all flesh had corrupted his way upon the earth.
>
> And God said unto Noah, *The end of all flesh is come before me; for the earth is filled with violence through them; and, behold, I will destroy them with the earth. . . .*
>
> And, behold, I, even I, do bring a flood of waters upon the earth, to destroy all flesh, wherein is the breath of life, from under heaven; and every thing that is in the earth shall die.
>
> *But with thee will I establish my covenant; and thou shalt come into the ark, thou, and thy sons, and thy wife, and thy sons' wives with thee.* (Genesis 6:11–13, 17–18)

These were His instructions to Noah pertaining to the construction of the huge ship, as recorded in Genesis chapter 6:

> Make thee an ark of *gopher wood; rooms* shalt thou make in the ark, and shalt pitch it within and without with pitch.
>
> And this is the fashion which thou shalt make it of: *The length of the ark shall be three hundred cubits, the breadth of it fifty cubits, and the height of it thirty cubits.*
>
> A *window* shalt thou make to the ark, and in a cubit shalt thou finish it above; and the *door* of the ark shalt thou set in the side thereof; with *lower, second, and third stories* shalt thou make it. (Genesis 6:14–16)

A bit of analysis of these instructions may help to put the enormous challenge they posed in perspective. First, a dimensional definition. *The Merriam-Webster's Collegiate Dictionary,* eleventh edition, defines *cubit* as "any of various ancient units of length based on the length of the forearm from the elbow to the tip of the middle finger and usu. equal to about 18 inches [46 centimeters]." Other dictionaries refine that overall definition. The *LDS Bible Dictionary* defines a cubit as "The distance from the elbow to the tip of the finger, normally about 17½ inches, or 444.25 millimeters (approximately 44.43 cm.)."[3]

---

3. "Weights and Measures: Cubit," *LDS Bible Dictionary,* p. 789. A more complete definition:

> The cubit (Heb. 'ammâ; Akkad. ammātu; Lat. cubitus) was the distance from elbow to fingertip. This 'natural cubit' (AV 'cubit of a man', RSV 'common cubit',

So, using the 17½-inch definition as a calculation basis, the ark probably was about 437½ feet long, 73 feet wide, and 43¾ feet tall. It had three levels, or stories, a window about a foot-and-a-half down from the top, and a door in one side. To visualize the ark's size in modern terms:

+ The ark was about a football field and a half in *length* (an NCAA field is 300' from goal-line to goal-line)
+ The ark was slightly less than half a football field in *width* (an NCAA field is 160' from sideline to sideline)
+ The ark's height was equal to the cumulative *height* of seven-and-a-quarter six-feet-tall men standing on top of one another—about a five-story building

In summary: the ark was HUGE![4]

The ark was to be made of "gopher wood," which some suggest is the wood of the cypress tree (*Cupressus sempervirens*), a coniferous evergreen tree. It was to be "pitched" (sealed with tree sap or other resinous substance) on both the inside and outside of the ship's exterior walls (Genesis 6:14).

Imagine how many thousands of trees had to be felled, hauled down out of the mountains, de-branched and de-barked, cut into boards, cut to proper lengths, and positioned onto the hull of the ark, plus the thousands more that were used to create the rooms in the ark's three stories! How many man-hours were required to perform all that labor? What equipment did they have to do all that fabricating and manufacturing?

And contemplate how many thousands of gallons of pitch it must have taken to seal those millions of board-feet planks, both inside and out. How many man-hours did it take to extract or make the pitch, and how many

---

Dt. 3:11) was used to indicate the general size of a person (4 cubits the height of a man; cf. 1 Sa. 17:4; 1 Ch. 11:23) or object (Est. 5:14; Zc. 5:2). It described depth (Gn. 7:20) or distance (Jn. 21:8).

A more precisely defined cubit was used for exact measurement. This *standard Hebrew cubit* was 17.5 inches (44.45 cm), slightly shorter than the common Egyp. cubit of 17.6 inches (44.7 cm). "Weights and Measures," Tyndale House Publishers: *The Illustrated Bible Dictionary*, vol. 3, pp. 1635–6.

4.   However, in comparison: The USS RONALD REAGAN (CVN-76), a Nimitz-class aircraft carrier launched in 2001, is reported to be 1,040' long and 252' wide: about two-and-a-half times larger than Noah's ark (NavSource Online: Aircraft Carrier Photo Archive: USS Ronald Reagan).

"Huge in ancient terms is even "more huge" when seen through modern perspectives!

hours to apply it? How many thousands of containers were needed to carry the pitch?

Today, no one knows if Noah had special status in his community. Was he wealthy? Did he have servants or employees, who helped in manufacturing the ark? Such a project as building Noah's ark most definitely was in the same league as the Egyptian Pharaohs erecting their gigantic pyramids. It would have required a qualified work-force of thousands!

Obviously, Noah and his ark-building project were objects of scoffing and derision during much of the 120–year construction period. If the giants were attempting to murder Noah, the builders may have had to defend their work like the Jews had to defend the construction of the Jerusalem city walls in the days of Nehemiah, thousands of years later (see Nehemiah, chapters 4–6).

The scriptures give no inkling of how many hands helped build the ark; they only say that entry into the ark when the floods came was limited to eight souls. When one considers the magnitude of constructing that huge ark, gathering all the animals, housing and feeding them for more than a year—all with only a minuscule human workforce—it becomes unavoidably apparent that there must have been tremendous support and assistance made available from beyond the veil. As one of the highest angels, archangel Gabriel (who was Noah) was in position and apparently held the authority to summon and direct the efforts of those angelic forces.

GATHERING THE ANIMALS

The book of Genesis indicates that two different categories of animals were to be brought onto the ark: those that were "clean," and the remainder, which were considered "unclean."

Seven of each "clean" species were to be brought aboard (One wonders what the ratio of clean-species males-to-females was in the divine plan!) Only a single male and female of the other species was to enter the ark:

> Of every clean beast thou shalt take to thee by sevens, the male and his female: and of beasts that are not clean by two, the male and his female.
>
> Of fowls also of the air by sevens, the male and the female; to keep seed alive upon the face of all the earth. (Genesis 7:2–3)

This statement of the commandment differs from the directive recorded in Genesis 6:19–20, and also Genesis 7:8–9, which both speak of only two from each species entering the ark.

It is interesting to recognize that a distinction between clean and unclean animals was already operational in Noah's day, though the scriptural definition of clean and unclean beasts wasn't set forth until many centuries later, through Moses (see Leviticus 11:1–47 and Deuteronomy 14:1–20).

The scriptures give no indication of any search for animals being made by Noah and his sons. Rather, the Lord told Noah that "every sort *shall come unto thee*, to keep them alive" (Genesis 6:20). And Genesis 7:9 indicates that "There went in two and two unto Noah into the ark, the male and the female," seeming to do so of their own volition.

FOOD AND SANITATION CHALLENGES

But even if they were not required to seek out the animals, they did have the responsibility to acquire sufficient food for all of them, as well as for their human protectors. The Lord commanded Noah to

> Take thou unto thee of all food that is eaten, and thou shalt gather it to thee; and it shall be for food for thee, and for them.
>
> Thus did Noah; according to all that God commanded him, so did he. (Genesis 6:21–22)

Let's see: sufficient food for eight humans, plus adequate food for all the animal species on the face of the earth—enough to last for more than twelve months. That task introduces an entirely different parameter to the Latter-day Saint concept of food storage, doesn't it? A year's supply really meant a year's supply—not just a 72–hour kit in the garage.

No canned or packaged foods, no refrigeration, no electric food grinders, no rolling storage bins, no delivery services, no supermarket sales or coupons. No discounts for buying in bulk. Just grow it or find it, glean it or harvest it, haul it to the ark, store it in all those many dozens of separate rooms they had built in the ark on all three levels. There were no elevators, escalators or electricity-driven conveyor belts to expedite the food-handling tasks. Remember, too, that special menus for many of the different species were needed. And they had no computers to keep track of all the details!

And what would have to be done to handle the vast challenges of food preparation and delivery, and the tremendous clean-up requirements? Did they have fire on board the ark? Probably. Where to burn it, and how to keep firewood dry must have been initial challenges.

With all that rain coming down, there was plenty of fresh water for the first couple of months, and rain apparently continued throughout the year. But what did they have to do to catch and store it, and to deliver it throughout the ark for an entire year?

And who had to shovel the huge quantities of manure and droppings all those animals generated? How did they get it off the ark—did they haul their odoriferous loads up the stairs every day? And did the ark's increasingly fragrant ambience add to their sea-sickness and nausea?

Obviously, there was plenty of work to be done every day on board the ark and plenty of challenges to overcome. Noah and his family carried some tremendously heavy shipboard workloads in exchange for having their lives preserved!

Again, their doing all the work alone, without major levels of assistance from beyond the veil, seems unfathomable. (Oops—bad pun!) They must have been given angelic help—there's just no way that eight mortals, four of them women, could have performed all the necessary chores, month after month for more than a year!

Boarding Day—A Time of Mixed Emotions

Noah and his family, along with all the animals, were instructed by the Lord to board the ark a week before the rains would begin (Genesis 7:1–4). That momentous boarding day is described in Genesis, along with the detail that the Lord (himself?) closed the ark's great door:

> In the selfsame day entered Noah, and Shem, and Ham, and Japheth, the sons of Noah, and Noah's wife, and the three wives of his sons with them, into the ark;
>
> They, and every beast after his kind, and all the cattle after their kind, and every creeping thing that creepeth upon the earth after his kind, and every fowl after his kind, every bird of every sort.
>
> And they went in unto Noah into the ark, two and two of all flesh, wherein is the breath of life.
>
> And they that went in, went in male and female of all flesh, as God had commanded him: the LORD shut him in. (Genesis 7:13–16)

Think of the mixed emotions those eight mortal souls must have felt. "Noah was six hundred years old when the flood of waters was upon the earth" (Genesis 7:6). Undoubtedly, he dealt with a wide range of feelings that day. There must have been great relief for all eight of them to finally get the ark finished and stocked, and to get all the animals loaded. What an accomplishment! And theirs was the sure knowledge that they had been obedient to a huge, life-altering commandment from God. Indeed, Noah had been explicitly told by the Lord that "thee have I seen righteous before me in this generation" (Genesis 7:1).

But profound sorrow certainly must have been predominant in their minds and hearts, as well. Japheth, Shem, and Ham—and their wives—had all seen their children turn away from the truth and go astray. Noah, specifically, had been told by revelation that "the daughters of thy sons have sold themselves; for behold mine anger is kindled against the sons of men, for they will not hearken to my voice" (Moses 8:15).

As the great door of the ark swung shut, the eight knew, and probably ached, that their children and grandchildren were being left behind. And most likely Noah and his wife had been the parents of many other children in the five centuries which had passed before their three faithful sons were born. All their descendants were being left behind—abandoned—left to perish in the flood!

And most certainly Noah—the archangel Gabriel—had already joined with the hosts of heaven as they shed profound tears for the overwhelming wickedness of all of humanity. He knew full well of the hell which awaited them beyond the veil of death. (See again Moses 7:30–40.)

THE FLOOD

Then the flood began. Torrents of rain fell, incessantly, from above, pounding down upon the earth for forty days and nights. But the water not only came down—it also came up in large quantities from great reservoirs situated below the surface of the earth:

> It came to pass after seven days, that the waters of the flood were upon the earth.
>
> In the six hundredth year of Noah's life, in the second month, the seventeenth day of the month, the same day *were all the fountains of the great deep broken up, and the windows of heaven were opened.*
>
> And the rain was upon the earth forty days and forty nights. (Genesis 7:10–12)

As the water-level rose, the ark was lifted up and began moving upon the waters. A smooth voyage in that kind of stormy weather? Very, very unlikely! Seasickness? Very probably! Seasick animals too? Most likely! Not very pleasant thoughts to ponder, right?

How deep? 15 cubits above the mountain tops—almost 22 feet above the highest hills. Who knows how high the mountains were in that day across the world? This was centuries before the days of Peleg in which the earth was divided (Genesis 10:25). Perhaps some of the towering peaks of today had not yet been thrust up as the result of great oceanic plates shifting and sliding.

Some today speak of "local floods," but that's not the message of the scriptures, which assert that "all the high hills, that were under the whole heaven, were covered":

> And the flood was forty days upon the earth; and the waters increased, and bare up the ark, and it was lift up above the earth.
>
> And the waters prevailed, and were increased greatly upon the earth; and the ark went upon the face of the waters.

And the waters prevailed exceedingly upon the earth; and all the high hills, that were under the whole heaven, were covered.

Fifteen cubits upward did the waters prevail; and the mountains were covered. (Genesis 7:17–20)

How widespread was the cleansing of the earth—the destruction of man and beasts and fowls? The scriptural message was that it was total: only the eight aboard the ark remained.

And all flesh died that moved upon the earth, both of fowl, and of cattle, and of beast, and of every creeping thing that creepeth upon the earth, and every man:

All in whose nostrils was the breath of life, of all that was in the dry land, died.

And every living substance was destroyed which was upon the face of the ground, both man, and cattle, and the creeping things, and the fowl of the heaven; and they were destroyed from the earth: and Noah only remained alive, and they that were with him in the ark. (Genesis 7:21–23)

How long did the earth remain under water? The account says that "the waters prevailed upon the earth an hundred and fifty days" (Genesis 7:24). That apparently means that at that point (after what today would be called five 30–day months) *the turning point was reached—water ceased to increase the depth of the flood.* Genesis 8:1–3 indicates the waters were "asswaged" (to assuage means "to lessen the intensity of"), the rainfall "was restrained," and the fountains of the deep "were stopped":

And God remembered Noah, and every living thing, and all the cattle that was with him in the ark: and God made a wind to pass over the earth, and the waters asswaged;

The fountains also of the deep and the windows of heaven were stopped, and the rain from heaven was restrained;

And the waters returned from off the earth continually: and after the end of the hundred and fifty days the waters were abated.

But that doesn't mean the family was able to exit the ark at that point. It was a month-and-a-half more before the ark stopped floating around. Then another two-and-a-half months went by before the tops of any mountains could be seen. Then it was 40 days more before Noah opened the window on the ark and began sending out birds—a process that went on for three more weeks until the dove failed to return to the ark. But then, it still was almost four months more before God told Noah it was time to disembark:

And the ark rested in the seventh month, on the seventeenth day of the month, upon the mountains of Ararat.

And the waters decreased continually until the tenth month: in the tenth month, on the first day of the month, were the tops of the mountains seen.

And it came to pass *at the end of forty days*, that Noah opened the window of the ark which he had made:

And he sent forth a raven, which went forth to and fro, until the waters were dried up from off the earth.

Also he sent forth a dove from him, to see if the waters were abated from off the face of the ground;

But the dove found no rest for the sole of her foot, and she returned unto him into the ark, for the waters were on the face of the whole earth: then he put forth his hand, and took her, and pulled her in unto him into the ark.

And he stayed *yet other seven days*; and again he sent forth the dove out of the ark;

And the dove came in to him in the evening; and, lo, in her mouth was an olive leaf pluckt off: so Noah knew that the waters were abated from off the earth.

And he stayed *yet other seven days; and sent forth the dove; which returned not again unto him any more.*

And it came to pass in the *six hundredth and first year, in the first month, the first day of the month, the waters were dried up from off the earth:* and Noah removed the covering of the ark, and looked, and, behold, the face of the ground was dry.

And in the second month, on the seven and twentieth day of the month, was the earth dried. (Genesis 8:4–14)

In summary, the flood began on the "six hundredth year of Noah's life, in the second month, the seventeenth day of the month" (Genesis 7:11). It was on the twenty-seventh day of the second month, in Noah's 601st year, that they were finally able to leave the ark (Genesis 8:14), so Noah and his family *spent a year and ten days on the ark!* They truly must have been very, very, very, very ready to disembark!

WHERE IS MOUNT ARARAT?

Before leaving this chapter on Noah, it is appropriate to add some information concerning where his ark apparently landed as the flood receded.

The scriptural account says that "the ark rested . . . upon *the mountains of Ararat*" (Genesis 8:4). If one wishes to spend an interesting and intriguing afternoon wandering through the internet, one can easily do so by Googling "Mt. Ararat ark." Hundreds of articles filled with facts, fantasies, and speculations await him there. They serve, however, to provide quick information on the geographical area in which Mt. Ararat is located. A few snatches from those sites are pieced together here to describe the rugged area in which the ark apparently came to rest.

Mount Ararat [called "Agri Dagi" by local people, meaning "Mountain of Pain"] is located in Eastern Turkey about two miles from Iran's northern border. It is about 250 kilometers east of Erzurum, 160 kilometers north of Van, and 130 kilometers southeast of Kars. The main road connecting Turkey with Iran goes from Erzurum through Dogubayazit (just south of Ararat) to Tabriz.

Skirmishes involving Mt. Ararat, along the border between Turkey and Iran, have made the Turkish government reluctant to allow archaeological work on the mountain. The mountain's commanding altitude, and its location so close to an international border between two belligerent nations, make it a place of considerable military importance.

The summit of Mt. Ararat is 16,854 feet (5,137 meters) above sea level. It is the highest mountain in Turkey. By comparison, it is higher than any mountain in the continental United States (except for Alaska), or in Europe outside the Caucasus. A dormant volcano, it was shaken by a strong earthquake that took place on June 2, 1840.

The altitude of this mountainous region is significant. In any local flood, the ark would have been swept along toward the sea. Only a cataclysm like that described in Genesis chapters six through nine could have lifted Noah's ark to such a height.

The upper third of the mountain is covered with snow all the time; the last hundred meters of snow at the top have turned to ice. Below the snowline the slopes are covered with great blocks of black basalt rock. Shepherds tend their flocks of sheep and live on the lower parts of the mountain. Plains surrounding the mountain vary from 2,000 to 3,000 feet in altitude. The road up to the mountain is just barely navigable.

Searchers trying to determine if any remains of the ark still exist have concentrated their efforts on an area on the mount's northwest corner. There, at the height of about 15,300 feet (4,633 meters), nearly submerged in glacial ice, is either the remains of a huge boat or a very strange boat-shaped rock formation. Some traditions identify the south slope as being where the ark landed.

Experts want to utilize modern technology to explore the region, but the intelligence agencies of various involved nations won't release their closely guarded satellite images of the area or allow other explorations to be conducted.

Ararat is the newer Armenian name for Urartu. The original Hebrew account of Noah and the ark only included the consonants "rrt." Bible translators replaced them with the name "Ararat" or "Armenia."

Assyrian kings wrote about battles with Urartian tribes during an eight-century period from the 13th to the 6th centuries BC. The Medes finally destroyed Urartu in the sixth century BC.

The name Urartu then was lost to historians until archaeologists re-discovered it in the 1800s.

During the first and second millennia AD, the general region was known as Armenia and the mountain was known as Ararat. As Christianity spread in the first century AD, Christians of Apamea, in Phrygia, built the "monastery of the ark" where an annual feast celebrated the disembarcation of Noah and his family.[5]

THE DISEMBARKATION

Hallelujah! It was time to set foot upon dry land once again:

> God spake unto Noah, saying,
> Go forth of the ark, thou, and thy wife, and thy sons, and thy sons' wives with thee.
> Bring forth with thee every living thing that is with thee, of all flesh, both of fowl, and of cattle, and of every creeping thing that creepeth upon the earth; that they may breed abundantly in the earth, and be fruitful, and multiply upon the earth.
> Every beast, every creeping thing, and every fowl, and whatsoever creepeth upon the earth, after their kinds, went forth out of the ark. (Genesis 8:15–19)

What was Noah's first recorded act after coming off of the ark? "Noah builded an altar unto the LORD; and took of every clean beast, and of every clean fowl, and offered burnt offerings on the altar" (Genesis 8:20). So that's why there were an uneven number of each of the clean beasts taken on board the ark: so that an offering of every species could be made in a glorious act of worship as life on earth began anew! One wonders how many dozens, or hundreds, of burnt offerings were made at this time, as a symbolic gratitude-offering was made for each species.

The Joseph Smith Translation of this passage adds an interesting perspective of the above-cited passage. Here the italicized words are those added in the JST:

> And Noah builded an altar unto the Lord, and took of every clean beast, and of every clean fowl, and offered burnt offerings on the altar; *and gave thanks unto the Lord, and rejoiced in his heart.*
> *And the Lord spake unto Noah, and he blessed him. And* Noah smelled a sweet savor, and he said in his heart;
> *I will call on the name of the Lord, that he* will not again curse the ground any more for man's sake, for the imagination of man's heart is evil from his youth; and that *he* will *not* again smite any more every thing living, as *he* hath done, while the earth remaineth. (Joseph Smith Translation, Genesis 9:4–6. Compare Genesis 8:20–22.)

---

5.   Adapted from NoahsArkSearch.com and other related websites.

Then, "God blessed Noah and his sons." The manner in which this blessing was conveyed is not recorded. Did the Lord actually appear to them? Lay His hands upon their heads? Or was a voice heard from the heavens? What is known is that the blessing contained several elements. The first was a blessing of fertility, couched in a repeated commandment to bear more children:

> And God blessed Noah and his sons, and said unto them, *Be fruitful, and multiply, and replenish the earth.* . . .
> And you, be ye fruitful, and multiply; bring forth abundantly in the earth, and multiply therein. (Genesis 9:1, 7)

The second portion of the blessing was a blessing of protection, shielding Noah and his family from the animals they had brought through the flood: "And the fear of you and the dread of you shall be upon every beast of the earth, and upon every fowl of the air, upon all that moveth upon the earth, and upon all the fishes of the sea; into your hand are they delivered" (Genesis 9:2).

The third element of the blessing was a dietary instruction—a granting of permission to eat of the animals of the earth, as well as the plant life: "Every moving thing that liveth shall be meat for you; even as the green herb have I given you all things" (Genesis 9:3). But with that blessing came a limitation: they were not to partake of blood: "But flesh with the life thereof, which is the blood thereof, shall ye not eat" (Genesis 9:4).

The fourth part of the blessing was a protective principle, basically dealing with the consequences of taking human life: "And surely your blood of your lives will I require; at the hand of every beast will I require it, and at the hand of man; at the hand of every man's brother will I require the life of man. *Whoso sheddeth man's blood, by man shall his blood be shed: for in the image of God made he man*" (Genesis 9:5–6). Today, advocates of requiring the death penalty for murderers hark back to this and similar passages in the Bible.

The Joseph Smith Translation treats this passage, adding significant insights. (In the following passage, the JST additions are shown in italics.)

> But, *the blood of all flesh which I have given you for meat, shall be shed upon the ground, which taketh life thereof, and the blood* ye shall not eat.
> And surely, *blood shall not be shed, only for meat, to save your lives; and the blood* of every beast will I require *at your hands.*
> *And* whoso sheddeth man's blood, by man shall his blood be shed; *for man shall not shed the blood of man.*
> *For a commandment I give,* that every man's brother *shall preserve* the life of man, for in *mine own image have I* made man.
> *And a commandment I give unto you,* Be ye fruitful and multiply; bring

forth abundantly on the earth, and multiply therein.

And God spake unto Noah, and to his sons with him, saying, And I, behold, I *will* establish my covenant with you, *which I made unto your father Enoch, concerning* your seed after you (Joseph Smith Translation, Genesis 9:10–15. Compare Genesis 9:3–9.)

And finally, the fifth blessing element was the Lord's solemn covenant that He never again would cleanse the earth by flood. Previously, when Noah offered up a specimen of each of the clean beasts, the record told of the Lord's reaction to those offerings:

And the LORD smelled a sweet savour; and the LORD said in his heart, *I will not again curse the ground any more for man's sake;* for the imagination of man's heart is evil from his youth; neither will I again smite any more every thing living, as I have done.

While the earth remaineth, *seedtime and harvest, and cold and heat, and summer and winter, and day and night shall not cease.* (Genesis 8:21–22)

Then, in this fifth element of the Lord's blessing upon Noah and his sons, the Lord turned His resolve into a covenant to never again destroy the earth by a flood. Note that the covenant wasn't made just with Noah and his sons, it also was made with "every beast of the earth."

And God spake unto Noah, and to his sons with him, saying,

And I, behold, *I establish my covenant with you, and with your seed after you;*

And with every living creature that is with you, of the fowl, of the cattle, and of every beast of the earth with you; from all that go out of the ark, to every beast of the earth.

And I will establish my covenant with you; neither shall all flesh be cut off any more by the waters of a flood; neither shall there any more be a flood to destroy the earth. (Genesis 9:8–11)

As sometimes is the case with the covenants the Lord makes with man, a token of the eternal efficacy of the covenant was established. In this case it was the rainbow, which would be a sign and remembrance of the covenant's eternal nature:

And God said, *This is the token of the covenant which I make between me and you and every living creature that is with you, for perpetual generations:*

I do set my bow in the cloud, and it shall be for a token of a covenant between me and the earth.

And it shall come to pass, when I bring a cloud over the earth, that the bow shall be seen in the cloud:

And *I will remember my covenant, which is between me and you and every living creature of all flesh;* and the waters shall no more become a flood to destroy all flesh.

And the bow shall be in the cloud; and I will look upon it, that I may remember the everlasting covenant between God and every living creature of all flesh that is upon the earth.

And God said unto Noah, *This is the token of the covenant, which I have established between me and all flesh that is upon the earth.* (Genesis 9:8–17)

The Joseph Smith Translation of this passage adds interesting insights concerning this covenant. (As above, in this JST passage the added words are shown in italics.) It says,

And the bow shall be in the cloud; and I will look upon it, that I may remember the everlasting covenant, *which I made unto thy father Enoch; that, when men should keep all my commandments, Zion should again come on the earth, the city of Enoch which I have caught up unto myself.*

And this is mine everlasting covenant, that when thy posterity shall embrace the truth, and look upward, then shall Zion look downward, and all the heavens shall shake with gladness, and the earth shall tremble with joy;

And the general assembly of the church of the first-born shall come down out of heaven, and possess the earth, and shall have place until the end come. And this is mine everlasting covenant, which I made with thy father Enoch.

And the bow shall be in the cloud, and I will establish my covenant unto thee, which I have made between *me* and *thee,* for every living creature of all flesh that *shall be* upon the earth.

And God said unto Noah, This is the token of the covenant which I have established between me and *thee; for* all flesh that *shall be* upon the earth. (Joseph Smith Translation, Genesis 9:21–25. Compare Genesis 9:16–17.)

NOAH'S CONTINUING RIGHTEOUSNESS
BEFORE THE LORD

Numerous scriptural passages reflect Noah's favorable standing before God Almighty, and the resulting promises God made to him:

1. "But Noah found grace in the eyes of the LORD" (Genesis 6:8).
2. "Noah was a just man and perfect in his generations, and Noah walked with God" (6:9).
3. "Thus did Noah; according to all that God commanded him, so did he" (6:22).
4. "The LORD said unto Noah, Come thou and all thy house into the ark; for thee have I seen righteous before me in this generation" (7:1).
5. "Noah did according unto all that the LORD commanded him" (7:5).
6. "And God remembered Noah, and every living thing" (8:1).
7. "And the LORD smelled a sweet savour; and the LORD said in his heart, I will not again curse the ground any more for man's sake; for the imagination of man's heart *is* evil from his youth; neither will I

again smite any more every thing living, as I have done. While the earth remaineth, seedtime and harvest, and cold and heat, and summer and winter, and day and night shall not cease" (Genesis 8:21–22).

8. "And God blessed Noah and his sons, and said unto them, Be fruitful, and multiply, and replenish the earth" (9:1).

9. "These are the families of the sons of Noah, after their generations, in their nations: and by these were the nations divided in the earth after the flood" (10:32).

10. "And Noah and his sons hearkened unto the Lord, and gave heed, and they were called the sons of God" (Moses 8:13).

11. "And it came to pass that Noah prophesied, and taught the things of God, even as it was in the beginning" (Moses 8:16).

12. "Thus Noah found grace in the eyes of the Lord; for Noah was a just man, and perfect in his generation; and he walked with God, as did also his three sons, Shem, Ham, and Japheth" (Moses 8:27).

An Unfortunate Incident with Long-range Consequences

Daily life began anew. Life began moving forward for the eight of them. Ham had a son, whom he named Canaan. Noah became a husbandman— one who plows and cultivates the land. Apparently, several years later, as his crops began to mature, a privacy incident caused Noah to react in anger and pronounce a prophecy concerning his descendants—a foretelling that came to pass as time unfolded:

And the sons of Noah, that went forth of the ark, were Shem, and Ham, and Japheth: and Ham is the father of Canaan.

These are the three sons of Noah: and of them was the whole earth overspread.

And he drank of the wine, and was drunken; and he was uncovered within his tent.

And Ham, the father of Canaan, saw the nakedness of his father, and told his two brethren without.

And Shem and Japheth took a garment, and laid it upon both their shoulders, and went backward, and covered the nakedness of their father; and their faces were backward, and they saw not their father's nakedness.

And Noah awoke from his wine, and knew what his younger son had done unto him.

And he said, *Cursed be Canaan; a servant of servants shall he be unto his brethren.*

And he said, *Blessed be the LORD God of Shem; and Canaan shall be his servant.*

> *God shall enlarge Japheth, and he shall dwell in the tents of Shem; and Canaan shall be his servant.* (Genesis 9:18–27)

Was Noah's exclamation the pronouncing of a curse upon his son Ham, and consequently upon his grandson Canaan, or was it his way of expressing, in a moment of anger, a previously unarticulated family-relationship situation that he knew would come to pass? Who can say for sure? This author prefers the latter viewpoint.

How interesting it is to note that of all the significant events that transpired in Noah's 950 years of obedience to the Lord and service to mankind, only this single, foolish incident is what is preserved of his personal life! Why?

No more details are related in the scriptures concerning the latter years of Noah's life except the following:

> And Noah lived after the flood three hundred and fifty years.
>
> And all the days of Noah were nine hundred and fifty years: and he died. (Genesis 9:28–29)

THE TABLE OF NATIONS

But the account of Noah's impact upon mankind can't end without registering the spread of mankind across the world once more after Noah and his family emerged from the ark.

Genesis 10:1–32 is often referred to as the table of nations because it indicates the areas which were settled by the descendants of Japheth, Ham, and Shem following the great flood. Another passage of scripture, 1 Chronicles 1:1–27, is also pertinent to this listing. Entire books have been written on the subject, along with numerous commentaries. There is only space here for a brief summary of the post-flood settlement patterns—in this case drawn from three Bible-study volumes. First, from the *HarperCollins Bible Commentary*:

> As an ethnological statement, Genesis 10 has grouped and related peoples in perplexing ways that have been the subject of considerable examination. One recent study has suggested that the distinguishing features of the three lines of descent are sociological, based on distinct ways of life, group characteristics, and professions: Shem's descendants comprise the non-sedentary, migratory segment of the population, the nomadic tribes; the descendants of Ham, the sedentary, agrarian population of village and town; and the descendants of Japheth, the maritime nations, the seafaring inhabitants of islands and coastal areas.[6]

---

6.   Mays, James L., General Editor. *HarperCollins Bible Commentary* (San Francisco: HarperSanFrancisco), 2000, p. 90.

Next, an observation from *The Archaeological Study Bible:*

> The list of Noah's descendants contains 70 names—a number that symbolized for the ancients totality and completion. It should be noted that the list is incomplete and apparently representative. The author penetrated selectively into various lines in order to achieve the final number.[7]

And finally, a brief summary from the *Life Application Bible:*

Bible Nations Descended from Noah's Sons

Shem: Hebrews, Chaldeans, Assyrians, Persians, Syrians
Ham: Canaanites, Egyptians, Philistines, Hittites, Amorites
Japheth: Greeks, Thracians, Scythians

Shem's descendants were called Semites. Abraham, David, and Jesus descended from Shem.

Ham's descendants settled in Canaan, Egypt, and the rest of Africa.

Japheth's descendants settled for the most part in Asia Minor.[8]

For a more thorough verse-by-verse commentary on Genesis chapter 10, see the *HarperCollins Study Bible.*[9]

OTHER SCRIPTURAL TRIBUTES AND ALLUSIONS TO NOAH

Certainly, Noah is one of the pivotal and widely recognized individuals in all the Latter-day Saint standard works. Listed below are the most significant of the passages which speak of him, in addition to his basic Genesis account, found in the scriptures. For lack of allotted space, they are summarized here in very brief phrases.

FROM THE OLD TESTAMENT

1 Chronicles 1:1–4: "Adam, . . . Methuselah, Lamech, Noah, Shem, Ham, and Japheth."

Isaiah 54:8–9: "As I have sworn that the waters of Noah should no more go over the earth."

---

7. *Archaeological Study Bible: An Illustrated Walk Through Biblical History and Culture* (Grand Rapids, Michigan: Zondervan), 2005, p. 18.

8. *Life Application Bible: King James Version* (Wheaton, IL: Tyndale House Publishers, Inc., 1989), p. 23.

9. *HarperCollins Study Bible: New Revised Standard Version* (New York: HarperCollinsPublishers, 1993), pp. 16–18.

Ezekiel 14:13–14: "Noah, Daniel, and Job . . . should deliver . . . their . . . souls by righteousness."

FROM THE NEW TESTAMENT

Matthew 24:36–39: "As the days of Noe were, so shall also the coming of the Son of man be."

Luke 3:36–38: "Arphaxad, which was the son of Sem, which was the son of Noe."

Luke 17:24–27: "They did eat, drink, . . . until the day Noe entered into the ark, and the flood came."

Hebrews 11:7: "By faith Noah, . . . prepared an ark to the saving of his house."

1 Peter 3:18–20: "God waited in the days of Noah, while the ark was a preparing."

2 Peter 2:4–5: "God . . . spared not the old world, but saved Noah, . . . bringing in the flood."

FROM THE BOOK OF MORMON

Alma 10:22: "Not be by flood, as were the people in the days of Noah, but . . . by famine."

3 Nephi 22:8–9: "I have sworn that the waters of Noah should no more go over the earth."

Ether 6:7: "their vessels being tight like unto a dish, . . . like unto the ark of Noah."

Ether 13:2–3: "after the waters had receded from off the face of this land it became a choice land."

FROM THE DOCTRINE AND COVENANTS

D&C 84:14–16: "Melchizedek, . . . [priesthood] through the lineage of his fathers, even till Noah."

D&C 107:52: "Noah was ten years old when he was ordained under the hand of Methuselah."

D&C 133:52–56: "The year of my redeemed is come; . . . and Noah also, and they . . . before him."

D&C 138:6–10: "for this cause was the gospel preached also to them that are dead."

D&C 138:28: "the spirits in prison, . . . disobedient . . . in the days of Noah."

D&C 138:38–41: "The great and mighty ones . . . Noah, who gave warning of the flood."

FROM THE PEARL OF GREAT PRICE

Moses 7:42–52: "Enoch saw that Noah built an ark; and that the Lord smiled upon it."

Moses 7:60: "To fulfil the oath which I have made unto you concerning the children of Noah."

Moses 8:2–3: "from his loins should spring all the kingdoms of the earth (through Noah),"

Abraham 1:25–27: "Priesthood, . . . the Pharaohs would fain claim it from Noah, through Ham."

CHAPTER 5

MELCHIZEDEK

THE KING OF SALEM, THE PRINCE OF PEACE, THE PRIEST OF THE MOST HIGH GOD

Think about it. Latter-day Saints repeat the name of Melchizedek more often than the names of all the other prophets discussed in this book—Adam, Seth, Enoch, Noah, Abraham, Isaac, Jacob, and Joseph—put together. They say his name constantly in priesthood meetings, sacrament meetings, stake and general Conferences, institute classes—everywhere Latter-day Saints congregate.

Unfortunately, about half the Saints mispronounce it. They reverse the vowel sounds of the second and fourth syllables. The correct pronunciation is Mel–KIZ–uh–deck, *not* Mel-KEZ-uh-dick! (The second and fourth syllables should rhyme with "his" and "check," respectively.)

Equally unfortunate is that the scriptures tell less about Melchizedek than any of the others, though there are passages that mention and refer to him in all four of the LDS standard works.

MELCHIZEDEK IN ABRAM'S DAY— THE GENESIS ACCOUNT

Genesis chapter 14 tells about Melchizedek while describing one of the mid-life adventures in the life of Abram (later, Abraham). It tells how four powerful kings, whose kingdoms centered in the areas of modern-day Iraq and Iran, waged war against five lesser kings whose kingdoms centered in the southern area of what today is modern Israel, particularly the areas near the Dead Sea. The five lesser kings had previously been vassal states of the four kings, but had rebelled against them.

A fierce battle was fought in the Dead Sea area, and the five lesser kings were defeated. The forces of the four conquering kings sacked the villages of Sodom and Gomorrah (located near the southern shores of the Dead Sea), then carried away their loot and the conquered inhabitants as they marched homeward. Among their captives "they took Lot, Abram's brother's son, who dwelt in Sodom, and his goods, and departed" (Genesis 14:12). Lot was the son of Abram's brother Haran (Genesis 11:27–31).

Word of Lot's capture was brought to his uncle, "Abram the Hebrew." Though he was more than seventy-five years old (Genesis 12:4), Abram immediately enlisted his servants and the help of powerful neighbors to pursue the marauders. They stalked the invaders more than one-hundred-fifty miles northward to Dan, then another sixty-plus miles east towards Damascus. They caught them there and ambushed them, securing Lot's release and regaining his servants, companions, and goods:

> And there came one that had escaped, and told Abram the Hebrew; for he dwelt in the plain of Mamre the Amorite, brother of Eschol, and brother of Aner: and these were confederate with Abram.
>
> And *when Abram heard that his brother was taken captive, he armed his trained servants, born in his own house, three hundred and eighteen,* and pursued them unto Dan.
>
> And he divided himself against them, he and his servants, by night, and smote them, and pursued them unto Hobah, which is on the left hand of Damascus.
>
> *And he brought back all the goods, and also brought again his brother Lot, and his goods, and the women also, and the people.* (Genesis 14:13–16)

On their way homeward, they came to Salem (modern-day Jerusalem), where the returning heroes were warmly received by the area's local king, Melchizedek. Abram recognized Melchizedek as "the priest of the most high God":

> And the king of Sodom went out to meet him after his return from the slaughter of Chedorlaomer, and of the kings that were with him, at the valley of Shaveh, which is the king's dale.
>
> And *Melchizedek king of Salem* brought forth bread and wine: and *he was the priest of the most high God.*
>
> And he blessed him, and said, *Blessed be Abram of the most high God, possessor of heaven and earth:*
>
> And blessed be the most high God, which hath delivered thine enemies into thy hand. And *he gave him tithes of all.* (Genesis 14:17–20)

And that is all that the Bible records about Melchizedek, the man! Perhaps more details need to be read into the above account than appear at first glance. It appears that Abram and Melchizedek already knew each other prior to this meeting, and were well acquainted with the roles each other were fulfilling in the Lord's kingdom. As will be seen later in this chapter, the Doctrine and Covenants asserts that it was Melchizedek who ordained Abram to the priesthood (see D&C 84:14), presumably prior to this meeting. Melchizedek already knew that Abram was being abundantly blessed by the most high God. Likewise, Abram already knew Melchizedek was the "priest of the most high God"—the Lord's representative upon the earth for that era.

The above Genesis passage indicates that Abram "gave him [Melchizedek] tithes of all," but it doesn't say when those tithes were being paid. Obviously, Abram hadn't come to this spontaneous gathering ready to deliver flocks and herds to Melchizedek—he and his followers had been suddenly recruited and had pursued the enemy forces over a long distance with little time for preparation. And the Genesis account clearly states that Abraham took no loot when they conquered the northern armies (Genesis 14:23), so he wasn't paying tithes of any confiscated bounty. It is likely that Abram had previously brought his tithes and offerings to Melchizedek and that he continued the practice throughout his life. They lived in close proximity to one another—there was only about a twenty-five-mile distance between the Hebron and Jerusalem areas.

INFORMATION ABOUT MELCHIZEDEK FROM THE BOOK OF MORMON

Obviously, Melchizedek's fame was widespread in Old Testament times, and that fame carried over, down through the centuries, into the Book of Mormon. About 1800 years later, when Alma and Amulek were preaching to the people of Ammonihah, Alma preached a powerful sermon on priesthood authority which included a number of interesting historical facts about Melchizedek—it tells how he brought his people back from wickedness to righteousness, and how he maintained peaceful relations with surrounding tribes to the extent he was known as the "prince of peace":

> Humble yourselves even as the people in the days of *Melchizedek, who was also a high priest after this same order which I have spoken, who also took upon him the high priesthood forever.*
>
> And *it was this same Melchizedek to whom Abraham paid tithes;* yea, even our father Abraham paid tithes of one-tenth part of all he possessed. . . .
>
> Now this Melchizedek was a king over the land of Salem; and his people had waxed strong in iniquity and abomination; yea, they had all gone astray; they were full of all manner of wickedness;
>
> But *Melchizedek having exercised mighty faith, and received the office of the high priesthood according to the holy order of God, did preach repentance unto his people.* And behold, they did repent; and Melchizedek did establish peace in the land in his days; therefore he was called the prince of peace, for *he was the king of Salem; and he did reign under his father.*
>
> Now, there were many before him, and also there were many afterwards, but *none were greater; therefore, of him they have more particularly made mention.* (Alma 13:14–15, 17–19)

Previously, in this same discourse, Alma had explained that the holy priesthood, which is "without beginning of days or end of years, being prepared from eternity to all eternity," was operational prior to the Creation of this earth. He indicated that many in premortality were called to the priesthood and ordained to be high priests in that holy order, and then cited Melchizedek's people as good examples of proper priesthood conduct:

> My brethren, I would cite your minds forward to the time when the Lord God gave these commandments unto his children; and I would that ye should remember that *the Lord God ordained priests, after his holy order, which was after the order of his Son, to teach these things unto the people.*
>
> *And those priests were ordained after the order of his Son, in a manner that thereby the people might know in what manner to look forward to his Son for redemption.*
>
> And this is the manner after which they were ordained—*being called and prepared from the foundation of the world according to the foreknowledge of God, on account of their exceeding faith and good works;* in the first place being left to choose good or evil; therefore they having chosen good, and exercising exceedingly great faith, are *called with a holy calling, yea, with that holy calling which was prepared with, and according to, a preparatory redemption for such.* . . .
>
> And thus being called by this holy calling, and ordained unto the high priesthood of the holy order of God, to teach his commandments unto the children of men, that they also might enter into his rest—
>
> This high priesthood being after the order of his Son, which order was from the foundation of the world; or in other words, being without beginning of days or end of years, being prepared from eternity to all eternity, according to his foreknowledge of all things—
>
> Now they were ordained after this manner—being called with a holy calling, and ordained with a holy ordinance, and *taking upon them the high priesthood of the holy order, which calling, and ordinance, and high priesthood, is without beginning or end*—
>
> Thus they become high priests forever, after the order of the Son, the Only Begotten of the Father, who is without beginning of days or end of years, who is full of grace, equity, and truth. And thus it is. Amen.
>
> Now, as I said concerning the holy order, or this high priesthood, *there were many who were ordained and became high priests of God;* and it was on account of their exceeding faith and repentance, and their righteousness before God, they choosing to repent and work righteousness rather than to perish; . . .
>
> Yea, humble yourselves *even as the people in the days of Melchizedek, who was also a high priest after this same order which I have spoken, who also took upon him the high priesthood forever.*

And it was this same Melchizedek to whom Abraham paid tithes; yea, even
our father Abraham paid tithes of one-tenth part of all he possessed.

Now these ordinances were given after this manner, that thereby the
people might look forward on the Son of God, it being a type of his order, or
it being his order, and this that they might look forward to him for a remis-
sion of their sins, that they might enter into the rest of the Lord. (Alma
13:1–3, 6–10, 14–16)

INFORMATION ON MELCHIZEDEK FROM THE JOSEPH SMITH TRANSLATION OF THE BIBLE

The inspired translation made of the book of Genesis in the Bible contains an informative passage on Melchizedek. It speaks of his great ministry and describes blessings and powers made available to man through the
Melchizedek Priesthood. (In the JST passage cited below, the additions to
the Biblical text of Genesis 14 are shown in italics.)

And Melchizedek lifted up his voice and blessed Abram.

Now Melchizedek was a man of faith, who wrought righteousness; and
when a child he *feared God, and stopped the mouths of lions, and quenched the
violence of fire.*

*And thus, having been approved of God, he was ordained an high priest
after the order of the covenant which God made with Enoch,*

*It being after the order of the Son of God; which order came, not by man,
nor the will of man; neither by father nor mother; neither by beginning of days
nor end of years; but of God;*

*And it was delivered unto men by the calling of his own voice, according to
his own will, unto as many as believed on his name.*

*For God having sworn unto Enoch and unto his seed with an oath by him-
self; that every one being ordained after this order and calling should have power,
by faith, to break mountains, to divide the seas, to dry up waters, to turn them
out of their course;*

*To put at defiance the armies of nations, to divide the earth, to break every
band, to stand in the presence of God; to do all things according to his will,
according to his command, subdue principalities and powers; and this by the will
of the Son of God which was from before the foundation of the world.*

*And men having this faith, coming up unto this order of God, were trans-
lated and taken up into heaven.*

*And now, Melchizedek was a priest of this order; therefore he obtained
peace in Salem, and was called the Prince of peace.*

*And his people wrought righteousness, and obtained heaven, and sought
for the city of Enoch which God had before taken, separating it from the earth,
having reserved it unto the latter days, or the end of the world;*

And hath said, and sworn with an oath, that the heavens and the earth should come together; and the sons of God should be tried so as by fire.

And this Melchizedek, having thus established righteousness, was called the king of heaven by his people, or, in other words, the King of peace.

And he lifted up his voice, and he blessed Abram, being the high priest, and the keeper of the storehouse of God;

Him whom God had appointed to receive tithes for the poor.

Wherefore, Abram paid unto him tithes of all that he had, of all the riches which he possessed, which God had given him more than that which he had need.

And it came to pass, that God blessed Abram, and gave unto him riches, and honor, and lands for an everlasting possession; according to the covenant which he had made, and according to the blessing wherewith Melchizedek had blessed him. (Joseph Smith Translation, Genesis 14:25–40. Compare Genesis 14.)

EARLY PRIESTHOOD LINES OF AUTHORITY

In addition to the insights Alma taught concerning Melchizedek, The Doctrine and Covenants tells even more about him. One of the most interesting items of information it conveys is that it was Melchizedek who bestowed the priesthood upon Abraham. Apparently Melchizedek traced his own line of priesthood authority back to Noah:

Abraham received the priesthood from Melchizedek, who received it through the lineage of his fathers, even till Noah;

And from Noah till *Enoch,* through the lineage of their fathers;

And from Enoch to *Abel,* who was slain by the conspiracy of his brother, who received the priesthood by the commandments of God, by the hand of his father *Adam,* who was the first man—

Which priesthood continueth in the church of God in all generations, and is without beginning of days or end of years. (D&C 84:14–17)

Verses from that same section indicate that Melchizedek's line of priesthood authority later continued down through the years to Moses, who received his ordination from his father-in-law, Jethro:

And the sons of *Moses, according to the Holy Priesthood which he received under the hand of his father-in-law, Jethro;*

And Jethro received it under the hand of *Caleb;*

And Caleb received it under the hand of *Elihu;*

And Elihu under the hand of *Jeremy;*

And Jeremy under the hand of *Gad;*

And Gad under the hand of *Esaias;*

And Esaias received it under the hand of *God.*

Esaias also lived in the days of Abraham, and was blessed of him—

Which Abraham received the priesthood from Melchizedek, who received it through the lineage of his fathers, even till Noah. (D&C 84:6–14)

An Ancient Name Change for
the Higher Priesthood

Section 107 of the Doctrine and Covenants explains that Church leaders in ancient times (*after* the time of Melchizedek, but *before* the days of King David), decided to "nickname" the higher priesthood "the Melchizedek Priesthood." This may have happened about the same time the decision was made to substitute the name LORD for Jehovah in the ancient scriptures. The Doctrine and Covenants passage states that

> There are, in the church, two priesthoods, namely, the Melchizedek and Aaronic, including the Levitical Priesthood.
>
> Why the first is called the Melchizedek Priesthood is because *Melchizedek was such a great high priest.*
>
> Before his day it was called *the Holy Priesthood, after the Order of the Son of God.*
>
> But out of *respect or reverence to the name of the Supreme Being, to avoid the too frequent repetition of his name, they, the church, in ancient days, called that priesthood after Melchizedek, or the Melchizedek Priesthood.* (D&C 107:1–4)

That adopted name for the higher priesthood apparently was in effect by the time King David wrote the 110th Psalm. In the unique style of several Old Testament prophecies concerning either or both the first and second comings of Christ to this earth, this prophecy portrays the Lord, who is Jehovah, speaking of himself in third person. Here, in verse four, Jesus Christ is spoken of as being "a priest for ever after the order of Melchizedek," which seems to indicate that the name change had been made prior to King David's day:

> The LORD said unto my Lord, Sit thou at my right hand, until I make thine enemies thy footstool.
>
> The LORD shall send the rod of thy strength out of Zion: rule thou in the midst of thine enemies.
>
> Thy people shall be willing in the day of thy power, in the beauties of holiness from the womb of the morning: thou hast the dew of thy youth.
>
> The LORD hath sworn, and will not repent, *Thou art a priest for ever after the order of Melchizedek.*
>
> The Lord at thy right hand shall strike through kings in the day of his wrath.
>
> He shall judge among the heathen, he shall fill the places with the dead bodies; he shall wound the heads over many countries.
>
> He shall drink of the brook in the way: therefore shall he lift up the head. (Psalm 110:1–7)

The author of the New Testament book of Hebrews quoted this psalm.

In doing so, he referred to Christ as a "high priest after the order of Melchisedec":

> Every high priest taken from among men is ordained for men in things pertaining to God, that he may offer both gifts and sacrifices for sins: . . .
>
> And no man taketh this honour unto himself, but he that is called of God, as was Aaron.
>
> So also Christ glorified not himself to be made an high priest; but he that said unto him, Thou art my Son, to day have I begotten thee.
>
> As he saith also in another place, Thou art a priest for ever after the order of Melchisedec.
>
> Who in the days of his flesh, when he had offered up prayers and supplications with strong crying and tears unto him that was able to save him from death, and was heard in that he feared;
>
> Though he were a Son, yet learned he obedience by the things which he suffered;
>
> And being made perfect, he became the author of eternal salvation unto all them that obey him;
>
> Called of God an high priest after the order of Melchisedec. (Hebrews 5:1, 4–10)

He previously had referred to the Savior as "the Apostle and High Priest of our profession, Christ Jesus; Who was faithful to him that appointed him" (Hebrews 3:1–2).

Doctrine and Covenants section 76, while describing the glorious blessings of those who will attain exaltation in the celestial kingdom, makes an interesting allusion to "the order of Melchizedek," linking it to earlier titles for the priesthood:

> They are they who are priests and kings, who have received of his fulness, and of his glory;
>
> And are priests of the Most High, after the order of Melchizedek, which was after the order of Enoch, which was after the order of the Only Begotten Son.
>
> Wherefore, as it is written, they are gods, even the sons of God—
>
> Wherefore, all things are theirs, whether life or death, or things present, or things to come, all are theirs and they are Christ's, and Christ is God's. (D&C 76:56–59)

Another Doctrine and Covenants section refers to "the Priesthood which is after the order of Melchizedek, which is after the order of mine Only Begotten Son" (D&C 124:123).

THE MELCHIZEDEK PRIESTHOOD HOLDS THE KEYS TO THE KNOWLEDGE OF GOD

This chapter is not intended to be a treatise on the many aspects of priesthood authority and administration. However, it should be recognized that the higher priesthood, "the holiest order of God," the priesthood which now is inseparably associated with the name of Melchizedek, holds great significance today, as it has throughout the history of this earth. It holds the keys to the knowledge of God and to the sacred ordinances which open the way for man to return to His presence:

> *Which priesthood continueth in the church of God in all generations, and is without beginning of days or end of years.*
>
> And the Lord confirmed a priesthood also upon Aaron and his seed, throughout all their generations, which priesthood also continueth and abideth forever with *the priesthood which is after the holiest order of God.*
>
> And this greater priesthood administereth the gospel and *holdeth the key of the mysteries of the kingdom, even the key of the knowledge of God.*
>
> Therefore, in the ordinances thereof, the power of godliness is manifest.
>
> *And without the ordinances thereof, and the authority of the priesthood, the power of godliness is not manifest unto men in the flesh;*
>
> *For without this no man can see the face of God, even the Father, and live.* (D&C 84:17–22)

Several verses from Doctrine and Covenants Section 107 serve to summarize the powers and authority of the priesthood that bears the greatly respected name of Melchizedek. This author has inserted numbers one through eight to highlight the various specific powers which they ennumerate:

> [1] The Melchizedek Priesthood holds *the right of presidency,* and [2] has *power and authority over all the offices in the church in all ages of the world,* [3] to *administer in spiritual things.* (D&C 107:8)

And also:

> The power and authority of the higher, or Melchizedek Priesthood, is [4] *to hold the keys of all the spiritual blessings of the church*—[5] To have the privilege *of receiving the mysteries of the kingdom of heaven,* [6] to have the *heavens opened* unto them, [7] to commune with the *general assembly* and *church of the Firstborn,* and [8] to enjoy the *communion and presence of God the Father, and Jesus the mediator of the new covenant.* (D&C 107:18–19)

And again, that highly significant indication from the book of Abraham, which speaks of God, seated upon his throne, revealing the key words of the priesthood unto Melchizedek, as unto others treated in this book, needs to be included here in this chapter on Melchizedek:

> *Fig. 3.* Is made to represent God, *sitting upon his throne,* clothed with power and authority; with a crown of eternal light upon his head; *representing also the grand Key-words of the Holy Priesthood, as revealed to* Adam in the

Garden of Eden, as also to Seth, Noah, *Melchizedek*, Abraham, and all to whom the Priesthood was revealed. (Abraham, Facsimile 2, Figure 3)

Why Is the Name of Melchizedek Held in Such High Esteem?

So, in retrospect, why is the name of Melchizedek held in such high esteem throughout the scriptures, and in the Church today?

1. He was the "king of Salem" (Genesis 14:18).
2. He was "the priest of the most high God" (Genesis 14:18).
3. He exercised mighty faith and received the office of the high priesthood according to the holy order of God (Alma 13:18).
4. He preached repentance to his people, and they repented (Alma 13:18).
5. He established peace in his land to the extent that he was called "the prince of peace" (Alma 13:18).
6. He helped establish and maintain the principle of tithing (JST Genesis 14:37–39).
7. "None were greater" than he, so he receives more-particular mention (Alma 13:19).
8. He ordained Abraham to the priesthood (D&C 84:6–14).
9. His priesthood line of authority reaches back through Noah all the way to Adam (D&C 84:14–17).
10. His priesthood line of authority continued down to Moses (D&C 84:6–14).
11. In ancient times, Church leaders renamed the holy priesthood the Melchizedek Priesthood to preserve the sacredness of the priesthood's original name (D&C 107:1–4).
12. Jesus Christ was called a "high priest after the order of Melchisedec" (Hebrews 5:1, 4–10).
13. Melchizedek received the grand key-words of the holy priesthood along with other ancient prophets and patriarchs (Abraham, Facsimile 2, Figure 3).
14. His name is the most-often spoken of all the names of the ancient prophets and patriarchs.

Reasons enough for him to be held in highest esteem down through all the ongoing ages of time!

CHAPTER 6

ABRAHAM

"ABRAHAM OBEYED MY VOICE, AND KEPT MY CHARGE, MY COMMANDMENTS, MY STATUTES, AND MY LAWS"

ABRAM'S RICH HERITAGE

How fortunate Latter-day Saints are to have so much scriptural information available about this great prophet and his times! Not only are there 15 chapters devoted to his life in the book of Genesis, there are five rich chapters in the book of Abraham which are easily accessible. In addition to the numerous allusions to Abraham and his descendants in both the Old and New Testaments, references to Abraham are rich and plentiful in the Book of Mormon and the Doctrine and Covenants. The challenge is to pull all of that information together into a meaningful and useable manuscript. Hopefully, this chapter will be a step in that direction.

Old Testament accounts begin to fit into historical molds that tally with archaeological findings and other external evidences after the flood in Noah's day. For instance, the genealogical pedigree chart for Abram stretches back to Noah's son, Shem. Here is how it is preserved in Genesis chapter 11:

These are the generations of *Shem*: Shem was an hundred years old, and begat *Arphaxad* two years after the flood: . . .

And Arphaxad lived five and thirty years, and begat *Salah*: . . .

And Salah lived thirty years, and begat *Eber*: . . .

And Eber lived four and thirty years, and begat *Peleg*: . . .

And Peleg lived thirty years, and begat *Reu*: . . .

And Reu lived two and thirty years, and begat *Serug*: . . .

And Serug lived thirty years, and begat *Nahor*: . . .

And Nahor lived nine and twenty years, and begat *Terah*: . . .

And Terah lived seventy years, and begat *Abram*, Nahor, and Haran. (Genesis 11:10–26. See also 1 Chronicles 1:17–27.)

As was done for Adam and his posterity, a generation chart for Shem's descendants serves to condense much of the above information:

Generation	Name	Shem's Age when Born	Father's Age when Born	Age at Death
1	Shem			600
2	Arphaxad	100	100	438
3	Salah	135	35	433
4	Eber	165	30	464
5	Peleg	195	30	239
6	Reu	225	30	239
7	Serug	257	32	230
8	Nahor	287	30	148
9	Terah	316	29	205
10	Abram	386	70	175

FAMILY RELATIONSHIPS

When did Abram live? One chronological listing gives his approximate date of birth at about 2166 BC and his death date at 1991 BC.[1] Family details began to be provided in more detail while Abram was still a youth and living with his parents. According to the scriptural record, Terah was the father of three sons, of which Abram was the firstborn. Abram's younger brother, Haran, married and became the father of three children: Lot, Milcah, and Ischah, but died at a relatively young age:

> Terah lived seventy years, and begat Abram, Nahor, and Haran.
> Now these are the generations of Terah: Terah begat Abram, Nahor, and Haran; and Haran begat Lot.
> And Haran died before his father Terah in the land of his nativity, in Ur of the Chaldees.[2] (Genesis 11:26–28)

---

1. This chronological listing will be reproduced in full later in this chapter.

2. Ur, today, is the modern Tell el-Mukayyar, a city in Iraq near the mouth of the Euphrates River as it flows into the Persian Gulf. It is situated south of the River on its right bank, about 9.9 miles (16 kilometers) from Nasiriyah, Iraq and close to the site of ancient Eridu. The city was well situated on both land and water routes for trade moving to and from Arabia. Ur very possibly was the largest city in the world from about 2030 to 1980 BC, with an estimated population at that time of 65,000 inhabitants. The largely intact ruins of a seventy-foot-tall Ziggurat (a temple of Nanna—the moon diety in Sumerian mythology) still stand in the area.

The Genesis account tells of Abram's marriage to Sarai. It also tells of his brother Nahor's marriage to Abram's niece: Milcah—the daughter of Abram's deceased brother Haran. "Abram and Nahor took them wives: the name of Abram's wife was Sarai; and the name of Nahor's wife, Milcah, the daughter of Haran, the father of Milcah, and the father of Iscah. But Sarai was barren; she had no child" (Genesis 11:29–30; see Abraham 2:2).

Sarai was ten years younger than Abram (Genesis 17:17). Apparently Terah had more than one wife, for later in the Abraham account, one learns that Sarai was Abraham's half-sister: Terah was her father, though Abraham's mother was not Sarai's mother (Genesis 20:12).

INSIGHTS CONCERNING ABRAM'S FAMILY FROM THE BOOK OF ABRAHAM

Latter-day Saints are privileged to have rich insights to Abram's early life through the Pearl of Great Price book of Abraham—an ancient record relatively unknown to the rest of the world. Chapter 1 of that record provides significant details concerning events in Abram's life[3] that transpired in Ur. It begins with Abraham relating his desire to hold the holy priesthood after the order of the Son of God—a blessing he perceived should be given to him as a result of his birthright as Terah's firstborn son.

> In the land of the Chaldeans, at the residence of my fathers, I, Abraham, saw that it was needful for me to obtain another place of residence;
>
> And, finding there was greater happiness and peace and rest for me, *I sought for the blessings of the fathers, and the right whereunto I should be ordained to administer the same;* having been myself a follower of righteousness, desiring also to be one who possessed great knowledge, and to be a greater follower of righteousness, and to possess a greater knowledge, and to be a father of many nations, a prince of peace, and desiring to receive instructions, and to keep the commandments of God, *I became a rightful heir, a High Priest, holding the right belonging to the fathers.*
>
> *It was conferred upon me from the fathers; it came down from the fathers,* from the beginning of time, yea, even from the beginning, or before the foundation of the earth, down to the present time, even *the right of the*

---

3. Abram's name was changed by the Lord to "Abraham" when he was more than a hundred years old. The Bible leaves his name as Abram up to that point, but the book of Abraham gives his name as Abraham throughout its pages. The two names usually will switch in this chapter depending on which book is the source document being discussed.

firstborn, or the first man, who is Adam, or first father, through the fathers unto me.

I sought for mine appointment unto the Priesthood according to the appointment of God unto the fathers concerning the seed. (Abraham 1:1–4)

Note, from the above, that Abram was seeking to receive the priesthood, but was not yet ordained. In the verses above he apparently is speaking of his right as his father's first-born son to receive the priesthood, rather than his actually having been ordained. Indeed, the Doctrine and Covenants indicates that he actually received his ordination many years later, from Melchizedek (see D&C 84:14–16).

The book of Abraham account, as it continues, indicates that at least some of his forefathers had fallen away and had turned to idolatry. Which ones had done so is not known. The above chart indicates that the men of most of the generations back to Seth were still alive when Abram was a young man, though whether they lived in close proximity to Ur of the Chaldees is not known:

My fathers having turned from their righteousness, and from the holy commandments which the Lord their God had given unto them, unto the worshiping of the gods of the heathen, utterly refused to hearken to my voice;

For their hearts were set to do evil, and were wholly turned to the god of Elkenah, and the god of Libnah, and the god of Mahmackrah, and the god of Korash, and the god of Pharaoh, king of Egypt;

Therefore they turned their hearts to the sacrifice of the heathen in offering up their children unto these dumb idols, and hearkened not unto my voice, *but endeavored to take away my life by the hand of the priest of Elkenah.* The priest of Elkenah was also the priest of Pharaoh. (Abraham 1:5–7)

At that time (shortly before the beginning of the second millennium BC), Egypt had extended its political power and religious influence up and across the fertile-crescent areas of the Tigris and Euphrates Rivers. From the book of Abraham account, it is obvious that Egyptian power was strong in Ur, and that human sacrifices, couched in the guise of religious rites, were being used to stamp out opposition from adherents to differing religious beliefs:

Now, at this time *it was the custom of the priest of Pharaoh, the king of Egypt, to offer up upon the altar which was built in the land of Chaldea, for the offering unto these strange gods, men, women, and children.*

And it came to pass that the priest made an offering unto the god of Pharaoh, and also unto the god of Shagreel, even after the manner of the Egyptians. Now the god of Shagreel was the sun.

Even the thank-offering of a child did the priest of Pharaoh offer upon the altar which stood by the hill called Potiphar's Hill, at the head of the plain of Olishem.

Now, this priest had offered upon this altar three virgins at one time, who were the daughters of Onitah, one of the royal descent directly from the loins of Ham. *These virgins were offered up because of their virtue; they would not bow down to worship gods of wood or of stone, therefore they were killed upon this altar,* and it was done after the manner of the Egyptians. (Abraham 1:8–11)

In the book of Abraham Facsimile No. 1, a drawing is preserved which shows a bedlike altar the Egyptian priests were using as they attempted to take Abram's life:

And it came to pass that *the priests laid violence upon me, that they might slay me also,* as they did those virgins upon this altar; and that you may have a knowledge of this altar, I will refer you to the representation at the commencement of this record.

It was made after the form of a bedstead, such as was had among the Chaldeans, and it stood before the gods of Elkenah, Libnah, Mahmackrah, Korash, and also a god like unto that of Pharaoh, king of Egypt.

That you may have an understanding of these gods, I have given you the fashion of them in the figures at the beginning, which manner of figures is called by the Chaldeans Rahleenos, which signifies hieroglyphics. (Abraham 1:12–14)

As the priests laid hands on Abram, he offered a fervent prayer, which brought immediate protection. An angel appeared and freed his hands. At the same time, he was granted a vision in which he saw Jehovah and received life-changing instructions:

And as they lifted up their hands upon me, that they might offer me up and take away my life, behold, I lifted up my voice unto the Lord my God, and *the Lord hearkened and heard, and he filled me with the vision of the Almighty,* and *the angel of his presence stood by me, and immediately unloosed my bands;*

And his voice was unto me: Abraham, Abraham, behold, *my name is Jehovah, and I have heard thee, and have come down to deliver thee, and to take thee away from thy father's house, and from all thy kinsfolk, into a strange land* which thou knowest not of;

And this because they have turned their hearts away from me, to worship the god of Elkenah, and the god of Libnah, and the god of Mahmackrah, and the god of Korash, and the god of Pharaoh, king of Egypt; therefore I have come down to visit them, and to destroy him who hath lifted up his hand against thee, Abraham, my son, to take away thy life.

Behold, I will lead thee by my hand, and *I will take thee, to put upon thee my name, even the Priesthood of thy father, and my power shall be over thee.*

As it was with Noah so shall it be with thee; but *through thy ministry my name shall be known in the earth forever,* for I am thy God. (Abraham 1:15–19)

True to the words of Jehovah, spoken in Abram's glorious vision, the pagan altar and the priest were destroyed (Abraham 1:20). Also, a severe famine was brought upon the land. Terah and his family suffered from the famine along with all the other inhabitants—their suffering was so intense that Terah repented and turned away from his idolatry (Abraham 1:29–30). The record goes on to say that "the Lord God caused the famine to wax sore in the land of Ur, insomuch that Haran, my brother, died" (Abraham 2:1).

It should be noted that at this time, perhaps because of Terah's repentance, that Abram was given charge of the sacred records of his forefathers. This passage is especially interesting because it reveals that Terah, while strongly influenced by the pagan beliefs he had embraced, had been influential in the Egyptian priests' decision to take Abram's life. Obviously, he had some major reasons to repent:

Accordingly a famine prevailed throughout all the land of Chaldea, and my father was sorely tormented because of the famine, and he repented of the evil which he had determined against me, to take away my life.

But *the records of the fathers, even the patriarchs, concerning the right of Priesthood, the Lord my God preserved in mine own hands; therefore a knowledge of the beginning of the Creation, and also of the planets, and of the stars, as they were made known unto the fathers, have I kept even unto this day.* (Abraham 1:30–31)

Abraham's Visions of the Heavens and of All the Lord's Creations

One of the most profound explanations of eternal truths provided in the scriptures was revealed to Abram, as recorded in chapter 3 of the book of Abraham. The record doesn't say when this glorious revelation, or group of revelations, was granted to him. It tells us that he had been given a Urim and Thummim while still in Ur (Abraham 3:1). It also says that he was told by the Lord that "I show these things unto thee before ye go into Egypt, that ye may declare all these words" (Abraham 3:15). So it's not known if these revelations were given in Ur, in Haran, or while Abram was traveling between those places or down towards Egypt.

At any rate, a verse-by-verse itemization of chapter 3 is included at this point in Abram's life story so that various doctrinal insights can be pointed out. Of course, the scriptural record should be read as this doctrinal outline is considered.

1. The Urim and Thummim are given to Abram (Abraham 3:1).
2. Many great stars are near the throne of God (3:2).
3. Kolob is a governing star near to the throne of God (3:3).
4. Kolob governs the stars in this earth's order (3:3).
5. The Lord can speak by the Urim and Thummim (3:4).
6. Kolob's times, seasons, and revolutions are after the Lord's time (3:4).
7. One day on Kolob equals a thousand years on this earth (3:4).
8. An intermediate star level exists between Kolob and earth (3:5).
9. Abram was given understanding of the time reckoning of this earth (3:6–7).
10. Abram was given knowledge of the planets between earth and Kolob (3:8–9).
11. Kolob governs the planets in this earth's order (3:9).
12. Abram was given knowledge of all the stars between earth and the throne of God (3:10).
13. Abram talked with the Lord face to face (3:11).
14. The Lord showed Abram the works He had created (3:11–12).
15. The Lord touched Abram's eyes to enable him to see beyond the veil (3:12).
16. Terms: Shinehah, Kokob, Olea, Kokaubeam (3:13).
17. The Lord will multiply Abram's seed like the stars (3:14).
18. Abram was to declare these things in Egypt (3:15).
19. Kolob is the greatest of all the Kokaubeam shown to Abram (3:16).
20. If there is a planet or star, another may exist above it (3:17).
21. The Lord will accomplish what He decides to do (3:17–18).
22. One spirit may be more intelligent than another (3:18).
23. Spirits are eternal, without beginning or end (3:18).
24. The Lord is more intelligent than all the spirits (3:19).
25. The Lord sent His angel to deliver Abram from the priest (3:20).
26. The Lord dwells in the midst of all the spirits (3:21).
27. The Lord came down to Abram to declare his creations (3:21).
28. The Lord is wiser than all of his creations (3:21).
29. The Lord rules in the heavens and earth over all the intelligences (3:21).
30. In the beginning, the Lord came down in the midst of all the intelligences (3:21).
31. The Lord showed Abram the intelligences organized before this earth's Creation (3:22).

32. The Lord chose premortal spirits to be His rulers on earth (3:22–23).
33. Abraham was chosen before he was born (3:23).
34. God stood among the premortal spirits and proposed the Creation of this earth (3:24).
35. Probation is a purpose of this earth's Creation (3:25).
36. Glories for those who keep their first and second estates (3:26).
37. Premortal choosing between Jesus and Lucifer (3:27).
38. Lucifer and his followers didn't keep their first estate (3:28).

THE MOVE FROM UR TO HARAN

The Genesis account says:

> Terah took Abram his son, and Lot the son of Haran his son's son, and Sarai his daughter in law, his son Abram's wife; and they went forth with them from Ur of the Chaldees, to go into the land of Canaan; and they came unto Haran, and dwelt there.
>
> And the days of Terah were two hundred and five years: and Terah died in Haran. (Genesis 11:31–32)

But much more insight is available in the book of Abraham account. It was Abram who made the decision to move to Haran, and to take his wife Sarai and his nephew Lot with him. That decision was made in response to a revelation from on high: "Now the Lord had said unto me: *Abraham, get thee out of thy country, and from thy kindred, and from thy father's house, unto a land that I will show thee*" (Abraham 2:3). Terah, no longer exercising parental authority over Abram, finally decided to follow them:

> Therefore I left the land of Ur, of the Chaldees, to go into the land of Canaan; and I took Lot, my brother's son, and his wife, and Sarai my wife; and also my father followed after me, unto the land which we denominated *Haran*. (Abraham 2:4)

Their route? Some Bible-history map-makers propose that they traveled west by northwest for about 400 miles to Mari, then trudged north by northwest another 200 miles or so to Haran.

Others propose that they crossed over from the Euphrates to the Tigris River and followed it up north to Nineveh, then went west to Haran. Either way, their journey was about 600 miles long (975 kilometers). Obviously, they were moving from one "major city" to another, as they sought to escape the ravages of the widespread famine by relocating to Haran.[4]

---

4. Haran was located in the foothills of the Zagros Mountains, about 60 miles directly east of Carchemish (the famous battlefield), and about 160 miles directly east from the eastern-most tip of the Mediterranean Sea. The area

EVENTS IN HARAN

The status of Abram and his family changed quite radically as various events transpired while they were in Haran. First, the famine ended (Abraham 2:5). Second, Terah prospered there ("there were many flocks there"), but turned back to his idolatry (ibid.). Years later, when Abram moved to the south, Terah "continued in Haran" (ibid.). Third, Abram and Lot also prospered there, acquiring many flocks and servants: "all their substance that they had gathered, and the souls that they had gotten" (Genesis 12:5).

But then, in answer to Abram's prayer for guidance, Jehovah appeared to him and issued unto him a life-changing mission call:

> The Lord appeared unto me, and said unto me: Arise, and take Lot with thee; for *I have purposed to take thee away out of Haran*, and to **make of thee a minister to bear my name in a strange land** *which I will give unto thy seed after thee for an everlasting possession*, when they hearken to my voice. (Abraham 2:6)

THE ABRAHAMIC COVENANT

The verses that follow, as found in both the Pearl of Great Price and the Bible, are known as The Abrahamic Covenant—a covenant that the Lord, Jehovah, made with Abram but that also extends to all mankind. They are so important they deserve verse-by-verse outlining and examination. The first passage is from the book of Abraham:

1. Jehovah is the Lord, the God of Abraham (Abraham 2:7–8).
2. Jehovah exercises great power over the elements (2:7).
3. Jehovah's foreknowledge (2:8).
4. Jehovah will guide, protect, and supervise Abram (2:8).

---

today is known as Carrhae; it is a district of the Sanliurfa Province in southeast Turkey. In ancient times it was a major commercial, religious and cultural center in Mesopotamia. Tyre was one of its main trading partners. The city was regarded as the home of the Mesopotamian moon-god Sin in the days of the Babylonians and on to Roman times. The town is now defunct, with only a small village nearby, but the ruins are regarded as a valuable archaeological site. The Battle of Carrhae was fought there in 53 BC between forces of the Parthian Empire and the Roman Republic.

Jehovah's 15 Promises

1. a land (2:6).
2. a great nation of Abram's posterity (2:9).
3. to bless Abram above measure (2:9).
4. to make Abram's name great among all nations (2:9).
5. that Abram will be a blessing unto his posterity (2:9).
6. that Abram's seed will bear the ministry and priesthood unto all nations (2:9).
7. Abram's posterity will be blessed through his name (2:10).
8. Those who receive the Gospel will be called by Abram's name (2:10).
9. Those who accept the Gospel will be considered as part of Abram's posterity (2:10).
10. Those who accept the Gospel will bless Abram as their father (2:10).
11. He will bless them that bless Abram (2:11).
12. He will curse them that curse Abram (2:11).
13. The priesthood shall continue in Abram and his posterity (2:11).
14. By Abram's literal seed shall all families be blessed with the gospel (2:11).
15. The blessings of the Gospel are salvation and life eternal (2:11).

As wonderful as the Biblical record of this event is, comparing it to modern revelations makes it easy to see what a blessing it is to have these additional insights, like the ones cited. The Genesis account lacks many key details:

> Now the LORD had said unto Abram, Get thee out of thy country, and from thy kindred, and from thy father's house, unto a land that I will shew thee:
>
> And *I will make of thee a great nation, and I will bless thee, and make thy name great; and thou shalt be a blessing:*
>
> And *I will bless them that bless thee, and curse him that curseth thee: and in thee shall all families of the earth be blessed.* (Genesis 12:1–3)

What was Abram's response to his mission call, to the instruction to leave Haran, and to these glorious promises?

> Now, after the Lord had withdrawn from speaking to me, and withdrawn his face from me, I said in my heart: *Thy servant has sought thee earnestly; now I have found thee;*
>
> Thou didst send thine angel to deliver me from the gods of Elkenah, and *I will do well to hearken unto thy voice,* therefore let thy servant rise up and depart in peace. (Abraham 2:12–13)

JOURNEYING SOUTH TO CANAAN

So I, Abraham, departed as the Lord had said unto me, and Lot with me; and *I, Abraham, was sixty and two years old when I departed out of Haran.*[5]

And I took Sarai, whom I took to wife when I was in Ur, in Chaldea, and Lot, my brother's son, and all our substance that we had gathered, and the souls that we had won in Haran, and *came forth in the way to the land of Canaan,* and dwelt in tents as we came on our way. (Abraham 2:14–15)

As the group traveled southward, Abram on several occasions built altars and offered sacrifices unto the Lord. When he did so in Jershon, he "prayed that the famine might be turned away from my father's house, that they might not perish" (Abraham 2:17).

When he offered sacrifice near Shechem, he "called on the Lord devoutly," and he again had the Lord appear to him. He recorded that "the Lord appeared unto me in answer to my prayers, and said unto me: Unto thy seed will I give this land" (Abraham 2:18–19). This event also was recorded in Genesis: "And the LORD appeared unto Abram, and said, Unto thy seed will I give this land" (Genesis 12:7). Another altar was built and a sacrifice was offered near Bethel (Genesis 12:8; Abraham 2:20).

Apparently the famine that was being felt back in Haran, five hundred miles to the north, was also ravaging the land of Canaan: "And there was a famine in the land: and Abram went down into Egypt to sojourn there; for the famine was grievous in the land" (Genesis 12:10; Abraham 2:21).

ABRAM IN EGYPT

Both the Genesis and Abraham accounts record a revelation given to Abram—a unique communication that shows the profound foreknowledge of God and his determination to keep his covenant to be with Abram and protect him. The Lord said unto Abram:

Behold, Sarai, thy wife, is a very fair woman to look upon; Therefore it shall come to pass, when the Egyptians shall see her, they will say—She is his wife; and they will kill you, but they will save her alive; therefore see that ye do on this wise:

Let her say unto the Egyptians, she is thy sister, and thy soul shall live.

And it came to pass that I, Abraham, told Sarai, my wife, all that the Lord had said unto me—Therefore say unto them, I pray thee, thou art my

---

5.   Note a minor chronology discrepancy between the book of Abraham and the Genesis account: the first records that Abram was 62 when he left Haran (above); the account in Genesis 12:4 says he was 75 when he departed from there.

sister, that it may be well with me for thy sake, and my soul shall live because of thee. (Abraham 2:22–25; Genesis 12:11–13)

Sure enough, the potential problem revealed to Abram came to pass. Sarai must have been extremely attractive for a woman in her sixties, because

When Abram was come into Egypt, the Egyptians beheld the woman that she was very fair. The princes also of Pharaoh saw her, and commended her before Pharaoh: and the woman was taken into Pharaoh's house.

And he entreated Abram well for her sake: and he had sheep, and oxen, and he asses, and menservants, and maidservants, and she asses, and camels. (Genesis 12:14–16)

The Lord, in His omnipotent wisdom, used this ruse not only to save Abram's life but to allow him to acquire wealth through the largesse of the Egyptians. However, the Lord also protected Sarai. Obviously, the couple's separation went on for a time, but finally "the LORD plagued Pharaoh and his house with great plagues because of Sarai Abram's wife" (Genesis 12:17). At some point she must have found it necessary to reveal her married status to the Pharaoh (perhaps to turn away his advances?), because he immediately confronted Abram with the angry challenge: "What is this that thou hast done unto me? why didst thou not tell me that she was thy wife? Why saidst thou, She is my sister? so I might have taken her to me to wife: now therefore behold thy wife, take her, and go thy way" (Genesis 12:18–19).

So "Pharaoh commanded his men concerning him: and they sent him away, and his wife, and all that he had" (Genesis 12:20). But by this time, apparently, the famine had abated, and it was time for them to return to the land of Canaan.

What had Abraham been doing in the weeks or months that went by while they were in Egypt besides increasing his flocks and herds and gaining other material wealth? A clue is found in the earlier instruction, recorded in Abraham chapter 3, where the Lord told Abram, "I show these things unto thee before ye go into Egypt, that ye may declare all these words" (Abraham 3:15). Perhaps Abram, the missionary, sought opportunities to preach to his Egyptian acquaintances concerning his God, Jehovah, and concerning His glorious creations and His plan of salvation.

Two explanations provided for Facsimile Number 3 in the book of Abraham provide further light:

Fig. 1. Abraham sitting upon Pharaoh's throne, by the politeness of the king, with a crown upon his head, representing the Priesthood, as emblematical of the grand Presidency in Heaven; with the scepter of justice and judgment in his hand. . . .

Abraham is reasoning upon the principles of Astronomy, in the king's court.
(Abraham Facsimile 3, Figures 1 and item 7)

THE RETURN TO CANAAN,
AND ABRAM'S SEPARATION FROM LOT

The preparations were made, and Abram, Sarai, Lot, and all their servants made ready to leave Egypt and move their tents and shepherd their animals northward over the hundreds of miles back to Bethel, their chosen destination. How far was their journey? The question can't be answered because the Biblical record doesn't state where they sojourned in Egypt.[6]

The record tells of their arrival in Bethel following their northward journey, and of the difficulties which soon arose after their arrival there:

> And Abram went up out of Egypt, he, and his wife, and all that he had, and Lot with him, into the south.
>
> *And Abram was very rich in cattle, in silver, and in gold.*
>
> And he went on his journeys from the south even to Beth-el, unto the place where his tent had been at the beginning, between Beth-el and Hai;
>
> Unto the place of the altar, which he had made there at the first: and there Abram called on the name of the LORD.
>
> *And Lot also, which went with Abram, had flocks, and herds, and tents.*
>
> *And the land was not able to bear them, that they might dwell together: for their substance was great, so that they could not dwell together.*
>
> And there was a strife between the herdmen of Abram's cattle and the herdmen of Lot's cattle: and the Canaanite and the Perizzite dwelled then in the land. (Genesis 13:1–7)

Abram took steps to resolve the problem, which had the potential to grow into much more serious proportions. The magnanimity of his character is evident from his willingness to allow Lot to choose where he wanted to move to, even though the fertile Jordan River valley was a far more attractive choice than remaining in the more barren hill country:

---

6. Perhaps they had been staying in Memphis—the ancient city founded about 3100 BC. It was the capital of Lower Egypt until around 2200 BC. Population estimates for the city during the Old-Kingdom period range from 30,000 down to 6,000 inhabitants. The ruins of Memphis, today, are located about twelve miles south of the modern city of Cairo, on the west bank of the Nile River. Another possibility as to where they were during their stay in Egypt might be Zoar—situated in the far more fertile area of the Nile delta. Shortly after returning to Canaan, when he was choosing where to locate his home, Lot commented on the lushness of the valley there (see Genesis 13:10).

And Abram said unto Lot, *Let there be no strife, I pray thee, between me and thee, and between my herdmen and thy herdmen; for we be brethren.*

Is not the whole land before thee? separate thyself, I pray thee, from me: *if thou wilt take the left hand, then I will go to the right; or if thou depart to the right hand, then I will go to the left.*

And Lot lifted up his eyes, and beheld all the plain of Jordan, that it was well watered every where, before the LORD destroyed Sodom and Gomorrah, *even as the garden of the LORD, like the land of Egypt, as thou comest unto Zoar.*

Then Lot chose him all the plain of Jordan; and Lot journeyed east: and they separated themselves the one from the other.

Abram dwelled in the land of Canaan, and Lot dwelled in the cities of the plain, and pitched his tent toward Sodom. (Genesis 13:8–12)

It should be recognized that the land of Canaan already was populated. Abram and Lot were superimposing their holdings into other areas where previous inhabitants had already chosen the best spots. As will be seen, Canaan wasn't just populated, it had been conquered and had been compelled to be a vassal state to kings situated further north—in Mesopotamia's Fertile Crescent (the areas which today are Iraq and parts of Iran).

Nevertheless, the Lord chose this occasion to repeat his promise to give the entire land to Abram's future descendants:

The LORD said unto Abram, after that Lot was separated from him, Lift up now thine eyes, and look from the place where thou art northward, and southward, and eastward, and westward:

For all the land which thou seest, to thee will I give it, and to thy seed for ever.

And *I will make thy seed as the dust of the earth:* so that if a man can number the dust of the earth, then shall thy seed also be numbered.

Arise, walk through the land in the length of it and in the breadth of it; for I will give it unto thee. (Genesis 13:14–17)

The Lord's promise wasn't just concerning land—it also was the prophetic promise that Abram would have an amazingly abundant posterity. And the promise was being made to a man, probably in his eighties, who as yet was childless!

As Abram and Lot had journeyed down to Egypt and then returned from there to Canaan, they most likely had passed through or near the area where Hebron now stands. Abram must have recognized it as an area where he might be able to settle. The record shows that after Lot departed towards Sodom, "Abram removed his tent, and came and dwelt in the plain of *Mamre, which is in Hebron,* and built there an altar unto the LORD" (Genesis 13:18).

Rescuing Lot, and the
Priesthood Blessings of Melchizedek

Genesis chapter 14 is the history of Abram's valiant rescue of his nephew, Lot. The account of the attack of the four northern kings on the five southern-Canaan vassal kings has already been retold in the previous chapter and won't be repeated in detail here. What is most significant is that when Abram's victorious "mini-army" was returning with the inhabitants of Sodom whom they had rescued, they were met, fed and honored by Melchizedek, the "king of Salem" and "the priest of the most high God" (Genesis 14:18).

The blessing pronounced by Melchizedek upon Abram indicates that the priestly king was well-acquainted with Abram and knew his eternal potential: *"Blessed be Abram of the most high God, possessor of heaven and earth"* (Genesis 14:19). Those aren't the words of one just getting acquainted with another that day for the first time. And Abram gave to Melchizedek "tithes of all" (Genesis 14:20; see also Alma 13:15), which he wouldn't be doing if this were a first-time encounter.

Why is that previous acquaintanceship important? Because the Doctrine and Covenants indicates that it was Melchizedek who ordained Abram into the priesthood: *"Abraham received the priesthood from Melchizedek, who received it through the lineage of his fathers, even till Noah; And from Noah till Enoch, through the lineage of their fathers"* (D&C 84:14–15). When?

Not at that time, in those agitated circumstances.

That priesthood would have been the higher priesthood, "the priesthood which is after the holiest order of God" (D&C 84:18). The same Doctrine and Covenants section explains that

> this greater priesthood administereth the gospel and *holdeth the key of the mysteries of the kingdom, even the key of the knowledge of God.*
>
> Therefore, in the ordinances thereof, the power of godliness is manifest.
>
> And without the ordinances thereof, and the authority of the priesthood, the power of godliness is not manifest unto men in the flesh;
>
> *For without this no man can see the face of God, even the Father, and live.*
> (D&C 84:19–22)

By this time, Abram had been visited several times by Jehovah, and had specifically reported that *"I, Abraham, talked with the Lord, face to face, as one man talketh with another"* back when he received the information conveyed in Abraham chapter 3 (Abraham 3:11). So, had Abram possessed the holy priesthood all this time? From while he still dwelt in Ur? or Haran? or when he first passed through Canaan en route to Egypt? Or is there some unifying or chronological relationship hinted at in the Figure 3 explanation of Facsimile 2 in the book of Abraham?

> *Fig. 3*: Is made to represent God, sitting upon his throne, clothed with power and authority; with a crown of eternal light upon his head; representing also *the grand Key-words of the Holy Priesthood, as revealed to Adam in the Garden of Eden,* as also to Seth, Noah, *Melchizedek, Abraham,* and all to whom the Priesthood was revealed.

These are questions for which Latter-day Saints, at present, are without an answer. However, they're good items for to put on a list of questions to ask when one arrives on the other side!

THE LORD'S NEW COVENANTS WITH ABRAM

Rarely discussed but highly significant, Genesis chapter 15 is the account of new promises which Jehovah made with Abraham. The Lord opened His communication with Abram by appearing to him in a vision: "the word of the LORD came unto Abram in a vision, saying, *Fear not, Abram: I am thy shield, and thy exceeding great reward* (Genesis 15:1).

Abram was ready with questions about the promises he had previously received concerning his having a posterity: "Lord GOD, what wilt thou give me, seeing I go childless, and the steward of my house is this Eliezer of Damascus? . . . Behold, to me thou hast given no seed: and, lo, one born in my house is mine heir" (Genesis 15:2–3).

As in other key chapters, the Lord's messages to Abram are so profound that they deserve individual listings to guide in the reading of the scriptural passage:

1. Jehovah is a shield and a reward (15:1).
2. Abram's heir would be his direct offspring (15:4).
3. Abram's posterity would be as numerous as the stars (15:5).
4. Jehovah counted Abram's belief in him as righteousness (15:6).
5. It was Jehovah that brought Abram out of Ur (15:7).
6. Jehovah brought Abram to Canaan to give him the land as an inheritance (15:7).
7. A prophecy of Abram's descendants' four-hundred-year Egyptian captivity (15:13).
8. Egypt will be judged for their afflicting the people of Israel (15:13–14).
9. The Israelites will leave Egypt with great substance (15:14).
10. The Israelites will return to Canaan in the fourth generation after being in Egypt (15:16).
11. Abram will live a long life and die peacefully (15:15).

12. The Lord again covenanted with Abram concerning the land of his inheritance (15:18).
13. The Lord partially defined the boundaries of Israel's promised land in the last days (15:18).
14. The Lord stipulated some of the peoples whose lands would be within the boundaries of Israel's promised land in the last days (15:19–21).

The partial defining of the prophesied last-days boundaries of Abram's descendants—the House of Israel—may lie at the heart of much of the opposition which the modern-day nation of Israel continually draws from its Arab neighbors. The boundaries set forth in this chapter would seemingly include portions or all of Israel, Egypt, Jordan, Syria, Lebanon, and Iraq. See Deuteronomy 11:24: "Every place whereon the soles of your feet shall tread shall be yours: from the wilderness and Lebanon, from the river, the river Euphrates, even unto the uttermost sea shall your coast be." (See also Ezekiel 47:13–23 and 48:1–29.)

A passage recorded in Joseph Smith's inspired translation of the Bible adds insights on this event. It tells us that Abraham saw Jesus Christ, the Son of God, in vision, and was aware of the resurrection process. (In the passage cited below, additions to the Genesis account are shown in italics.)

And Abram said, Lord God, how wilt thou give me this land for an everlasting inheritance?

And the Lord said, Though thou wast dead, yet am I not able to give it thee?

And if thou shalt die, yet thou shall possess it, for the day cometh, that the Son of Man shall live; but how can he live if he be not dead? he must first be quickened.

And it came to pass, that Abram looked forth and saw the days of the Son of Man, and was glad, and his soul found rest, and he believed in the Lord; and the Lord counted it unto him for righteousness. (Joseph Smith Translation, Genesis 15:9–12; compare Genesis 15:1–6)

THE BIRTH OF ISHMAEL

Ten years passed after Abram settled his family near Hebron. Abram was now about eighty-five years old (Genesis 16:3, 16). Sarai, his wife, knowing that she had been barren and apparently was past the age of childbearing, but also knowing of the Lord's promise to Abram that he would have an heir who would literally be the fruit of his loins, suggested that Abram take her maid as a substitute wife. At that time, a married woman who was unable to have children often was shamed by her peers, and was expected to give a female servant to her husband in order to produce heirs.

It was understood that children born by the servant would be considered to be children of the wife. By mating with the servant, Abram was following the accepted custom of the day. But Abram's mating with Hagar was more than the following of custom: Doctrine and Covenants 132, verses 34 and 65, indicate that the Lord commanded Sarai and Abraham to follow that course of action.

Hagar, Sarai's servant and handmaid, was Egyptian (probably a young servant brought back with them from Egypt ten years previous). Unfortunately, when she was with child, Hagar's pride caused her difficulties with her mistress:

> Now Sarai Abram's wife bare him no children: and she had an handmaid, an Egyptian, whose name was Hagar.
>
> And Sarai said unto Abram, Behold now, the LORD hath restrained me from bearing: I pray thee, go in unto my maid; it may be that I may obtain children by her. And Abram hearkened to the voice of Sarai.
>
> And Sarai Abram's wife took Hagar her maid the Egyptian, after Abram had dwelt ten years in the land of Canaan, and gave her to her husband Abram to be his wife.
>
> And he went in unto Hagar, and she conceived: and when she saw that she had conceived, her mistress was despised in her eyes.
>
> And Sarai said unto Abram, My wrong be upon thee: I have given my maid into thy bosom; and when she saw that she had conceived, I was despised in her eyes: the LORD judge between me and thee.
>
> But Abram said unto Sarai, Behold, thy maid is in thy hand; do to her as it pleaseth thee. And when Sarai dealt hardly with her, she fled from her face. (Genesis 16:1–6)

Hagar fled south, heading back to Egypt, through Shur.[7] While stopped at a watering hole, she was intercepted by an angel sent by Jehovah:

> The angel of the LORD found her by a fountain of water in the wilderness, by the fountain in the way to Shur.
>
> And he said, Hagar, Sarai's maid, whence camest thou? and whither wilt thou go? And she said, I flee from the face of my mistress Sarai.
>
> And the angel of the LORD said unto her, Return to thy mistress, and submit thyself under her hands. (Genesis 16:7–9)

And then the angel conveyed a prophetic message from the Lord, words of consolation which reach down in time to the present day. The

---

7. Shur was a wilderness area east of the Red Sea. It adjoined the Egyptian border. At that time it may have been a small border settlement located 150 to 200 miles south of Hebron. She would have had to cross a lot of barren desert terrain to reach the border.

angel, speaking for Jehovah, said unto her:

1. Hagar will have many descendants: a multitude (16:10).
2. The babe within her will be a son (16:11).
3. She was to name him Ishmael—meaning, "God hears" (16:11).
4. Jehovah was aware of her and had heard her (16:11).
5. Ishmael will be a wild man, constantly fighting with others (16:12).
6. Ishmael will live among his brethren (16:12).

In obedience to the angel's instruction, Hagar returned and bore Abram a son, which he named Ishmael. Abram was eighty-six when his son arrived. More will be said of Ishmael later in this chapter.

What became of the descendants of Ishmael, in fulfillment of the angel's prophecies? Little is known. He married an Egyptian woman (Genesis 21:21), participated in Abraham's funeral at Machpelah (Genesis 25:9), and lived to be 137 years old (Genesis 25:17).

Genesis 25:16–18 and 1 Chronicles 1:29–31 briefly tell of his sons and where they settled. Jewish and Muslim traditions regard Ishmael as the ancestor of the desert-dwelling tribes. Arabs regard him as their forefather. According to Muslim traditions, he and his mother, Hagar, are buried in the sacred Ka'aba in Mecca.

A NEW MANIFESTATION BROADENS THE ABRAHAMIC COVENANT

Thirteen years pass. Abram is 99 years old; Ishmael is 13. Jehovah once again appears to Abram (Genesis 17:1).

1. Jehovah identifies himself as God Almighty (17:1).
2. Perfection is commanded of Abram (17:1).
3. A covenant between Jehovah and Abram (17:2, 4).
4. Abram's posterity to be greatly multiplied (17:2).
5. Abram prostrated himself before Jehovah (17:3).
6. Abram to be the father of many nations (17:4).
7. A name change: from Abram to Abraham (17:5).
8. Abraham to have many descendants (17:6).
9. Nations and kings will descend from Abraham (17:6).
10. Jehovah will re-establish this covenant with Abraham's descendants (17:7).
11. The covenant is to be forever (17:7).
12. The covenant: Jehovah is to be the God of Abraham and his descendants (17:8).

13. The land of Canaan is to be an everlasting possession for Abraham's descendants. (17:8).

14. Jehovah's commandment: Abraham and his descendants are to keep this covenant. (17:9–10).

15. Jehovah's commandment: every male shall be circumcised (17:10).

16. Circumcision is to be a token of the covenant (17:11).

17. When and to whom circumcision is to be performed (17:12–13).

18. Circumcision to be an everlasting sign of the covenant (17:13).

19. Uncircumcised males are to be "cut off" (excommunicated; denied membership rights) from his people (17:14).

20. To be uncircumcised is to break the Abrahamic covenant (17:14).

21. Another name change: from Sarai to Sarah (17:15).

22. Sarah will bear Abraham a son (17:16).

23. Sarah will be a mother of nations and kings (17:16).

24. Abraham doubted God's promise of another son, and thought his line would only come through Ishmael (17:17–18).

25. Sarah will bear a son, to be called Isaac (17:19).

26. Jehovah will re-establish His covenant with Isaac and his descendants (17:19).

27. Blessings and prophetic promises for Ishmael (17:20).

28. Jehovah's covenant line will be through Isaac (17:21).

29. Isaac will be born next year (17:21).

Then the conversation was ended, and Jehovah departed. Clearly, this was an in-person visit here on earth, for the scripture records that "he left off talking with him, and *God went up from Abraham*" (Genesis 17:22).

What a remarkable experience! Jehovah, Himself, appeared once again. He restated his covenant with Abraham, making it clear that the most central point of the covenant was that He, Jehovah, would be and serve as the God of Abraham and all Abraham's descendants. They, in turn, were to accept Him as their God—to worship Him and Him only, to rely on Him, to obey His instructions and commandments, to rejoice in His blessings and protection, to enjoy the watchful companionship that He desired of them. Circumcision was established as the everlasting token of that covenant relationship.

Names were changed. No longer was he to be known as *Abram*, [pronounced AY-brum] meaning "exalted father." Now and forever more he was to be known as *Abraham*, [pronounced AY-bruh-ham] meaning "father of a multitude." This multitude would come through his thirteen-year-old son *Ishmael* [pronounced ISH-may-uhl], whose name means "God hears," and the birth of another son, *Isaac* [pronounced I-zik], meaning "he laughs," was promised to take place the following year at the same date as the receiving of this glorious revelation. *Sarai's* name was changed to *Sarah* [pronounced SAIR-uh], which means "princess."

Abraham responded willingly and promptly to the Lord's instructions concerning circumcision, seeing to it that the required token of the covenant was carried out among all his household and retinue of servants that same day. No doubt that action was a matter of considerable discussion in the days that followed!

> And Abraham took Ishmael his son, and all that were born in his house, and all that were bought with his money, every male among the men of Abraham's house; and circumcised the flesh of their foreskin in the selfsame day, as God had said unto him.
>
> And *Abraham was ninety years old and nine*, when he was circumcised in the flesh of his foreskin.
>
> And Ishmael his son was thirteen years old, when he was circumcised in the flesh of his foreskin.
>
> In the selfsame day was Abraham circumcised, and Ishmael his son.
>
> And all the men of his house, born in the house, and bought with money of the stranger, were circumcised with him. (Genesis 17:23–27)

Another passage in Joseph Smith's inspired translation of the Bible adds additional insights to the Genesis chapter 17 renewing of the Abrahamic Covenant. It shows that the ordinance of baptism was revealed to Abraham, and also that age eight was designated as the age at which children become accountable before God. (In the passage cited below, additions in the JST are indicated in italics.)

> And *it came to pass, that* Abram fell on his face, *and called upon the name of the Lord.*
>
> And God talked with him, saying, *My people have gone astray from my precepts, and have not kept mine ordinances, which I gave unto their fathers;*
>
> *And they have not observed mine anointing, and the burial, or baptism wherewith I commanded them;*
>
> *But have turned from the commandment, and taken unto themselves the washing of children, and the blood of sprinkling;*
>
> *And have said that the blood of the righteous Abel was shed for sins; and have not known wherein they are accountable before me.* . . .
>
> And I will establish *a covenant of circumcision with thee, and it shall be* my covenant between me and thee, and thy seed after thee, in their generations; *that thou mayest know for ever that children are not accountable before me until they are eight years old.*
>
> *And thou shall observe to keep all my covenants wherein I covenanted with thy fathers; and thou shall keep the commandments which I have given thee with*

mine own mouth, and I will be a God unto thee and thy seed after thee. (Joseph
Smith Translation, Genesis 17:3–7, 11–12; compare Genesis 17:3–12)

THE LORD VISITS ABRAHAM AND THE DESTRUCTION OF SODOM IS ANTICIPATED

Several days or a few short weeks later, Jehovah once again visited Abraham, this time along with two other heavenly beings. They apparently came
dressed in typical Canaanite garb, but Abraham recognized his Master and
responded graciously to His presence:

> *The LORD appeared unto him in the plains of Mamre:* and he sat in the
> tent door in the heat of the day;
>   And he lift up his eyes and looked, and, lo, three men stood by him:
> and when he saw them, he ran to meet them from the tent door, and bowed
> himself toward the ground,
>   And said, *My Lord, if now I have found favour in thy sight, pass not away,
> I pray thee, from thy servant:*
>   Let a little water, I pray you, be fetched, and wash your feet, and rest
> yourselves under the tree:
>   And I will fetch a morsel of bread, and comfort ye your hearts; after
> that ye shall pass on: for therefore are ye come to your servant. And they
> said, So do, as thou hast said. (Genesis 18:1–5)

Abraham scampered to see that cakes were baked, and that a young calf
was selected, dressed, and cooked, while the three visitors waited patiently
in the shade of a nearby tree—obviously for a long time. During the course
of their meal, several significant items were discussed:

1. Sarah will give birth to a son (18:10).
2. The Lord discerns thoughts and attitudes (18:10–13, 15).
3. Nothing is too difficult for the Lord to accomplish (18:14).
4. The Lord would return and enable Sarah's fertility (18:14).

So, the first of the reasons for the Lord's visit to Abraham was accomplished: to reiterate His recent promise that Abraham and Sarah would give
birth to a son within the year. Then, as the three visitors were leaving, the
second purpose of their visit was addressed: to decide if the wickedness of
Sodom was so great that its inhabitants should be destroyed. The following verses provide remarkable insights into the Lord's decision-making processes:

1. The Lord's self-analysis and pondering (18:17).
2. Abraham's descendants will become a great nation (18:18).
3. All the nations of the earth will be blessed through Abraham's lineage
    (18:18).

4. The Lord foreknew Abraham would be obedient (18:19).
5. The Lord's personal visit to Sodom to evaluate its fate (18:20–21).
6. The Lord will consider counter-proposals and barter concerning his decisions (18:22–33).

JUDGMENTS UPON SODOM AND GOMORRAH, AND LOT'S ESCAPE

It appears that the two angels who had accompanied Jehovah in his visit to Abraham continued to Sodom. Lot, having discernment, invited them into his home and sheltered them for the night. But as the evening progressed, the men of Sodom came to the house and demanded that the two men be brought out so they could have homosexual relations with them:

> Before they lay down, the men of the city, even the men of Sodom, compassed the house round, both old and young, all the people from every quarter:
>
> And they called unto Lot, and said unto him, "Where are the men which came in to thee this night? bring them out unto us, that we may know them." (Genesis 19:4–5)

Lot sought to dissuade the mob, seeking to protect the two whom he knew to be God's messengers. He was pressed so hard, he even made the unimaginable decision to offer his two young daughters in their stead. What a terrible challenge that would be for any father!

> I pray you, brethren, do not so wickedly.
>
> Behold now, I have two daughters which have not known man; let me, I pray you, bring them out unto you, and do ye to them as is good in your eyes: only unto these men do nothing; for therefore came they under the shadow of my roof. (Genesis 19:7–8)

The Joseph Smith Translation of this passage in the Bible provides further insights concerning this confrontation. (In the passage cited below, additions to the Genesis text are shown in italics.)

> *And they said unto him, Stand back. And they were angry with him.*
>
> *And they said among themselves, This one man came in to sojourn among us, and he will needs now make himself to be a judge; now we will deal worse with him than with them.*
>
> *Wherefore they said unto the man, we will have the men, and thy daughters also; and we will do with them as seemeth us good.*
>
> *Now this was after the wickedness of Sodom.*
>
> And Lot said, Behold now, I have two daughters which have not known man; let me, I pray you, *plead with my brethren that I may not* bring them out unto you; and ye shall *not* do unto them as seemeth good in your eyes;

For God *will not justify his servant in this thing; wherefore, let me plead with my brethren, this once only, that* unto these men ye do nothing, *that they may have peace in my house;* for therefore came they under the shadow of my roof.

And they were angry with Lot and came near to break the door, but the *angels of God, which were holy men,* put forth their hand and pulled Lot into the house unto them, and shut the door (Joseph Smith Translation, Genesis 19:9–15. Compare Genesis 19:5–10.)

But the unruly ruffians wouldn't be deterred. Finally, the two angels used their miraculous powers to defend the entire household: "they smote the men that were at the door of the house with blindness, both small and great: so that they wearied themselves to find the door." (Genesis 19:11)

It appears that this wicked confrontation was the act that sealed the fate of the city. The two angels told Lot:

Hast thou here any besides? son in law, and thy sons, and thy daughters, and whatsoever thou hast in the city, bring them out of this place:

For *we will destroy this place, because the cry of them is waxen great before the face of the LORD; and the LORD hath sent us to destroy it.* (Genesis 19:12–13)

Lot went to the homes of his sons-in-law and warned them of the impending devastation of the city, pleading for them to bring out his daughters and all their families and to escape. But they somehow thought Lot was mocking them and refused his frantic pleas. As dawn came, there was no alternative—those who were to survive had to flee. And then transpired a horrendous event that has been remembered worldwide throughout history:

And when the morning arose, then the angels hastened Lot, saying, Arise, take thy wife, and thy two daughters, which are here; lest thou be consumed in the iniquity of the city.

And while he lingered, *the men laid hold upon his hand, and upon the hand of his wife, and upon the hand of his two daughters; the LORD being merciful unto him: and they brought him forth, and set him without the city.*

And it came to pass, when they had brought them forth abroad, that he said, *Escape for thy life; look not behind thee, neither stay thou in all the plain; escape to the mountain, lest thou be consumed.*

And Lot said unto them, Oh, not so, my Lord:

Behold now, *thy servant hath found grace in thy sight, and thou hast magnified thy mercy, which thou hast shewed unto me in saving my life;* and I cannot escape to the mountain, lest some evil take me, and I die:

Behold now, this city is near to flee unto, and it is a little one: Oh, let me escape thither, (is it not a little one?) and my soul shall live.

And he said unto him, *See, I have accepted thee concerning this thing also, that I will not overthrow this city, for the which thou hast spoken.*

Haste thee, escape thither; for I cannot do any thing till thou be come thither. Therefore the name of the city was called Zoar.

The sun was risen upon the earth when Lot entered into Zoar.

Then the LORD rained upon Sodom and upon Gomorrah brimstone and fire from the LORD out of heaven;

And he overthrew those cities, and all the plain, and all the inhabitants of the cities, and that which grew upon the ground.

But his wife looked back from behind him, and she became a pillar of salt. (Genesis 19:15–26)

The scriptural account relates that Abraham got up that morning and watched from afar as the cities were destroyed. But the concept is set forth that Lot and his daughters were saved from the flames as a result of Abraham's pleas to the Lord the previous day: "It came to pass, when God destroyed the cities of the plain, *that God remembered Abraham, and sent Lot out of the midst of the overthrow,* when he overthrew the cities in the which Lot dwelt" (Genesis 19:29).

Then follows a brief but significant account of the beginning of two famous tribal lines which had interplay with Abraham's descendants for many hundreds of years—throughout Old Testament history. Recognizing that the entire down-line of their father's family had been destroyed in the flames, Lot's two young daughters plotted to seduce their father so that seed would be born that would preserve the family's bloodlines:

And Lot went up out of Zoar, and dwelt in the mountain, and his two daughters with him; for he feared to dwell in Zoar: and he dwelt in a cave, he and his two daughters.

And the firstborn said unto the younger, Our father is old, and there is not a man in the earth to come in unto us after the manner of all the earth:

Come, let us make our father drink wine, and we will lie with him, that we may preserve seed of our father.

And they made their father drink wine that night: and the firstborn went in, and lay with her father; and he perceived not when she lay down, nor when she arose.

And it came to pass on the morrow, that the firstborn said unto the younger, Behold, I lay yesternight with my father: let us make him drink wine this night also; and go thou in, and lie with him, that we may preserve seed of our father.

And they made their father drink wine that night also: and the younger arose, and lay with him; and he perceived not when she lay down, nor when she arose.

Thus were both the daughters of Lot with child by their father.

*And the firstborn bare a son, and called his name Moab: the same is the
father of the Moabites unto this day.*

*And the younger, she also bare a son, and called his name Benammi: the
same is the father of the children of Ammon unto this day* (Genesis 19:30–
38).

Wouldn't it be interesting to know of the conversations between Lot and
his daughters as their seductions came to fruition? The name Moab [pro-
nounced MOH-ab] means "from my father."

Concerning these two tribal groups, the *Revell Bible Dictionary* says:

The Ammonites inhabited territory that is now modern Jordan, and
maintained a capital at Rabbah, modern Amman. They traced their ancestry to Ben Ammi, a son of Abraham's nephew Lot (about 1985 BC). Thus
the Israelites initially viewed them as near relatives, and were prohibited
from invading their territory (Deut. 2:19). However, the Ammonites joined
Moab in hiring Balaam to curse Israel. This act of hostility led to their ban-
ishment from the assembly of Israel and to God's command, "Do not seek
peace or good relations with them" (Deut. 23:3–6).

Conflict between Israel and Ammon persisted from the time of Israel's
conquest of Canaan until the time of the Maccabees, two centuries before
Christ.[8]

RELATIONSHIPS WITH ABIMELECH, KING OF GERAR

Very shortly after the destruction of Sodom and Gomorrah, Abraham
and Sarah took a trip to "the south country." Today this probably would
be viewed as a camping-in-the-desert vacation. They stayed in two places:
first they "dwelled between Kadesh and Shur."[9] Then they came back north,
further into Canaan, and stayed in Gerar. This was an area about ten miles
inland from the Mediterranean, about fifty miles west by southwest of their
home near Hebron.

Apparently they ran into the same predicament they'd encountered in
Egypt, almost twenty-five years previous (see Genesis 12:1–20). In those
days, kings were considered as having the right to any woman of their choice
within the bounds of their kingdoms, and they obviously were willing to
exercise those rights. If a husband were to stand in the way, he could easily

8.   *The Revell Bible Dictionary* (New York: Wynwood Press, 1984), p. 56.

9.   Kadesh-barnea was a town about 50 miles inland from the Mediterranean Sea,
further south than the southern tip of the Dead Sea. Shur would be the Wilderness of Shur, west of the River of Egypt which was regarded as the border-line
between Canaan and Egypt.

be disposed of, so Sarah again was reminded to speak of Abraham as her brother, which he indeed was—her half-brother since they both claimed Terah as their father (see Genesis 20:12). Abraham's wife was eighty-nine years old, but she still must have been beautiful, for "Abimelech king of Gerar sent, and took Sarah" (Genesis 20:2).

Now a drama was played out between God and two righteous men. (Note that even though Abimelech was exercising his "kingly rights with the women," he still was considered righteous in the Lord's eyes.) There are some significant doctrinal insights in these verses, so they will again receive verse-by-verse outlining and analysis:

1. God's warning to Abimelech (20:3).
2. Abimelech's defense and assertion of his righteousness (20:4–5).
3. Jehovah's acknowledgment of Abimelech's righteousness (20:6).
4. Jehovah's protection of Abimelech's and Sarah's virtue (20:6).
5. Jehovah's alternative courses offered to Abimelech (20:7).
6. Abimelech's sharing of Jehovah's warning with his servants (20:8).
7. Abimelech's complaint to Abraham (20:9–10).
8. Abraham's response to Abimelech (20:11–13).
9. Abimelech's acts of repentance and reconciliation (20:14–16).
10. Abraham's prayers in Abimelech's behalf (20:17).
11. The Lord responds to and grants the prayers of His prophets (20:17).
12. The Lord can control human fertility (20:18).

THE MIRACULOUS BIRTH OF ISAAC AND THE SEPARATION OF HAGAR AND ISHMAEL

The Lord keeps His promises! When He visited with Abraham and Sarah, just prior to the destruction of Sodom and Gomorrah, He promised that "At the time appointed I will return unto thee, according to the time of life, and Sarah shall have a son" (Genesis 18:14). The scripture is very pointed in its assertion that Jehovah did exactly as He promised: He returned and somehow generated the necessary physical changes so that Abraham and Sarah would be able to come together and Sarah—poor, all-her-life-barren Sarah—would be able to become pregnant: "The LORD visited Sarah as he had said, and the LORD did unto Sarah as he had spoken. For Sarah conceived, and bare Abraham a son in his old age, at the set time of which God had spoken to him" (Genesis 21:1–2).

Task completed, right on schedule—the Lord does all things well! Abraham was one hundred, Sarah was ninety when the birth took place. This birth truly was miraculous!

And Abraham called the name of his son that was born unto him,
whom Sarah bare to him, Isaac.

And Abraham circumcised his son Isaac being eight days old, as God
had commanded him.

And Abraham was an hundred years old, when his son Isaac was born
unto him.

And she said, Who would have said unto Abraham, that Sarah should
have given children suck? for I have born him a son in his old age.

And the child grew, and was weaned: and Abraham made a great feast
the same day that Isaac was weaned. (Genesis 21:3–8)

And then it happened. Ishmael now was sixteen or seventeen (who
knows how long it was before Isaac was weaned?), and he acted like a typical jealous teenager: he made fun of the weaning celebration. Sarah, who
had cast Hagar out because of Hagar's haughty pride when she was carrying the unborn Ishmael, had put up with allowing the woman's return
before Ishmael's birth, doing so for her husband's sake. But resentments
still simmered over the years, apparently, and they came to a head at this
feast.

And Sarah saw the son of Hagar the Egyptian, which she had born
unto Abraham, mocking.

Wherefore she said unto Abraham, Cast out this bondwoman and her
son: for the son of this bondwoman shall not be heir with my son, even with
Isaac.

And the thing was very grievous in Abraham's sight because of his son.
(Genesis 21:9–11)

But then, probably in answer to Abraham's fervent prayers, God gave
him directions:

1. Don't grieve over Ishmael and Hagar (21:12).
2. Follow Sarah's wishes: send them away (21:12).
3. The Abrahamic covenant will flow through Isaac (21:12).
4. A nation will come from Ishmael also, because he too is a descendant of
   Abraham (21:13).

So Abraham sent Hagar and Ishmael away. The account reads like
Ishmael was a small child rather than a nearly mature teenager, but he was
already fourteen when Isaac was born. It's uncertain where Abraham was
living at this time; it may have been in the west towards Gerar, or back
in the vicinity of Hebron, or forty miles southwest of Hebron near Beer-
sheba.[10]

---

10. The country in the area is rather rugged and mountainous: Hebron's altitude is

And Abraham rose up early in the morning, and took bread, and a bottle of water, and gave it unto Hagar, putting it on her shoulder, and the child, and sent her away: and she departed, and wandered in the wilderness of Beer-sheba.

And the water was spent in the bottle, and she cast the child under one of the shrubs.

And she went, and sat her down over against him a good way off, as it were a bowshot: for she said, Let me not see the death of the child. And she sat over against him, and lift up her voice, and wept. (Genesis 21:14–16)

1. An angel represented God, saying God has heard Ishmael (21:17).
2. A great nation will come from Ishmael (21:18).
3. God opened Hagar's eyes to find water (21:19).
4. God was with Ishmael (21:20–21).

The wilderness of Paran, where Ishmael dwelled, was about 150 miles due south of Hebron, in the Sinai Peninsula, just northwest of the northern tip of the Gulf of Aqaba. To this day, it remains a very barren desert.

BUSINESS COVENANTS BETWEEN ABRAHAM AND ABIMELECH

The record of the business dealings between Abraham and Abimelech, King of Gerar, in the latter part of Genesis chapter 21, still stands as a good example of how to do business today. They sought to establish trust and confidence between the two of them, and took the necessary steps to resolve differences and conflicts:

1. Abimelech's request for an oath of trustworthiness from Abraham (21:22–24).
2. Abraham's complaint that control of his well had been taken by force (21:25–26).
3. The two made a business covenant (21:27).
4. Abraham sought an acknowledgment that a well his men had dug belonged to him (21:28–30).
5. Naming the site as a memorial of their covenants together (21:31–32).
6. Marking the site by planting a grove in Beer-sheba and saying a (dedicatory?) prayer (21:33).

A passage in Joseph Smith's inspired translation of the Bible indicates

---

3,040 feet; Beer-sheva's is 1,013 feet. Gerar, down in the near-sea-level coastal plain, is only 180 feet. Those who owned flocks and herds would move them to find adequate pasture-land at the various times of the year.

that Abimelech and his assistant were the ones who planted the grove there, and that they called upon the Lord from that place. (In the following passage, additions in the JST are shown in italics.)

> Then Abimelech, and Phicol, the chief captain of his hosts, rose up, *and they planted a grove in Beer-sheba*, and called there on the name of the Lord; and they returned unto the land of the Philistines.
>
> And Abraham *worshipped the everlasting God, and* sojourned in the land of the Philistines many days. (Joseph Smith Translation, Genesis 21:31–32)

In place names, the Hebrew word "beer" (pronounced BEE-air) means "well," so *Beer-sheba* meant "the well of Sheba" or "well of the oath." The end of chapter 21 indicates that "Abraham sojourned in the Philistines' land many days" (Genesis 21:34), so Abraham apparently was renting land in the King of Gerar's extended domain or paying tribute for the use of it. The coastal plain later came to be known as the Philistine plain after aggressive colonists settled there about 1200 BC.

JEHOVAH'S TESTING OF ABRAHAM AND ISAAC

One of the most heart-rending events in all scripture is the account of how the Lord tried the faith of his trusted servant, Abraham. One day, while he was dwelling in Beer-sheva, Abraham suddenly received this startling commandment:

> It came to pass after these things, that *God did tempt Abraham*, and said unto him, Abraham: and he said, Behold, here I am.
>
> And he said, *Take now thy son, thine only son Isaac, whom thou lovest, and get thee into the land of Moriah; and offer him there for a burnt offering upon one of the mountains which I will tell thee of.* (Genesis 22:1–2)

How painful it is to imagine the host of conflicting thoughts that must have raged in Abraham's mind and heart as he dutifully began to fulfill this strange commandment. Abraham saddled an ass, and then took his beloved son Isaac and two young men helpers on a three-day journey northward to Mt. Moriah—the same hill where Solomon's temple stood a thousand years later. Today, right in the midst of the city of Jerusalem, the Muslim "Dome of the Rock" stands atop that hill. The site is now considered one of the most sacred spots on earth by a majority of the earth's inhabitants: specifically, Christians, Muslims, and Jews.

Abraham, who knew Jehovah intimately, who had walked and conversed with him on many occasions, and who had been promised by him that his posterity through Isaac would fill the earth, must have been in a terrible quandary as he bound his son to the altar and raised the knife to take his life. Perhaps he was recalling how he had been in that same position back in Ur and had been saved by God's intervention just seconds before his life was to be forfeited. Would that now happen again? Suddenly, Jehovah spoke from the heavens: "The angel of the LORD called unto him out of heaven, and said, Abraham, Abraham: and he said, Here am I. And he said, Lay not thine hand upon the lad, neither do thou any thing unto him. *For now I know that thou fearest God, seeing thou hast not withheld thy son, thine only son from me*" (22:11–12).

And Abraham lifted up his eyes, and saw a ram caught in a thicket by his horns. He took the ram and offered it up for a burnt offering in the stead of his son (Genesis 22:13–14). Then Jehovah spoke to Abraham a second time:

1. Jehovah's promise to bless Abraham (22:16–17).
2. Jehovah will multiply Abraham's seed immeasurably (22:17).
3. Abraham's seed will possess the gates of their enemies (22:17).
4. All the nations of the earth will be blessed through Abraham's seed (22:18).

So, undoubtedly feeling greatly relieved and again greatly blessed, Abraham and the three young men made their way back to their tents in Beer-sheva.

Insights on the Testing of Abraham. Various scriptural passages give pertinent insights concerning God's motives as he tested Abraham on Mt. Moriah. First, the commandment for Abraham to sacrifice his son Isaac stands as a similitude of the future choice God the Father would have to make in sending his son Jesus to sacrifice his life for all mankind (see John 3:16–17). The Book of Mormon prophet Jacob observed that "for this intent we keep the law of Moses, it pointing our souls to him; and for this cause it is sanctified unto us for righteousness, *even as it was accounted unto Abraham in the wilderness to be obedient unto the commands of God in offering up his son Isaac, which is a similitude of God and his Only Begotten Son*" (Jacob 4:5).

Second, Abraham's faith in the future resurrection is exhibited in the roll call of the faithful in the book of Hebrews:

> By faith Abraham, when he was tried, offered up Isaac: and he that had received the promises offered up his only begotten son,
> Of whom it was said, That in Isaac shall thy seed be called:
> *Accounting that God was able to raise him up, even from the dead; from whence also he received him in a figure.* (Hebrews 11:17–19)

Third, James saw the incident as a manifestation of Abraham's faith, as well as his works:

Was not Abraham our father justified by works, when he had offered
Isaac his son upon the altar?

Seest thou how faith wrought with his works, and by works was faith
made perfect?

And the scripture was fulfilled which saith, *Abraham believed God, and
it was imputed unto him for righteousness: and he was called the Friend of God.*
(James 2:21–23)

Fourth, a Doctrine and Covenants passage regards the testing incident
as an instance of chastening—a part of God's process for refining those who
will be found worthy to come into his kingdom: "I will own them, and they
shall be mine in that day when I shall come to make up my jewels. Therefore,
*they must needs be chastened and tried, even as Abraham, who was commanded
to offer up his only son.* For all those who will not endure chastening, but deny
me, cannot be sanctified" (D&C 101:3–5; see also D&C 136:31).

And fifth, part of the challenge of the saints in mortality is to faithfully keep all God's words and commandments, which Abraham faithfully
sought to obey:

Marvel not at these things, for *ye are not yet pure; ye can not yet bear my
glory; but ye shall behold it if ye are faithful in keeping all my words that I have
given you,* from the days of Adam to *Abraham,* from *Abraham* to Moses,
from Moses to Jesus and his apostles, and from Jesus and his apostles to
Joseph Smith, whom I did call upon by mine angels, my ministering servants, and by mine own voice out of the heavens, to bring forth my work.
(D&C 136:37)

SARAH'S DEATH AND BURIAL

The scriptural life stories of Abraham and Sarah skip ahead a couple
of decades, then report the passing of Sarah, the great matriarch, at the age
of 127. By this time, the family had left the territories controlled by King
Abimelech and was once again dwelling in Hebron. The announcement of
her passing was as follows:

And Sarah was an hundred and seven and twenty years old: these were
the years of the life of Sarah.

And Sarah died in Kirjath-arba; the same is Hebron in the land of
Canaan: and Abraham came to mourn for Sarah, and to weep for her. (Genesis 23:1–2)

Abraham set out to purchase an appropriate burial place for his wife
from the sons of Heth, owners of a field and cave in the area. The way they
greeted him indicates the high esteem held for him by those who lived
nearby: "Hear us, my lord: thou art a mighty prince among us: in the choice

of our sepulchers bury thy dead; none of us shall withhold from thee his sepulchre, but that thou mayest bury thy dead" (Genesis 23:6). Abraham finally negotiated with Ephron the Hittite, purchasing the field that contained the cave of Machpelah, and all the trees in the field, for the substantial sum of four hundred shekels of silver:

> And the field of Ephron, which was in Machpelah, which was before Mamre, the field, and the cave which was therein, and all the trees that were in the field, that were in all the borders round about, were made sure
>
> Unto Abraham for a possession in the presence of the children of Heth, before all that went in at the gate of his city.
>
> And after this, Abraham buried Sarah his wife in the cave of the field of Machpelah before Mamre: the same is Hebron in the land of Canaan.
>
> And the field, and the cave that is therein, were made sure unto Abraham for a possession of a burying place by the sons of Heth. (Genesis 23:17–20)

ABRAHAM'S LATER YEARS, DEATH, AND BURIAL

Abraham was 137 years old when his wife Sarah passed away. He died at the age of 175, so the last 38 years of his life are mostly unrecorded.

Genesis chapter 24 relates that when "Abraham was old, and well stricken in age" he prevailed upon his servant to go back to Mesopotamia and find a wife for his son Isaac from among his kinfolk there. The interesting details of that quest and the resulting marriage will be left for the next chapter, which deals with the life of Isaac. That chapter does report, however, that "the LORD had blessed Abraham in all things"—a truly profound observation (Genesis 24:1).

Abraham remarried—this time to a woman named Keturah. She must have been younger—still of childbearing age—because she bore him six sons (and who knows how many daughters; the daughters are rarely mentioned in Old Testament times):

> Then again Abraham took a wife, and her name was Keturah.
>
> And she bare him Zimran, and Jokshan, and Medan, and Midian, and Ishbak, and Shuah. (Genesis 25:1–2)

Some of the next generations of two of the sons, Jokshan and Midian, are then listed:

> And Jokshan begat Sheba, and Dedan. And the sons of Dedan were Asshurim, and Letushim, and Leummim.
>
> And the sons of Midian; Ephah, and Epher, and Hanoch, and Abida, and Eldaah. All these were the children of Keturah. (Genesis 25:3–4)

As his last days were approaching, Abraham generously gave gifts to each of his sons who came through Keturah and then sent them off to make their own ways as young adults. However, he reserved the bulk of his estate to pass on to his son Isaac:

> And Abraham gave all that he had unto Isaac.
> But unto the sons of the concubines,[11] which Abraham had, Abraham gave gifts, and sent them away from Isaac his son, while he yet lived, east-ward, unto the east country. (Genesis 25:5–6)

Then came the time of Abraham's passing:

> *These are the days of the years of Abraham's life which he lived, an hundred threescore and fifteen years.*
>
> Then Abraham gave up the ghost, and *died in a good old age, an old man, and full of years;* and was gathered to his people. (Genesis 25:7–8)

The final words about Abraham in the Genesis biographical account were that

> His sons Isaac and Ishmael buried him in the cave of Machpelah, in the field of Ephron the son of Zohar the Hittite, which is before Mamre;
> The field which Abraham purchased of the sons of Heth: there was Abraham buried, and Sarah his wife. (Genesis 25:9–10)

In modern times, this burial site was a popular tourist attraction in Israel for many years until the conflicts between the Jews and Palestinians made it relatively unsafe for tourists to visit in Hebron, a Palestinian-controlled city.

A CHRONOLOGICAL SUMMARY OF ABRAHAM'S LIFE

The exact dating of events four thousand years ago is still beyond reach, though archaeological findings are adding supporting data. Approaching dates that early from different sources has led to various outcomes, and chronologies differ by as much as 200–300 years back in the days of Abraham. One chronological chart, which holds to the earlier dating view, is found in *The Revell Bible Dictionary* and re-created on the following page.[12]

---

11. The term "concubines," mentioned above, is generally understood to mean Hagar and Keturah—those previously reported in the Genesis account.

12. *The Revell Bible Dictionary* (New York: Wynwood Press, 1990), p. 12.

Event	Genesis Passage	New Testament Commentary	Abram's Age	Approx. Date BC
Abram's birth.	11:26			2166
His call by God.	12:1–3	Heb. 11:8		
His entry into Canaan.	12:4–9	Acts 7:2–32	75	2091
Abram in Egypt.	12:10–20			
Abram and Lot separate.	13:1–18			
Abram rescues Lot.	14:1–17			
Abram pays tithes to Melchizedek.	14:18–24	Heb. 7:1–10		
Abram given formal covenant.	15:1–21	Rom. 4:1–17 Gal. 3:6–25 Heb. 6:13–20	85	2081
Abram fathers Ishmael.	16:1–16		86	2080
Abraham given circumcision, promised son by Sarah	17:1–27	Rom. 4:18–25 Heb. 11:11–12	99	2067
Abraham pleads for Sodom.	18:1–33			
Sodom destroyed. Lot saved.	19:1–38			
Abraham in Gerar.	20:1–18			
Isaac born.	21:1–7		100	2066
Hagar, Ishmael sent away.	21:8–34	Gal. 4:21–31	103	2063
Abraham to sacrifice Isaac.	22:1–24	Heb. 11:17–29 James 2:20–24		
Sarah dies, buried in Hebron.	23:1–20		137	2029
A bride chosen for Isaac.	24:1–67		140	2026
Abraham dies, buried in Hebron.	25:1–11		175	1991

Abraham Now Is a Resurrected and Exalted Being

Several scriptural passages bear witness that Abraham now is a resurrected being who dwells in heaven in God's celestial realms. For this author, at least, that knowledge serves as a reassuring source of faith that others may someday follow in his footsteps and attain the same glorious reward.

It is interesting to note that all the passages that address this subject link Abraham, Isaac, and Jacob together—all receiving the same eternal reward.

For instance, the Savior, while commenting on the faith of a Roman centurion in Capernaum, made a unique reference to their final status: "I say unto you, That *many shall come from the east and west, and shall sit down with Abraham, and Isaac, and Jacob, in the kingdom of heaven* (Matthew 8:11).

The Book of Mormon prophet Alma said, "Behold, my brethren, do ye suppose that such an one can have a place *to sit down in the kingdom of God, with Abraham, with Isaac, and with Jacob, and also all the holy prophets, whose garments are cleansed and are spotless, pure and white?*" (Alma 5:24).

On another occasion Alma closed a sermon with these words: "May the Lord bless you, and keep your garments spotless, *that ye may at last be brought to sit down with Abraham, Isaac, and Jacob, and the holy prophets who have been ever since the world began, having your garments spotless even as their garments are spotless, in the kingdom of heaven to go no more out*" (Alma 7:25).

Nephi, whose words are recorded in the book of Helaman, taught that "We see that whosoever will may lay hold upon the word of God, ... *And land their souls, yea, their immortal souls, at the right hand of God in the kingdom of heaven, to sit down with Abraham, and Isaac, and with Jacob, and with all our holy fathers, to go no more out*" (Helaman 3:29–30).

Statements in the Doctrine and Covenants also refer to Abraham's having entered into his exaltation, such as this one in Doctrine and Covenants 132: "Abraham received all things, whatsoever he received, by revelation and commandment, by my word, saith the Lord, and hath entered into his exaltation and sitteth upon his throne. . . . and as touching Abraham and his seed, out of the world they should continue; both in the world and out of the world should they continue as innumerable as the stars" (D&C 132:29–30; see also verses 49 and 57, and D&C 137:1, 5).

COMMENTS ABOUT ABRAHAM
IN OTHER SCRIPTURES

There are hundreds of other references to Abraham, scattered throughout the Latter-day Saint standard works—far too many for all to be compiled in this volume. However, some of the most interesting and pertinent passages are briefly summarized in the abbreviated list below:

FROM THE OLD TESTAMENT

Exodus 2:23–24: "God remembered his covenant with Abraham, with Isaac, and with Jacob."

Exodus 3:6: "I am the God of thy father, the God of Abraham, the God of Isaac, and . . . Jacob."

Exodus 3:14–16: "The LORD God of your fathers, the God of Abraham, . . . sent me unto you."

Exodus 6:2–4: "I appeared unto Abraham, . . . but by . . . JEHOVAH was I not known to them."

Exodus 32:11–14: "Remember Abraham, Isaac, and Israel, thy servants, to whom thou swarest ."

Joshua 24:2–3: "I took your father Abraham . . . and multiplied his seed, and gave him Isaac."

Nehemiah 9:7–8: "Thou art the LORD the God, who didst choose Abram, . . . broughtest him forth."

Psalms 105:7–11: "Which covenant he made with Abraham, and his oath unto Isaac."

FROM THE NEW TESTAMENT

Matthew 3:9; Luke 3:8: "So all the generations from Abraham to David are fourteen generations."

Matthew 22:31–32: "I am the God of Abraham, and the God of Isaac, and the God of Jacob."

Luke 1:54–55: "His mercy; As he spake to our fathers, to Abraham, and to his seed for ever."

Luke 1:73–75: "The oath which he sware to our father Abraham, . . ."

Luke 13:28: "Ye shall see Abraham, and Isaac, and Jacob, . . . in the kingdom of God."

Luke 16:22–26: "The beggar died, and was carried by the angels into Abraham's bosom."

John 8:39–40: "If ye were Abraham's children, ye would do the works of Abraham."

John 8:52–53: "Art thou greater than our father Abraham, which is dead?"

John 8:55–58: "Your father Abraham rejoiced to see my day: and he saw it, and was glad."

Acts 3:25: "Ye are the children . . . of the covenant which God made . . . unto Abraham."

Acts 7:2: "The God of glory appeared unto our father Abraham, when he was in Mesopotamia."

Acts 7:8: "Abraham begat Isaac, and circumcised him the eighth day."

Acts 7:17–18: "When the time of the promise drew nigh, which God had sworn to Abraham, . . ."

Romans 4:1–3: "Abraham believed God, and it was counted unto him for righteousness."

Romans 4:16–17: "Abraham; who is the father of us all, . . . a father of many nations."

Romans 11:1–2: "I also am an Israelite, of the seed of Abraham, of the tribe of Benjamin."

Galatians 3:6–9: "Abraham believed God, and it was accounted to him for righteousness."

Hebrews 6:13–15: "God made promise to Abraham, . . . Saying, Surely blessing I will bless thee."

Hebrews 7:1–2: "Melchisedec, . . . met Abraham . . . and blessed him."

Hebrews 11:8–19: "By faith Abraham, when he was tried, offered up Isaac."

James 2:21–23: "Abraham believed God, and it was imputed unto him for righteousness."

1 Peter 3:5–6: "Holy women also, who trusted in God, . . . Even as Sara obeyed Abraham."

FROM THE BOOK OF MORMON

1 Nephi 6:4: "Mine intent is that I may persuade men to come unto the God of Abraham."

1 Nephi 15:18: "The . . . covenant the Lord made to our father Abraham, . . ."

2 Nephi 29:14: "I am God, and . . . I covenanted with Abraham . . . I . . . remember his seed forever."

Jacob 4:5: "It was accounted unto Abraham . . . to be obedient unto the commands of God."

Alma 13:15: "Our father Abraham paid tithes of one–tenth part of all he possessed."

Helaman 8:17–18: "There were many before the days of Abraham . . . called by the order of God."

3 Nephi 20:26–27: "Then fulfilleth the Father the covenant which he made with Abraham."

Mormon 9:11: "I will show unto you a God of miracles, even the God of Abraham."

Ether 13:11: "Are partakers . . . of the covenant which God made with their father, Abraham."

FROM THE DOCTRINE AND COVENANTS

D&C 84:14: Abraham received the priesthood from Melchizedek.

D&C 84:34: "They become the sons of Moses and of Aaron and the seed of Abraham, . . ."

D&C 98:32: "The law I gave unto . . . thy fathers, Joseph, and Jacob, and Isaac, and Abraham."

D&C 101:4: "Therefore, they must needs be chastened and tried, even as Abraham."

D&C 103:17: "For ye are the children of Israel, and of the seed of Abraham."

D&C 109:64: "Judah may begin to return to the lands which thou didst give to Abraham."

D&C 110:12: "Elias appeared, and committed the dispensation of the gospel of Abraham."

D&C 124:19: "My aged servant Joseph Smith, Sen., who sitteth with Abraham at his right hand."

D&C 124:58: "And as I said unto Abraham concerning the kindreds of the earth, . . ."

D&C 136:37: "Keeping all my words that I have given you, from the days of Adam to Abraham."

CHAPTER 7

ISAAC

ISAAC AND JACOB "HAVE ENTERED INTO THEIR
EXALTATION . . . AND SIT UPON THRONES,
AND ARE NOT ANGELS BUT ARE GODS."

A MIRACULOUS BIRTH

Of all the billions of people born into mortality on this earth, this man's birth certainly was one of the most unique! It was a miraculous event—prophesied, commanded, scheduled, and enabled by God Almighty, the great Jehovah!

In a series of heavenly manifestations, Jehovah prepared Isaac's father, Abram, for the glorious role he was to fulfill here on earth, telling him that he was to be the father of a vast posterity. He was to be the father of nations, and the entire earth was to be blessed through his posterity.

Yet Abram's wife, Sarai, was barren—childless throughout all her long married life. She longed for the blessing of motherhood, yet it was not granted to her. In despair, she finally sent Abram to her young Egyptian handmaid, Hagar, so an heir could be raised up for the family. Thus Ishmael was born, but it was not he that Jehovah had determined to be the heir through which the rich blessings of the Abrahamic covenant would be passed down to mankind.

When Abram was ninety-nine years old and Sarai was eighty-nine (Genesis 17:1), the Lord, Jehovah, once again appeared to Abram and reiterated the promised blessings of the covenant. But the Lord went beyond what had previously been promised. He made significant changes: he changed Abram's name (which meant "exalted father") to be Abraham (meaning "father of a multitude"). He changed Sarai's name to Sarah (meaning "princess"), and then gave very explicit instructions concerning a son who was to be born to them:

> God said unto Abraham, As for Sarai thy wife, thou shalt not call her name Sarai, but Sarah shall her name be.
>
> And *I will bless her, and give thee a son also of her: yea, I will bless her, and she shall be a mother of nations; kings of people shall be of her.*
>
> Then Abraham fell upon his face, and laughed, and said in his heart,

> Shall a child be born unto him that is an hundred years old? and shall Sarah, that is ninety years old, bear? . . .
>
> And God said, *Sarah thy wife shall bear thee a son indeed; and thou shalt call his name Isaac: and I will establish my covenant with him for an everlasting covenant,* and with his seed after him. . . . But *my covenant will I establish with Isaac,* which Sarah shall bear unto thee *at this set time in the next year.* (Genesis 17:15–17, 19, 21)

So Isaac's birth date was set, prophetically. It was to take place a year from that date: "at this set time in the next year."

A few days later, Jehovah and two angels, apparently all dressed in mortal apparel, came to Abraham as he sat in his tent. A meal was prepared for them, which they ate under a nearby tree. During the course of the meal the Lord asked Abraham,

> Where is Sarah thy wife? And he said, Behold, in the tent.
>
> And he said, *I will certainly return unto thee according to the time of life; and, lo, Sarah thy wife shall have a son.* And Sarah heard it in the tent door, which was behind him.
>
> Now Abraham and Sarah were old and well stricken in age; and it ceased to be with Sarah after the manner of women.
>
> Therefore Sarah laughed within herself, saying, After I am waxed old shall I have pleasure, my lord being old also?
>
> And the LORD said unto Abraham, Wherefore did Sarah laugh, saying, Shall I of a surety bear a child, which am old?
>
> *Is any thing too hard for the LORD? At the time appointed I will return unto thee, according to the time of life, and Sarah shall have a son.* (Genesis 18:9–14)

It appears that the Lord's phrase "I will return unto thee, according to the time of life" had reference to the time when the unborn child was to be conceived. Apparently, it would be necessary for the Lord to make some changes in Sarah's body so that she would be able to give birth to a child.

True to his word, the Lord did what he had promised to do. Weeks later, "*the LORD visited Sarah as he had said, and the LORD did unto Sarah as he had spoken. For Sarah conceived,*" (Genesis 21:1–2). He came at the appropriate time, for the child was born the next year, on the date the Lord had previously foretold. The scriptural record affirms that Sarah "bare Abraham a son in his old age, *at the set time of which God had spoken to him*" (Genesis 21:2).

Truly, the birth of Isaac was a miraculous event—prophesied, commanded, scheduled, and enabled by God Almighty, the great Jehovah! He even told them the name they were to give their child!

When did Isaac's birth occur? Some attempts at Bible chronology put the date about 2066 BC, but these are typically accompanied with the observation that all dates are approximate that far back in time.

What does the name *Isaac* mean—the name commanded by God Himself? The translation of the name is "laughter," or "he laughs." Perhaps it commemorates Sarah's laughter at the thought that she could have a baby long after she had passed the age of child-rearing (see Genesis 18:12; 21:6). Perhaps it stood for the joy his long-awaited birth brought to both his parents after their years of prayerful petitioning to God for that blessing.

ISAAC'S YOUTH

When Isaac was born, he already had a half-brother, Ishmael, who was born fourteen years before Isaac. However, the two boys didn't grow up together. Very early in Isaac's life, an event took place which caused them to be separated. When he was born, his mother chose to breast-feed him—a process which often continued for several years. When he finally was weaned, Abraham and Sarah gave a feast to celebrate the event:

Abraham was an hundred years old, when his son Isaac was born unto him.

And *Sarah said, God hath made me to laugh, so that all that hear will laugh with me.*

And she said, *Who would have said unto Abraham, that Sarah should have given children suck? for I have born him a son in his old age.*

And the child grew, and was weaned: and Abraham made a great feast the same day that Isaac was weaned.

And Sarah saw the son of Hagar the Egyptian, which she had born unto Abraham, mocking.

Wherefore she said unto Abraham, Cast out this bondwoman and her son: for the son of this bondwoman shall not be heir with my son, even with Isaac.

And the thing was very grievous in Abraham's sight because of his son.

And *God said unto Abraham, Let it not be grievous in thy sight because of the lad, and because of thy bondwoman; in all that Sarah hath said unto thee, hearken unto her voice; for in Isaac shall thy seed be called.*

And *also of the son of the bondwoman will I make a nation, because he is thy seed.*

And Abraham rose up early in the morning, and took bread, and a bottle of water, and gave it unto Hagar, putting it on her shoulder, and the child, and sent her away: and she departed. (Genesis 21:5–14)

So Isaac was raised as a protected only child, with wealthy parents who were well along in years. Along with his parents and numerous servants,

Isaac lived a semi-nomadic life in Canaan. They could grow crops on the southern plains during the November-March rainy season and then move to higher and cooler pasture lands during the hotter summer months.

The family was highly respected by the people of the area, harking back to Abraham's rescuing of Lot and the people of Sodom years before. Abraham was literate, a competent and prospering businessman, highly educated and well-traveled, as compared to other peoples of his day—traits he apparently sought to inculcate into his son's realms of experience.

Most importantly, Abraham had walked with God and was deemed worthy in His sight. Surely the passing on of this rich spiritual heritage to his cherished son was one of Abraham's highest personal objectives.

An overall look at Isaac's scriptural life story leads one to perceive him as quiet and mostly concerned with his own business unless he was specifically required to take action. Obviously, Abraham was determined to pass on his material property as well as his spiritual heritage to and through him.

THE MOUNT MORIAH EPISODE

The Lord's commandment to Abraham to offer Isaac as a human sacrifice was a challenging event in Isaac's life, just as it was for his father Abraham. The scriptures don't tell how old Isaac was when this event took place—it's only known that both Abraham and the attending angel spoke of him as being a "lad" (Genesis 22:5, 12). But Joseph was called a "lad" when he was 17 (Genesis 37:2), and Benjamin was called a "lad" by his older brothers (Genesis 43:8, 44:22, 30–34) even though he was the father of 10 children! (Genesis 46:21).

The Genesis account relates that Isaac went willingly on their three-day journey to Mt. Moriah, and that he asked a youthful, naive question when he observed that they brought no sacrificial lamb (Genesis 22:7). However, his trust in his father was sufficient that he allowed himself to be bound and laid on the altar:

> And it came to pass after these things, that *God did tempt Abraham*, and said unto him, Abraham: and he said, Behold, here I am.
>
> And he said, *Take now thy son, thine only son Isaac, whom thou lovest, and get thee into the land of Moriah; and offer him there for a burnt offering upon one of the mountains which I will tell thee of.*
>
> And Abraham rose up early in the morning, and saddled his ass, and took two of his young men with him, and Isaac his son, and clave the wood for the burnt offering, and rose up, and went unto the place of which God had told him.

Then on the third day Abraham lifted up his eyes, and saw the place afar off.

And Abraham said unto his young men, Abide ye here with the ass; and *I and the lad will go yonder and worship, and come again to you.*

And Abraham took the wood of the burnt offering, and laid it upon Isaac his son; and he took the fire in his hand, and a knife; and they went both of them together.

And Isaac spake unto Abraham his father, and said, My father: and he said, Here am I, my son. And he said, Behold the fire and the wood: but where is the lamb for a burnt offering?

And Abraham said, My son, *God will provide himself a lamb for a burnt offering:* so they went both of them together.

And they came to the place which God had told him of; and Abraham built an altar there, and laid the wood in order, and bound Isaac his son, and laid him on the altar upon the wood.

And Abraham stretched forth his hand, and took the knife to slay his son.

And the angel of the LORD called unto him out of heaven, and said, Abraham, Abraham: and he said, Here am I.

And he said, Lay not thine hand upon the lad, neither do thou any thing unto him: for now I know that thou fearest God, seeing thou hast not withheld thy son, thine only son from me.

And Abraham lifted up his eyes, and looked, and behold behind him a ram caught in a thicket by his horns: and Abraham went and took the ram, and offered him up for a burnt offering in the stead of his son.

And Abraham called the name of that place Jehovah-jireh: as it is said to this day, In the mount of the LORD it shall be seen.

And the angel of the LORD called unto Abraham out of heaven the second time,

And said, By myself have I sworn, saith the LORD, for because thou hast done this thing, and hast not withheld thy son, thine only son:

That in blessing I will bless thee, and in multiplying I will multiply thy seed as the stars of the heaven, and as the sand which is upon the sea shore; and thy seed shall possess the gate of his enemies;

And in thy seed shall all the nations of the earth be blessed; because thou hast obeyed my voice.

So Abraham returned unto his young men, and they rose up and went together to Beer-sheba; and Abraham dwelt at Beer-sheba. (Genesis 22:1–19)

Why might Abraham have been willing to sacrifice his son, Isaac? Perhaps the Apostle Paul, in his great roll call of faith in the book of Hebrews, had the answer: Abraham knew that there was to be a resurrection, and that God might use Isaac's death and resurrection as a type for the future death and resurrection of God the Father's firstborn son, Jesus Christ:

> By faith *Abraham*, when he was tried, offered up *Isaac:* and *he that had received the promises offered up his only begotten son,*
>
> Of whom it was said, That in Isaac shall thy seed be called:
>
> *Accounting that God was able to raise him up, even from the dead; from whence also he received him in a figure.* (Hebrews 11:17–19)

THE SELECTING OF A WIFE FOR ISAAC

Years passed. Isaac turned forty years old (Genesis 25:20). From Abraham's point of view, it was time for his son to get married and move out of the tent. But he didn't want him to marry one of the local girls who didn't worship Jehovah; he wanted Isaac to be wed to someone raised with his own beliefs and values. After all, the Abrahamic covenant had to be passed on through worthy descendants!

Sometime after the Mt. Moriah episode—but prior to the quest for a wife for Isaac reported in Genesis chapter 24—Abraham had received news concerning Nahor, his brother, and Nahor's family back in Mesopotamia.

A short review of the family's genealogy is appropriate at this point. Abraham's father, Terah, had three sons: Abraham, Nahor, and Haran. The youngest brother, Haran, fathered several children, including a son, Lot, and a daughter, Milcah, but he died fairly early in life. Nahor, the middle son, took Haran's daughter Milcah as his wife about the time Abraham married Sarai (See Genesis 11:26–29).

So, back to Abraham. The news that had come to Abraham told of eight of his nieces and nephews. Though Abraham didn't hear of any other daughters and granddaughters, he learned that Nahor and Milcah's youngest son, Bethuel, had a daughter named Rebekah, who was Abraham's grand-niece. Bethuel's family might be a good place to begin looking for an appropriate partner for his son:

> And it came to pass after these things, that it was told Abraham, saying, Behold, Milcah, she hath also born children unto thy brother Nahor;
>
> Huz his firstborn, and Buz his brother, and Kemuel the father of Aram,
>
> And Chesed, and Hazo, and Pildash, and Jidlaph, and *Bethuel.*
>
> And *Bethuel* begat *Rebekah.* (Genesis 22:20–23)

So Abraham summoned his most trusted servant and put him under solemn oath to go north to Mesopotamia, search out Nahor's children's and grandchildren's families, and, being guided by inspiration and an angel, find a potential bride for Isaac:

And *Abraham was old, and well stricken in age: and the LORD had blessed Abraham in all* things.

And Abraham said unto his eldest servant of his house, that ruled over all that he had, Put, I pray thee, thy hand under my thigh:

And *I will make thee swear by the LORD, the God of heaven, and the God of the earth, that thou shalt not take a wife unto my son of the daughters of the Canaanites, among whom I dwell:*

But *thou shalt go unto my country, and to my kindred, and take a wife unto my son Isaac.*

And the servant said unto him, Peradventure the woman will not be willing to follow me unto this land: must I needs bring thy son again unto the land from whence thou camest?

And Abraham said unto him, *Beware thou that thou bring not my son thither again.*

The LORD God of heaven, which took me from my father's house, and from the land of my kindred, and which spake unto me, and that sware unto me, saying, Unto thy seed will I give this land; *he shall send his angel before thee, and thou shalt take a wife unto my son from thence.*

And if the woman will not be willing to follow thee, then thou shalt be clear from this my oath: only bring not my son thither again.

And *the servant put his hand under the thigh of Abraham his master, and sware to him concerning that matter.* (Genesis 24:1–9)

The servant, in obedience to his master's request, took ten camels loaded with goods to be used as a dowry for the young lady he would select and journeyed to Mesopotamia. To where, exactly? To the city of Nahor, wherever that was (Genesis 24:10). Presumably, the "city" was named for the person who settled it, and presumably, that Nahor was Nahor the brother of Abraham. Most likely, it was in the general vicinity of Haran, about six hundred miles to the north—the city from which Abraham had departed almost a century previously. If news of Nahor's family had found its way down to Abraham, he undoubtedly had a better address than what is reported in the Genesis account.

Did the servant travel alone? Apparently not. An elderly man doesn't manage ten camels by himself, nor is he capable of protecting their cargos from thieves and marauders. Notice that when he asked for lodging, he asked for "us" (Genesis 24:23, 32).

How long a trip? At 20 miles per day it would have taken about 30 days. This was no small undertaking!

The servant, obviously a believer in Jehovah, as was Abraham his master, sought inspiration in finding the young woman for whom he was seeking. When he arrived in the designated area, he proposed a sign, asking the Lord to honor it and thus indicate the proper choice of a life-partner for Isaac:

> And he made his camels to kneel down without the city by a well of water at the time of the evening, even the time that women go out to draw water.
>
> And he said, *O LORD God of my master Abraham, I pray thee, send me good speed this day, and shew kindness unto my master Abraham.*
>
> *Behold, I stand here by the well of water; and the daughters of the men of the city come out to draw water:*
>
> *And let it come to pass, that the damsel to whom I shall say, Let down thy pitcher, I pray thee, that I may drink; and she shall say, Drink, and I will give thy camels drink also: let the same be she that thou hast appointed for thy servant Isaac; and thereby shall I know that thou hast shewed kindness unto my master.* (Genesis 24:11–14)

Most of the Christian world knows what happened next:

> And it came to pass, *before he had done speaking, that, behold, Rebekah came out,* who was born to Bethuel, son of Milcah, the wife of Nahor, Abraham's brother, with her pitcher upon her shoulder.
>
> *And the damsel was very fair to look upon, a virgin, neither had any man known her:* and she went down to the well, and filled her pitcher, and came up.
>
> And the servant ran to meet her, and said, Let me, I pray thee, drink a little water of thy pitcher.
>
> And she said, *Drink, my lord:* and she hasted, and let down her pitcher upon her hand, and gave him drink.
>
> And when she had done giving him drink, she said, *I will draw water for thy camels also,* until they have done drinking.
>
> And she hasted, and emptied her pitcher into the trough, and ran again unto the well to draw water, and drew for all his camels. (Genesis 24:15–20)

Pleased with her response, Abraham's servant inquired about lodging for himself and his fellow servants.

> And it came to pass, as the camels had done drinking, that *the man took a golden earring of half a shekel weight, and two bracelets for her hands of ten shekels weight of gold;*
>
> And said, *Whose daughter art thou? tell me, I pray thee: is there room in thy father's house for us to lodge in?*
>
> And she said unto him, *I am the daughter of Bethuel the son of Milcah, which she bare unto Nahor.*
>
> She said moreover unto him, We have both straw and provender enough, and room to lodge in. (Genesis 24:22–25)

Abraham's servant rejoiced and offered profound thanks for having received the answer to his prayerful requests:

The man bowed down his head, and *worshipped the LORD.*

And he said, *Blessed be the LORD God of my master Abraham, who hath not left destitute my master of his mercy and his truth: I being in the way, the LORD led me to the house of my master's brethren.* (Genesis 24:26–27)

Apparently he offered his prayer of thanksgiving vocally, for "the damsel ran, and told them of her mother's house these things." (Genesis 24:28) And shortly thereafter, when Rebekah's brother Laban came out to Abraham's servant, he greeted him with the words, "Come in, thou blessed of the LORD" (Genesis 24:31). Abraham's servants were invited into the house and were graciously welcomed and treated there. But when food was set before them, the head servant spoke up and said, "I will not eat, until I have told mine errand." When told to "Speak on," he began speaking. First he told them who he was, and what his mission was:

> I am Abraham's servant.
>
> And the LORD hath blessed my master greatly; and he is become great: and he hath given him flocks, and herds, and silver, and gold, and menservants, and maidservants, and camels, and asses.
>
> And Sarah my master's wife bare a son to my master when she was old: *and unto him hath he given all that he hath.*
>
> And my master made me swear, saying, Thou shalt not take a wife to my son of the daughters of the Canaanites, in whose land I dwell:
>
> But thou shalt go unto my father's house, and to my kindred, and take a wife unto my son.
>
> And I said unto my master, Peradventure the woman will not follow me.
>
> And he said unto me, *The LORD, before whom I walk, will send his angel with thee, and prosper thy way;* and thou shalt take a wife for my son of my kindred, and of my father's house:
>
> Then shalt thou be clear from this my oath, when thou comest to my kindred; and if they give not thee one, thou shalt be clear from my oath. (Genesis 24:34–41)

Then Abraham's servant told them of his prayer beside the well, when he had asked Jehovah for a sign that he might recognize the girl he had been sent to find, and how the answer had been received even before he finished his prayer:

> And I came this day unto the well, and said, *O LORD God of my master Abraham, if now* thou do prosper my way which I go:
>
> Behold, I stand by the well of water; and it shall come to pass, that when the virgin cometh forth to draw water, and I say to her, Give me, I pray thee, a little water of thy pitcher to drink;
>
> *And she say to me, Both drink thou, and I will also draw for thy camels: let*

the same be the woman whom the LORD hath appointed out for my master's son.

And *before I had done speaking in mine heart,* behold, Rebekah came forth with her pitcher on her shoulder; and she went down unto the well, and drew water: and I said unto her, Let me drink, I pray thee.

And she made haste, and let down her pitcher from her shoulder, and said, Drink, and I will give thy camels drink also: so I drank, and she made the camels drink also.

And I asked her, and said, Whose daughter art thou? And she said, The daughter of Bethuel, Nahor's son, whom Milcah bare unto him: and *I put the earring upon her face, and the bracelets upon her hands.*

And I bowed down my head, and worshipped the LORD, and blessed the LORD God of my master Abraham, which had led me in the right way to take my master's brother's daughter unto his son. (Genesis 24:33–48)

Then and there, right on the spot, he made his proposal of marriage: "And now if ye will deal kindly and truly with my master, tell me: and if not, tell me; that I may turn to the right hand, or to the left" (Genesis 24:49).

And the decision he requested was made right then too. Who knows if there was a long, pregnant pause at that point? How many glances passed from one face to another? How many nods? The Spirit must have burned in everyone's heart during the conversation, for then Bethuel and Laban answered, saying:

The thing proceedeth from the LORD: we cannot speak unto thee bad or good.

Behold, Rebekah is before thee, take her, and go, and let her be thy master's son's wife, as the LORD hath spoken. (Genesis 24:50–51)

Has anyone ever heard of a speedier "whirlwind" courtship, proposal, and acceptance than that? And they hadn't even seen the dowry!

And it came to pass, that, when Abraham's servant heard their words, *he worshipped the LORD, bowing himself to the earth.*

And the servant brought forth jewels of silver, and jewels of gold, and raiment, and gave them to Rebekah: he gave also to her brother and to her mother precious things. (Genesis 24:52–53)

The caravan was soon headed back to Canaan. Rebekah didn't come by herself—she had a nurse and damsels that came with her. Abraham's family wasn't the only family branch that had prospered; Nahor's kin, who had a home big enough to house all the visiting servants and their animals, exhibited signs of being well-to-do also, having servants of their own too.

Notice that before the travelers departed, Bethuel's family had been fully informed of the Abrahamic Covenant and of the glorious promises that were destined to flow through Isaac and his family:

> And they called Rebekah, and said unto her, Wilt thou go with this man? And she said, I will go.
>
> And they sent away Rebekah their sister, and *her nurse*, and Abraham's servant, and his men.
>
> And they blessed Rebekah, and said unto her, Thou art our sister, be thou the mother of thousands of millions, and let thy seed possess the gate of those which hate them.
>
> And Rebekah arose, and *her damsels*, and they rode upon the camels, and followed the man: and the servant took Rebekah, and went his way. (Genesis 24:58–61)

Another month, more or less, passed as they wended their way south, back through Canaan to their home in the south country. The account ends with a description of Isaac and Rebekah meeting one another:

> And Isaac came from the way of the well Lahai-roi; for he dwelt in the south country.
>
> And Isaac went out to meditate in the field at the eventide: and he lifted up his eyes, and saw, and, behold, the camels were coming.
>
> And Rebekah lifted up her eyes, and when she saw Isaac, she lighted off the camel.
>
> For she had said unto the servant, What man is this that walketh in the field to meet us? And the servant had said, *It is my master:* therefore she took a vail, and covered herself.
>
> And the servant told Isaac all things that he had done.
>
> And Isaac brought her into his mother Sarah's tent, and took Rebekah, and she became his wife; and he loved her: and Isaac was comforted after his mother's death. (Genesis 24:62–67)

ISAAC'S RELATIONSHIP WITH HIS FATHER DURING ABRAHAM'S FINAL YEARS

Sometime after Sarah died, Abraham married a woman named Keturah. Abraham still had some romance in him because the two of them managed to parent six sons (and possibly some daughters too). Their sons' names were "Zimran, and Jokshan, and Medan, and Midian, and Ishbak, and Shuah" (Genesis 25:2). Several of them became the forefathers of tribes which were prominent in later political affairs in Canaan reported in the Old Testament.

Isaac and Rebekah were living away from Abraham, near the "well Lahai-roi . . . in the south country" (Genesis 24:62), so Isaac probably had little or no connection with these younger half-brothers. How often he saw his father Abraham is not known, though Abraham lived for thirty-five years or more after Isaac's wedding.

When Abraham finally passed away, at the age of 175, he "*died in a good old age, an old man, and full of years*; and was gathered to his people" (Genesis 25:8). He truly had enjoyed the longevity blessing which Jehovah long before had promised him: "thou shalt go to thy fathers in peace; thou shalt be buried in a good old age" (Genesis 15:15).

What about inheritances? The scripture relates that "*Abraham gave all that he had unto Isaac*. But unto the sons of the concubines [Hagar and Keturah], which Abraham had, Abraham gave gifts, and sent them away from Isaac his son, while he yet lived, eastward, unto the east country" (Genesis 25:5–6).

That distribution of Abraham's many goods was in obedience to the Lord's commandments. Jehovah had instructed Abraham that "my covenant will I establish with Isaac" (Genesis 17:21), and "in Isaac shall thy seed be called" (Genesis 21:12).

Abraham's funeral and burial? "His sons Isaac and Ishmael buried him in the cave of Machpelah" (Genesis 25:9). Obviously, Abraham's death was anticipated in sufficient time that both of his sons could be there together for the burial, which of necessity would have had to take place very shortly after Abraham's passing. How well acquainted the two sons were, and how compatible they were with one another, is not reported, but it certainly would be interesting to know, wouldn't it?

The Birth of Dueling Twins: Esau and Jacob

Having children didn't come easily to Isaac and Rebekah. Almost two decades passed, and it appeared Rebekah would be childless. The problem became a matter of prayer for Isaac, and his prayers in her behalf eventually were answered: "Isaac intreated the LORD for his wife, because she was barren: and the LORD was intreated of him, and Rebekah his wife conceived" (Genesis 25:21).

Even after becoming pregnant, Rebekah found childbearing difficult. After she learned she would be the mother of twins, she found that "the children struggled together within her." When she pondered the turmoil within her womb and asked "why am I thus," she finally "went to enquire of the LORD." Her prayerful inquiry brought a revealed answer that would change the course of history. The LORD said unto her,

1. Two separate nations would come from the children in her womb (25:23).
2. Her two babies would be two different "manners" of people (25:23).
3. The two peoples would be of disproportionate strengths (25:23).

4. The descendants of the older twin would serve the descendants of the younger twin (25:23).

Sure enough, when the time of birth arrived, "there were twins in her womb" (Genesis 25:24).

> And the first came out red, all over like an hairy garment; and they called his name Esau.
>
> And after that came his brother out, and his hand took hold on Esau's heel; and his name was called Jacob: and *Isaac was threescore years old* when she bare them. (Genesis 25:25–26)

If Abraham died at age 175 (Genesis 25:7), and was 100 when Isaac was born (Genesis 21:5), and Isaac was 60 when his twin sons were born (Genesis 26:26), then Abraham didn't die until Esau and Jacob were 15 years old.

What did the twins' names mean? "Esau" means "hairy," "Jacob" means "supplanter." Both names are related to the twins' appearance and actions at the moment of their birth. The twins seemed to be rivals from the day they entered mortality—and on through their lifetimes. Esau's descendants, the Edomites, were rivals of the Israelites after they returned to Canaan following their four-hundred-year captivity in Egypt.

From the time of the twins' birth and early childhood, Rebekah could see that the Lord's prophetic words to her would come to pass. That knowledge would influence her actions later, at a critical time in the lives of all the family members.

As the twins grew, they followed different courses. "Esau was a cunning hunter, a man of the field; and Jacob was a plain man, dwelling in tents" (Genesis 25:27). In other words, one hunted for a living; the other herded animals and farmed.

The differences in their personalities became increasingly apparent as they matured. Bible scholars who have analyzed the Genesis life stories of Esau and Jacob have drawn some down-to-earth conclusions concerning their youthful personalities and attitudes, based on decisions they made later in their lives and the perceived social perceptions of their day. For instance, according to the *Jewish Study Bible*, "To the ancient Israelite, Esau's hunting, like his hairiness, suggested uncouthness and even a certain degree of danger. The uncouthness is also apparent in his blunt speech and impulsive behavior in the ensuing tale (vv. 30–34)."[1] Others observed that when Esau

---

1. Berlin, Adele and Marc Zvi Brettler, editors. *The Jewish Study Bible: Featuring the Jewish Publication Society Tanakh Translation—Torah, Nevi'im, Kethuvim* (New York: Oxford University Press, 1999), p. 53.

was faced with the challenge of important decisions, he tended to make his choices based on his immediate needs rather than considering the potential long-range effect. This tendency would be manifested in his selling his birthright to his brother for the price of a meal, and in the poor choices he made when selecting marriage partners, thereby angering his parents. He liked to be off by himself rather than mingling with others all the time.

Jacob, on the other hand, was developing more personal discipline and business skills. He was willing to work hard and long for the things he wanted, and he was able to take the long-term view of the ultimate results of his actions. He was more of a "people person" than his brother.

Surely each of their parents loved both their sons, but as time went by, they both had their favorite: "Isaac loved Esau, because he did eat of his venison: but Rebekah loved Jacob" (Genesis 25:28).

THE POTTAGE AND THE BIRTHRIGHT

Millions have heard, read, and retold the tale of the Isaac's two sons and the mess of pottage. This is the Biblical account:

> And Jacob sod pottage: and Esau came from the field, and he was faint:
>
> And Esau said to Jacob, Feed me, I pray thee, with that same red pottage; for I am faint: therefore was his name called Edom.
>
> And Jacob said, Sell me this day thy birthright.
>
> And Esau said, Behold, I am at the point to die: and what profit shall this birthright do to me?
>
> And Jacob said, Swear to me this day; and he sware unto him: and he sold his birthright unto Jacob.
>
> Then Jacob gave Esau bread and pottage of lentiles; and he did eat and drink, and rose up, and went his way: thus Esau despised his birthright. (Genesis 25:29–34)

Like millions of others, this author heard this Bible story many times in his childhood, but there were key words he didn't really understand. Many others probably had the same experience because the full meaning of the event is difficult to grasp. Hence—here are several other Bible translations and some definitions needed to fully understand the account of Esau selling his birthright.

"Jacob *sod pottage*," of Genesis 25:29 in the *King James* version, is translated differently in other Bible versions. The *Amplified* version: "Jacob was boiling pottage (lentil stew) one day." The *New American Standard* version: "When Jacob had cooked stew." The *New International Version* (NIV): "Once when Jacob was cooking some stew."

Sod is an archaic past tense of the verb "seethe;" it's a variation of that verb's past-tense "seethed," which means "boiled."

Red pottage: Genesis 25:30 records that "Esau said to Jacob, Feed me, I pray thee, with that same *red pottage*; for I am faint." The red pottage, or "red stuff," was a mess of lentils (verse 34).

Lentils are a widely cultivated Euroasian legume with flattened, edible seeds—a cousin of the pea and bean vegetable families. A nutritious vegetable protein, they are commonly used in Middle Eastern lands in soups, also in stews where lentils may be combined with meat and other vegetables.

Edom: ("Therefore was his name called Edom.") *Edom* is a word that means "red." The insertion of this phrase in the tale demonstrates the use of a popular literary device—an allusion to a well-known place or people. Since Esau's descendants later settled in Edom, it probably is an allusion to the red color of that area's sandstone cliffs.

Birthright: Genesis 25:31 says, "Sell me this day thy birthright." The birthright of that day consisted of several things that were considered parts of the inheritance rights usually reserved for the firstborn son. In this case, Jacob, in his purchase from Esau, apparently obtained a considerable estate that probably contained various items Isaac had previously inherited from Abraham:

1. The headship of the family, meaning the authority to preside in family affairs.
2. A land inheritance, including his parents' burial site.
3. Material goods and objects of value, including servants and large herds of animals.
4. A double portion of any inheritance allotted to others—twice the value, or more, of others' inheritances (See Deuteronomy 21:17: "But he shall acknowledge the son of the hated for the firstborn, *by giving him a double portion of all that he hath:* for he is the beginning of his strength; the right of the firstborn is his.")
5. Priesthood rights: from Adam down through Jacob and others, the Lord's main representative on the earth held the joint offices of high priest and presiding patriarch, and this office was conferred from father to son successively. This privilege continued to Jacob, not Esau.
6. Heirship to the privileges of the Abrahamic covenant. Jacob's grandfather, Abraham, had been promised that from his day on, all his worthy descendants would have the right, by lineage, to hold God's priesthood, and also that righteous individuals who came to Christ and accepted His gospel would be adopted into Abraham's lineage. They were to be

accounted "lawful heirs, according to the flesh" (D&C 86:8–10). Certainly this was the most important aspect of the inheritance Jacob purchased.

JEHOVAH'S FIRST APPEARANCE TO ISAAC

Once again, "there was a famine in the land, beside the first famine that was in the days of Abraham." (Genesis 26:1) The dry, parched earth wouldn't yield sufficiently to sustain Isaac and Rebekah where they dwelled. They contemplated doing what Abraham had done a century before—going down to Egypt where the Nile River would provide adequate irrigation water for their crops and animals. But Jehovah had a different destination for them. "The LORD appeared unto him, and said,"

1. Don't go to Egypt; go to Gerar (26:2).
2. Remain in that area and the Lord will be with you and bless you (26:3).
3. Gerar (not Egypt) is among the countries the Lord will give to Isaac and his descendants (26:3).
4. The Lord will perform the oath He made to Abraham (26:3).
5. The Lord will multiply Isaac's descendants (26:4).
6. The Lord will give Isaac's descendants all the promised countries in the Canaan area (26:4).
7. Through Isaac's descendants all nations shall be blessed (26:4).
8. Why? Because of Abraham's obedience (26:5).

THE "SHE'S MY SISTER" QUESTION, FOR THE THIRD TIME

When the Lord appears to you and gives you commandments, you do what He says! Abraham did. So did Isaac. The record shows that when the famine came upon them, instead of going down to Egypt, "Isaac went unto Abimelech king of the Philistines unto Gerar" and "Isaac dwelt in Gerar" (Genesis 26:1, 6). This meant that Isaac moved down from the highlands of central Canaan into the more-fertile coastal plain a few miles inland from the Mediterranean Sea.

That custom—that a king had the "right" to take any woman residing in his kingdom into his harem—must have caused a lot of people plenty of heartburn over the years. It shows up for the third time in Genesis 26 (previously in Genesis 12:10–20 and 20:1–18). This time it is Isaac with his attractive wife Rebekah instead of Abraham with his beautiful wife Sarah. But for the second time, it involves Abimelech, king of Gerar. And it's the same story: the king grabs the wife, she says her husband is her brother so he won't be assassinated, the king discovers what the problem is, and then he complains to the husband that he's been lied to.

Abimelech, the King of Gerar, must have been a very young man when Abraham came into his country many years before, but he was still exercising his kingly prerogative when Isaac came:

> And Isaac dwelt in Gerar:
>
> And the men of the place asked him of his wife; and he said, *She is my sister: for he feared to say, She is my wife; lest, said he, the men of the place should kill me for Rebekah; because she was fair to look upon.*
>
> And it came to pass, when he had been there a long time, that Abimelech king of the Philistines looked out at a window, and saw, and, behold, *Isaac was sporting with Rebekah his wife.*
>
> And Abimelech called Isaac, and said, *Behold, of a surety she is thy wife: and how saidst thou, She is my sister?* And Isaac said unto him, Because I said, *Lest I die for her.*
>
> And Abimelech said, What is this thou hast done unto us? *one of the people might lightly have lien with thy wife, and thou shouldest have brought guiltiness upon us.*
>
> And Abimelech charged all his people, saying, *He that toucheth this man or his wife shall surely be put to death.* (Genesis 26:6–11)

So even though his lusty desires were thwarted, Abimelech was a good-enough man to grant Isaac and Rebekah protection through his royal decree and to allow them to dwell within the boundaries of his kingdom during the duration of the famine. Because of his protection, Isaac and Rebekah prospered while living in Gerar:

> Then Isaac sowed in that land, *and received in the same year an hundredfold: and the LORD blessed him.*
>
> And the man waxed great, and went forward, and grew until he became very great:
>
> For he had possession of flocks, and possession of herds, and great store of servants: *and the Philistines envied him.*
>
> For all the wells which his father's servants had digged in the days of Abraham his father, the Philistines had stopped them, and filled them with earth. (Genesis 26:12–15)

That envy was sufficient that Abimelech eventually "said unto Isaac, Go from us; for thou art much mightier than we" (Genesis 26:16). Abimelech's motive obviously was more than jealousy—like any king protecting his holdings, he didn't want any faction of his population to grow so strong it could overthrow and usurp his kingdom. But Isaac wasn't fully expelled from the kingdom of Gerar. He still was allowed to dwell in an outlying area of the kingdom—a more barren area, but one where Isaac wouldn't be so conspicuous in his growing wealth and power.

And Isaac departed thence, and pitched his tent in the valley of Gerar, and dwelt there.

And Isaac digged again the wells of water, which they had digged in the days of Abraham his father; for the Philistines had stopped them after the death of Abraham: and he called their names after the names by which his father had called them.

And Isaac's servants digged in the valley, and found there a well of springing water.

And the herdmen of Gerar did strive with Isaac's herdmen, saying, The water is ours: and he called the name of the well Esek; because they strove with him.

And they digged another well, and strove for that also: and he called the name of it Sitnah.

And he removed from thence, and digged another well; and for that they strove not: and he called the name of it Rehoboth; and he said, For now the LORD hath made room for us, and we shall be fruitful in the land. (Genesis 26:17–22)

Several comments on the above passage are appropriate. First, the passage refers to "the Philistines" (Genesis 26:18; see also 21:32, 34; 26:8, 14, 15). Those weren't the same people who were known as the Philistines in the days of King David, though they lived in the same area. The later "Philistines," an aggressive Sea People, immigrated to the coastal plains of Canaan from Crete about 1200 BC. Second: note the meanings of the names of the wells Isaac's servants dug—Esek: strife; Sitnah: opposition; Rehoboth: broad open places. Third, note the continued emphasis on the need to find water and maintain a viable water supply: wells were dug; unused wells were stopped up; herdsmen fought to maintain adequate watering sources to care for their own animals. Water was precious then, as it is today. Fourth: this passage mentions travelers from a foreign country, yet, as things turned out, Isaac was the only one of the patriarchs who never went beyond Canaan.

THE LORD'S SECOND APPEARANCE TO ISAAC

This appearance of Jehovah took place after Isaac had moved from the Rehoboth-well area up to Beer-sheba (Genesis 26:23). "The LORD appeared unto him the same night, and said,"

1. Jehovah identifies himself as the God of Abraham (26:24; see Abraham 1:16).
2. Jehovah will be with Isaac and bless him (26:24).
3. Jehovah will multiply Isaac's descendants (26:24).
4. Multiplying Isaac's seed will be done for Abraham's sake (26:24).

The scriptural account relates that after being visited by Jehovah there in Beer-sheba and being assured that the Abrahamic covenant would be continued through him, Isaac "built an altar there, and called upon the name of the LORD and pitched his tent there: and there Isaac's servants digged a well" (26:25).

ANOTHER COVENANT WITH ABIMELECH, KING OF GERAR

Many years previous, obviously when King Abimelech was a much younger man, he and Abraham covenanted to live in peace with one another (see Genesis 21:22–34). The same scenario was repeated at this time with Isaac. Again, the covenanting process was initiated by Abimelech. Again, the king acknowledged that he recognized Isaac was blessed by Jehovah:

> Then Abimelech went to him from Gerar, and Ahuzzath one of his friends, and Phichol the chief captain of his army.
>
> And Isaac said unto them, Wherefore come ye to me, seeing ye hate me, and have sent me away from you?
>
> And they said, *We saw certainly that the LORD was with thee*: and we said, Let there be now an oath betwixt us, even betwixt us and thee, and *let us make a covenant with thee*;
>
> *That thou wilt do us no hurt*, as we have not touched thee, and as we have done unto thee nothing but good, and have sent thee away in peace: *thou art now the blessed of the LORD*.
>
> And he made them a feast, and they did eat and drink.
>
> And they rose up betimes in the morning, and *sware one to another*: and Isaac sent them away, and they departed from him in peace. (Genesis 26:26–31)

That same day, Isaac's servants came to him and announced that water had come into the well that they had been digging. Taking that as a good omen, Isaac named the well Beer-sheba, meaning "well of an oath." That name still is used by the inhabitants of the city that has grown up in that locale, almost 4,000 years later (Genesis 26:32–33).

ESAU TAKES WIVES AND MOVES TO EDOM

The Genesis account reports that when Esau was forty years old, he married two different women: "he took to wife Judith the daughter of Beeri the Hittite, and Bashemath the daughter of Elon the Hittite." His marrying these two pagan wives most certainly did not please his parents. The account says the two women "were a grief of mind unto Isaac and to Rebekah" (Genesis 26:34–35). Years later, when Rebekah and Isaac were discussing Jacob's marriage prospects, Rebekah expressed her exasperation concerning the two wives Esau had taken: "Rebekah said to Isaac, I am weary of my life because of the daughters of Heth: if Jacob take a wife of the daughters of Heth, such as these which are of the daughters of the land, what good shall my life do me?" (Genesis 27:46).

Some years later, Esau took himself a third wife:

> And Esau seeing that the daughters of Canaan pleased not Isaac his father;
>
> Then went Esau unto Ishmael, and took unto the wives which he had Mahalath the daughter of Ishmael Abraham's son, the sister of Nebajoth, to be his wife. (Genesis 28:8–9)

The record doesn't indicate how Isaac and Rebekah felt about Esau's choosing a daughter of Ishmael, Isaac's rival half-brother, to be another plural wife, but an educated guess would be they certainly didn't jump for joy over that marriage, either.

Time passed, and Esau's wives began bearing him children (There may have been some divorcing and remarrying on his part too; the list of his wives from Genesis 36 doesn't exactly match the list given above, from Genesis 26.) At any rate, it wasn't too long before he was the father of five sons:

> Esau took his wives of the daughters of Canaan; *Adah* the daughter of Elon the Hittite, and *Aholibamah* the daughter of Anah the daughter of Zibeon the Hivite;
>
> And *Bashemath* Ishmael's daughter, sister of Nebajoth.
>
> And Adah bare to Esau *Eliphaz*; and Bashemath bare *Reuel*;
>
> And Aholibamah bare *Jeush*, and *Jaalam*, and *Korah*: these are the sons of Esau, which were born unto him in the land of Canaan. (Genesis 36:2–5)

Esau was prospering, as were Isaac and Jacob. The time came when the area where they were living couldn't support all three of them, so Esau opted to move to the southeast, beyond the Salt Sea (the Dead Sea), to a place called Edom:

> And Esau took his wives, and his sons, and his daughters, and all the persons of his house, and his cattle, and all his beasts, and all his substance, which he had got in the land of Canaan; and went into the country from the face of his brother Jacob.
>
> For their riches were more than that they might dwell together; and the land wherein they were strangers could not bear them because of their cattle.
>
> Thus dwelt Esau in mount Seir: Esau is Edom. (Genesis 36:6–8)

ISAAC'S BLESSINGS FOR JACOB AND ESAU

It is difficult to assign an approximate date to the highly significant episode when Jacob received his father's birthright blessing. Recall that Isaac was forty when he married Rebekah, and sixty when twins Esau and Jacob were born. Esau took his first two wives when he was forty, so Isaac was about a hundred years old when those marriages occurred. Some more time has transpired, but Jacob was not yet married. Esau had at least five children. One could easily imagine that another fifteen years had gone by, though that, of course, would simply be a guess.

As chapter 27 of Genesis begins, "Isaac was old, and his eyes were dim, so that he could not see." He was so old, it appears, that he believed his death was fast approaching (Genesis 27:1–2, 41). He realized that he had not yet given his sons a father's blessing, and he recognized it was time to deal with matters pertaining to the passing on of his estate and defining matters relating to his sons' inheritances.

The account says that he sent word to Esau, who presumably was living with his wives in Edom, asking him to come make him a tasty venison dinner, and intimating that he would then give him a father's blessing.

> And it came to pass, that when Isaac was old, and his eyes were dim, so that he could not see, he called Esau his eldest son, and said unto him, My son: and he said unto him, Behold, here am I.
>
> And he said, Behold now, I am old, I know not the day of my death:
>
> Now therefore take, I pray thee, thy weapons, thy quiver and thy bow, and go out to the field, and take me some venison;
>
> And make me savoury meat, such as I love, and bring it to me, that I may eat; that my soul may bless thee before I die.
>
> And Rebekah heard when Isaac spake to Esau his son. And Esau went to the field to hunt for venison, and to bring it. (Genesis 27:1–5)

So, there was Rebekah, who overheard Isaac's request—she suddenly found herself confronted by what she recognized as a serious dilemma. Here was Isaac: old, blind or nearly so, feeling feeble and believing he rapidly was approaching his deathbed. Did he know of Esau's selling his birthright to Jacob, more than four or five decades ago?

If he did know of Esau's oath to Jacob, relinquishing his birthright privileges, would Isaac honor that sworn agreement, or would he ignore it?

Was Esau worthy of receiving the birthright blessing after being so headstrong that he had married outside of the covenant lineage, much to the disapproval of both his parents? Wasn't he flighty, irresponsible, not managing life well, not honoring nor bringing honor upon his parents?

In contrast, here with them was Jacob, living more worthily, remaining at home and increasingly shouldering the load as Isaac aged, preparing himself to be the one who would embrace and pass on the Abrahamic covenant which was, of necessity, the core of the birthright blessing. What of him?

What did God want to happen at this juncture? What of that profound revelation He gave her while the twins were still in her womb: "Two nations are in thy womb, and two manner of people shall be separated from thy bowels; and the one people shall be stronger than the other people; *and the elder shall serve the younger*" (Genesis 25:23). She'd seen the first part come to pass: the twins very definitely were "two manner of people"—as different as could be.

The birthright was the right of family authority, of leadership in the home and among the family's coming generations—both in mortality and throughout the eternities. Which twin was best suited for that responsibility? And was the younger to serve the older, or—as God had clearly revealed before their birth—was the elder to serve the younger?

Rebekah made her choice and acted decisively upon it, for it required immediate action:

> Rebekah spake unto Jacob her son, saying, Behold, I heard thy father speak unto Esau thy brother, saying,
>
> Bring me venison, and make me savoury meat, that I may eat, and *bless thee before the LORD* before my death.
>
> Now therefore, my son, obey my voice according to that which I command thee.
>
> Go now to the flock, and fetch me from thence two good kids of the goats; and I will make them savoury meat for thy father, such as he loveth:
>
> And thou shalt bring it to thy father, that he may eat, and that he may bless thee before his death.
>
> And Jacob said to Rebekah his mother, Behold, Esau my brother is a hairy man, and I am a smooth man:
>
> My father peradventure will feel me, and I shall seem to him as a deceiver; and I shall bring a curse upon me, and not a blessing.
>
> And his mother said unto him, Upon me be thy curse, my son: only obey my voice, and go fetch me them.
>
> And he went, and fetched, and brought them to his mother: and his mother made savoury meat, such as his father loved.
>
> And Rebekah took goodly raiment of her eldest son Esau, which were with her in the house, and put them upon Jacob her younger son:
>
> And she put the skins of the kids of the goats upon his hands, and upon the smooth of his neck:
>
> And she gave the savoury meat and the bread, which she had prepared, into the hand of her son Jacob. (Genesis 27:6–17)

Obviously, Jacob had to deceitfully play the role of his elder brother when he brought his father the venison he desired:

> And he came unto his father, and said, My father: and he said, Here am I; who art thou, my son?
>
> And Jacob said unto his father, I am Esau thy firstborn; I have done according as thou badest me: arise, I pray thee, sit and eat of my venison, that thy soul may bless me.
>
> And Isaac said unto his son, How is it that thou hast found it so quickly, my son? And he said, Because the LORD thy God brought it to me.
>
> And Isaac said unto Jacob, Come near, I pray thee, that I may feel thee, my son, whether thou be my very son Esau or not.
>
> And Jacob went near unto Isaac his father; and he felt him, and said, The voice is Jacob's voice, but the hands are the hands of Esau.
>
> And he discerned him not, because his hands were hairy, as his brother Esau's hands: so he blessed him.
>
> And he said, Art thou my very son Esau? And he said, I am.
>
> And he said, Bring it near to me, and I will eat of my son's venison, that my soul may bless thee. And he brought it near to him, and he did eat: and he brought him wine, and he drank.
>
> And his father Isaac said unto him, Come near now, and kiss me, my son.
>
> And he came near, and kissed him. (Genesis 27:18–27)

And then Isaac pronounced upon Jacob his birthright blessing:

1. God will give you water and the fatness of the earth (27:28).
2. People will serve you (27:29).
3. Nations will bow down to you (27:29).
4. You are to preside and rule over your family (27:29).
5. Those who curse you will be cursed (27:29).
6. Those who bless you will be blessed (27:29).

Imagine the grief and bitterness Esau felt when he learned that Jacob had taken his place and received his father's blessing:

> And it came to pass, as soon as Isaac had made an end of blessing Jacob, and Jacob was yet scarce gone out from the presence of Isaac his father, that Esau his brother came in from his hunting.
>
> And he also had made savoury meat, and brought it unto his father, and said unto his father, Let my father arise, and eat of his son's venison, that thy soul may bless me.
>
> And Isaac his father said unto him, Who art thou? And he said, I am thy son, thy firstborn Esau.
>
> And Isaac trembled very exceedingly, and said, Who? where is he that hath taken venison, and brought it me, and *I have eaten of all before thou camest, and have blessed him? yea, and he shall be blessed.*

And when Esau heard the words of his father, he cried with a great and exceeding bitter cry, and said unto his father, *Bless me, even me also, O my father.*

And he said, Thy brother came with subtilty, and hath taken away thy blessing.

And he said, *Is not he rightly named Jacob? for he hath supplanted me these two times: he took away my birthright; and, behold, now he hath taken away my blessing. And he said, Hast thou not reserved a blessing for me?*

And Isaac answered and said unto Esau, Behold, *I have made him thy lord, and all his brethren have I given to him for servants; and with corn and wine have I sustained him:* and what shall I do now unto thee, my son?

And Esau said unto his father, Hast thou but one blessing, my father? *bless me, even me also, O my father. And Esau lifted up his voice, and wept.* (Genesis 27:30–38)

And Isaac his father answered with blessings which primarily would characterize Esau's posterity. He said unto him,

1. Esau also will have water and the earth's fatness (27:39).
2. You will live by the sword (27:40).
3. You will serve your brother (27:40).
4. When you have dominion, you will be able to remove his yoke from you (27:40).

JACOB'S FLIGHT TO MESOPOTAMIA

Esau's bitterness was so overwhelming that he resolved to kill Jacob right after his father's death. Hearing of his plan, Rebekah hastened to send Jacob away while his brother cooled down:

And *Esau hated Jacob because of the blessing wherewith his father blessed him:* and Esau said in his heart, *The days of mourning for my father are at hand; then will I slay my brother Jacob.*

And these words of Esau her elder son were told to Rebekah: and she sent and called Jacob her younger son, and said unto him, *Behold, thy brother Esau, as touching thee, doth comfort himself, purposing to kill thee.*

Now therefore, my son, obey my voice; and arise, flee thou to Laban my brother to Haran;

And tarry with him a few days, until thy brother's fury turn away;

Until thy brother's anger turn away from thee, and he forget that which thou hast done to him: then I will send, and fetch thee from thence: why should I be deprived also of you both in one day? (Genesis 27:41–45)

Rebekah found that Isaac needed some convincing that rushing Jacob away was the right thing to do. She couched the matter in terms of finding a suitable marriage partner for Jacob. Rebekah said to Isaac, "I am weary of my life because of the daughters of Heth: if Jacob take a wife of the daughters of Heth, such as these which are of the daughters of the land, what good shall my life do me?" (Genesis 27:46). Isaac soon became convinced of her plan, apparently, because he counseled Jacob not to take a Canaanite wife, but rather to find one of Rebekah's nieces and marry her. And then he gave Jacob another blessing in which he acknowledged that the blessings of the Abrahamic Covenant were to be bestowed by the Lord upon Jacob, his son:

> And Isaac called Jacob, and blessed him, and charged him, and said unto him, *Thou shalt not take a wife of the daughters of Canaan.*
>
> Arise, go to Padan-aram, to the house of Bethuel thy mother's father; and *take thee a wife from thence of the daughters of Laban thy mother's brother.* (Genesis 28:1–2)

1. May God Almighty bless you (28:3).
2. May God make you fruitful and multiply you (28:3).
3. May God give the blessings of Abraham to you and your descendants (28:4).
4. May you inherit the promised land (28:4).

And then the life story of Isaac, recorded in the book of Genesis, came to a temporary end with these words:

> And Isaac sent away Jacob: and he went to Padan-aram unto Laban, son of Bethuel the Syrian, the brother of Rebekah, Jacob's and Esau's mother.
>
> When Esau saw that Isaac had blessed Jacob, and sent him away to Padan-aram, to take him a wife from thence; and that as he blessed him he gave him a charge, saying, *Thou shalt not take a wife of the daughters of Canaan;*
>
> And that *Jacob obeyed his father and his mother, and was gone to Padan-aram;*
>
> And Esau seeing that the daughters of Canaan pleased not Isaac his father;
>
> Then went *Esau unto Ishmael, and took unto the wives which he had Mahalath the daughter of Ishmael Abraham's son, the sister of Nebajoth, to be his wife.* (Genesis 28:5–9)

At this point the story leaves Isaac and Rebekah and follows Jacob on his journey northward. Yes, he finds a wife, in fact, more than one! Yes, Jacob and Esau are eventually reconciled. But for all those exciting details, you'll have to read the next chapter!

Though Isaac thought he was on his deathbed when he gave blessings to Isaac and Esau, he was not. He was still alive more than 20 years later, after Jacob had returned from Haran. Chapter 35 of Genesis finally reports his passing:

And Jacob came unto Isaac his father unto Mamre, unto the city of Arbah, which is Hebron, where Abraham and Isaac sojourned.

And the days of Isaac were an hundred and fourscore years.

And Isaac gave up the ghost, and died, and was gathered unto his people, *being old and full of days:* and his sons Esau and Jacob buried him. (Genesis 35:27–29)

NEW TESTAMENT TRIBUTES AND ALLEGORIES CONCERNING ISAAC

There are numerous references to Isaac scattered throughout the standard works, but in almost all cases, they refer to Abraham, Isaac, and Jacob in the same passage. The most significant of those references were previously quoted in the chapter on Abraham and will not be repeated here.

It should be noted that those passages repeatedly assert that Isaac, along with Abraham and Jacob, now are resurrected beings and are dwelling in the celestial realms.

However, In three different New Testament passages, the Apostle Paul pays specific tribute to Isaac, in each one depicting him in different roles in an allegorical setting. Those passages are cited below.

In his Epistle to the Romans, Paul differentiates between the descendants of Isaac and the descendants of his brother, Esau. While both lines are descended from Abraham, the House of Israel is based on Isaac's son Jacob, so the descendants of Esau are not part of the covenant line of Israel. Paul characterizes Esau's progeny as "children of flesh," as contrasted with Isaac's offsprings through Israel whom he describes as "children of God":

I have great heaviness and continual sorrow in my heart.

For I could wish that myself were accursed from Christ for my brethren, my kinsmen according to the flesh:

Who are Israelites; to whom pertaineth the adoption, and the glory, and the covenants, and Whose are the fathers, and of whom as concerning the flesh Christ came, who is over all,

God blessed for ever. Amen.

Not as though the word of God hath taken none effect. *For they are not all Israel, which are of Israel:*

Neither, because they are the seed of Abraham, are they all children: but, In Isaac shall thy seed be called.

That is, *They which are the children of the flesh, these are not the children of God: but the children of the promise are counted for the seed.*

For this is the word of promise, At this time will I come, and Sara shall have a son.

And not only this; but when Rebecca also had conceived by one, even by our father Isaac;

(For the children being not yet born, neither having done any good or evil, that the purpose of God according to election might stand, not of works, but of him that calleth;)

It was said unto her, The elder shall serve the younger.

As it is written, Jacob have I loved, but Esau have I hated. (Romans 9:2–13)

In the allegory in his Epistle to the Galatians, Paul used Isaac as a symbol of one who is born as a child of promise—being born after the Spirit, contrasting him with one that is bound by the Law of Moses:

Tell me, ye that desire to be under the law, do ye not hear the law?

For it is written, that *Abraham had two sons, the one by a bondmaid, the other by a freewoman.*

But he who was of the bondwoman was born after the flesh; but he of the freewoman was by promise.

Which things are an allegory: for these are the two covenants; the one from the mount Sinai, which gendereth to bondage, which is Agar.

For this Agar is mount Sinai in Arabia, and answereth to Jerusalem which now is, and is in bondage with her children.

But Jerusalem which is above is free, which is the mother of us all.

For it is written, Rejoice, thou barren that bearest not; break forth and cry, thou that travailest not: for the desolate hath many more children than she which hath an husband.

Now we, brethren, as Isaac was, are the children of promise.

But as then he that was born after the flesh persecuted him that was born after the Spirit, even so it is now.

Nevertheless what saith the scripture? Cast out the bondwoman and her son: for the son of the bondwoman shall not be heir with the son of the freewoman.

So then, brethren, *we are not children of the bondwoman, but of the free.* (Galatians 4:21–31)

In yet a different setting—the book of Hebrews—Paul includes Isaac in his famous roll call of faith, while also paying tribute to many other valiant individuals in the Old Testament. He lists Isaac in chronological order, right between Abraham and Jacob. Of the three of them: Abraham, Isaac, and Jacob, he said:

By faith *Abraham*, when he was called to go out into a place which he should after receive for an inheritance, obeyed; and he went out, not knowing whither he went.

By faith he sojourned in the land of promise, as in a strange country, *dwelling in tabernacles with Isaac and Jacob, the heirs with him of the same promise:*

For he looked for a city which hath foundations, whose builder and maker is God.

Through faith also *Sara* herself received strength to conceive seed, and was delivered of a child when she was past age, because she judged him faithful who had promised.

Therefore sprang there even of one, and him as good as dead, so many as the stars of the sky in multitude, and as the sand which is by the sea shore innumerable.

These all died in faith, not having received the promises, but having seen them afar off, and were persuaded of them, and embraced them, and confessed that they were strangers and pilgrims on the earth. . . .

By faith *Abraham,* when he was tried, offered up *Isaac:* and he that had received the promises offered up his only begotten son,

Of whom it was said, That *in Isaac shall thy seed be called:*

Accounting that God was able to raise him up, even from the dead; from whence also he received him in a figure.

By faith Isaac blessed Jacob and Esau concerning things to come.

By faith *Jacob,* when he was a dying, blessed both the sons of *Joseph;* and worshipped, leaning upon the top of his staff. (Hebrews 11:8–13, 17–21)

CHAPTER 8

JACOB

"A NATION AND A COMPANY OF NATIONS SHALL BE OF THEE, AND KINGS SHALL COME OUT OF THY LOINS"

Jacob, the younger of the twin sons of Isaac and Rebekah, is believed to have been born about 2006 BC. He and his older brother, Esau, were born in response to Isaac's prayer in behalf of Rebekah, who had been "barren" for almost twenty years. Prior to their coming forth, Rebekah had received a revelation indicating that "the elder shall serve the younger." According to the Biblical account, even within their mother's womb there was turmoil between the two, and at birth, as Esau emerged, Jacob's hand reached out and grasped his heel. Rebekah's revelation, plus his hand grasping his brother's heel at birth, caused the younger twin to be named Jacob, which meant "supplanter." (Genesis 25:20–26). His father was sixty years old when the twins were born.

Jacob purchased his hungry older brother's birthright for a bowl of stew in their youth, which indicated Esau's disdain for his birthright's importance (Genesis 25:27–34). Later, when the two twins were probably in their forties or fifties—and when Isaac was old, blind, and anticipating that his death was near—Jacob supplanted Esau by posing as his elder brother and receiving his father's blessing. This granted to Jacob the privileges of the family's birthright. Esau was so bitter about the matter that he vowed to murder his brother as soon as his father died. Knowing of this vow, his parents sent Jacob up to Mesopotamia to escape from Esau's wrath and to find himself a wife from among Rebekah's nieces—daughters of her brother, Laban (Genesis 27:1–28:4).

All of the above events were reported in detail in the chapter on Isaac and won't receive further coverage in this chapter.

JEHOVAH RENEWS THE ABRAHAMIC COVENANT WITH JACOB

This chapter begins the detailing of Jacob's life as he began his journey northward to Mesopotamia. Because there are so many of his life events recorded in the book of Genesis and other scriptures, his life will be treated in a more summarylike format than the lives of his forefathers, presented in the preceding chapters.

> And Isaac sent away Jacob: and he went to Padan-aram unto Laban, son of Bethuel the Syrian, the brother of Rebekah, Jacob's and Esau's mother. . . .
>
> And Jacob went out from Beer-sheba, and went toward Haran.[1] (Genesis 28:5, 10)

As Jacob began wending his way northward, and came about sixty miles to the place later called Beth-el, Jehovah appeared to him in a dream:

> And Jacob went out from Beer-sheba, and went toward Haran.
>
> And he lighted upon a certain place, and tarried there all night, because

---

1. One source tells us:

    Haran was the chief town of the region called Paddan-aram (Field of Aram) by later Israel.

    An earlier name appears to have been Aram of the Two Rivers (Gen. 24:10, R.V. marg.). This was one of the centers of the new Amorite settlement, and it is tempting to connect the journeys of the family of Abraham either directly or indirectly with the Amorite movement. Several lines of evidence lead to the conclusion that this can be done.

    For one thing, certain of the names of the ancestors and family of Abraham were also names of towns in the area of Haran: that is, Peleg, Serug, Nahor, and Terah (Gen. 11:16 ff.). The name of the city Haran sounds very much like that of one of Abraham's brothers, though the initial letter in the original language is slightly different. The identification of one name with an ancient town might be mere coincidence, but in this case there are at least four in the precise area from which Abraham came. These names were probably patriarchal clan names which either were given by the clans to towns they founded or were taken from the towns which they seized during the disturbances around 2000 BC.

    Further, the names Abram (in the form *Abamram*) and Jacob (in the form *Jacob-el*) are known as personal names among the Amorites. . . . Even more interesting is the light thrown on patriarchal customs by the archives of a later city of northern Mesopotamia named Nuzi. The customs reflected in these documents explain a number of patriarchal laws and practices that were obscure, and they demonstrate that patriarchal life as described in Genesis is that of the second millennium, and not of the first millennium, when Israelites were retelling the stories and putting them into writing. Thus, the relations between Jacob and Laban, the hitherto obscure "teraphim" (Gen. 31:19 ff.), Esau's sale of his birthright, patriarchal deathbed blessings, and so forth, are now seen in clearer perspective. (Taken from: *The Westminster Historical Atlas to the Bible* (Philadelphia: The Westminster Press, 1946), p. 25.)

the sun was set; and he took of the stones of that place, and put them for his pillows, and lay down in that place to sleep.

And he dreamed, and behold a ladder set up on the earth, and the top of it reached to heaven: and behold the angels of God ascending and descending on it.

And, behold, *the LORD stood above it,* and said, (Genesis 28:10–13)

1. Jehovah is the God of Abraham and Isaac (28:13).
2. Jehovah will give the land of Canaan to Jacob and his descendants (28:13).
3. Jacob's descendants will be as plentiful as the dust of the earth (28:14).
4. Jacob's descendants will spread in all directions (28:14).
5. All the families of the earth will be blessed by Jacob and his descendants (28:14).
6. Jehovah will be with Jacob and protect him (28:15).
7. Jehovah will bring Jacob back to Canaan (28:15).
8. Jehovah will remain with Jacob until He has fulfilled these promises (28:15).

When Jacob awoke, he set up a pillar of stone and anointed it. Then he made a solemn vow to the Lord:

And Jacob awaked out of his sleep, and he said, *Surely the LORD is in this place;* and I knew it not.

And he was afraid, and said, How dreadful is this place! *this is none other but the house of God, and this is the gate of heaven.*

And Jacob rose up early in the morning, and took the stone that he had put for his pillows, and set it up for a pillar, and poured oil upon the top of it.

And he called the name of that place Beth-el: but the name of that city was called Luz at the first.

And Jacob vowed a vow, saying, (Genesis 28:16–20)

1. God's obligations in the covenant (28:20–21).
2. Jacob's obligations in the covenant (28:21–22).

JACOB COVENANTS WITH LABAN FOR A WIFE: RACHEL

Jacob completed his six-hundred-mile journey to the outskirts of Haran in northern Mesopotamia and "came into the land of the people of the east." (Genesis 29:1) When he drew near to a field with a covered well, he asked nearby shepherds if they knew Laban the son of Nahor. They replied that they not only knew him, but that it was his daughter Rachel coming to water the sheep she was shepherding. Jacob rolled away the well's stone covering and helped her water her flock. Then he identified himself to her as a relative, telling her he was the son of Rebekah—her father Laban's sister. "When Laban heard the tidings of Jacob his sister's son, . . . he ran to meet him, and embraced him, and kissed him, and brought him to his house," telling him "Surely thou art my bone and my flesh" (Genesis 29:4–15).

This Laban was the same Laban who came out to greet Abraham's servant, coming to select a wife for Isaac—more than sixty years before (see Genesis 24:29–31). But the situation was different back then from how Jacob now was arriving. That servant had come with camels laden with precious things to offer as a dowry (Genesis 24:53); Jacob came empty-handed.

The story unfolds like a romance novel. First, the cast of characters is introduced:

> Laban had two daughters: the name of the elder was Leah, and the name of the younger was Rachel. Leah was tender eyed; but Rachel was beautiful and well favoured. (Genesis 29:16–17)

Then, the novel's plot begins to develop. Jacob stayed at Laban's home for a month, during which time his initial attraction for Rachel apparently blossomed into love. When Jacob negotiated with his uncle to be able to stay on in his home there in Haran, Jacob asked for Rachel's hand in marriage. Jacob obviously was aware that he had no dowry to offer, so he proposed that he "serve thee seven years for Rachel thy younger daughter." (Genesis 29:18) The proposal was accepted, with Laban saying "It is better that I give her to thee, than that I should give her to another man: abide with me." (Genesis 29:19)

The plot thickens as time rolls by, but quickly reaches the moment of climax:

> Jacob served seven years for Rachel; and they seemed unto him but a few days, for the love he had to her.
>
> And Jacob said unto Laban, Give me my wife, for my days are fulfilled, that I may go in unto her.
>
> And Laban gathered together all the men of the place, and made a feast. (Genesis 29:20–22)

Then Jacob is suddenly identified as the protagonist—the "good guy," and Laban is shown to be the antagonist—the "bad guy" who fails to keep his word:

> And it came to pass in the evening, that he took Leah his daughter, and brought her to him; and he went in unto her. . . .
>
> And it came to pass, that in the morning, behold, it was Leah: and he

said to Laban, What is this thou hast done unto me? did not I serve with thee for Rachel? wherefore then hast thou beguiled me?

And Laban said, It must not be so done in our country, to give the younger before the firstborn. (Genesis 29:23, 25–26)

One wonders: how long before the switch occurred did Leah know she was going to be the substitute bride? Perhaps one of the many important lessons one should learn from the Bible is to never allow one's bride to be delivered on the wedding night in an unlit tent!

Though Jacob was dismayed, Laban continued to drive a hard bargain. He proposed that Jacob give Leah a week-long honeymoon, and then he would give Jacob Rachel to be his wife, on the condition that Jacob provide him seven more years of free labor! Two handmaids would be thrown in to sweeten the deal—Zilpah would be Leah's servant; Bilhah would be Rachel's. Jacob agreed and served Laban another seven years (Genesis 29:23–30).

THE CHILDREN OF JACOB AND HIS WIVES

Chapters 29 and 30 definitely read like a romance novel or a long-running TV soap opera, with lots of pillow talk and sexy events taking place. The chapters are summarized here:

Jacob, then almost fifty years old, found himself with two wives, and tried to be a husband to both of them. However, for the first years of their marriages, Leah was fertile while Rachel was barren.

Leah gave Jacob his first four sons:

Child	Name	Name Means	Reference	Pronounced
Child 1	Reuben	"behold, a son"	29:32	ROO-ben
Child 2	Simeon	"one who hears"	29:33	SIM-ee-uhn
Child 3	Levi	"joined" or "pledged"	29:34	LEE-vi
Child 4	Judah	"hearing" or "praise"	29:35	JOO-duh

Bilhah, Rachel's handmaid, was the mother of sons five and six:

Child	Name	Name Means	Reference	Pronounced
Child 5	Dan	"he has vindicated"	30:1–6	DAN
Child 6	Naphtali	"wrestler"	30:7–8	NAF-tu-li

Zilpah, Leah's handmaid, was the mother of sons seven and eight:

Child	Name	Name Means	Reference	Pronounced
Child 7	Gad	"fortunate"	30:9–11	GAD
Child 8	Asher	"happy"	30:12–13	ASH-uhr

Leah gave Jacob his ninth and tenth sons (her fifth and sixth sons) and a daughter, Dinah:

Child	Name	Name Means	Reference	Pronounced
Child 9	Issachar	"hired worker"	30:14–18	IS-uh-kahr
Child 10	Zebulun	"exalted abode" or "honor"	30:19–20	ZEB-yoo-luhn
Child 11	Dinah		30:21	DI-nuh

Rachel gave Jacob his eleventh and twelfth sons:

Child	Name	Name Means	Reference	Pronounced
Child 12	Joseph	"may God add"	30:22–24	JOH-suhf
Child 13	Benjamin	"son of my right hand"	35:18	BEN-juh-min

The sons are listed in Genesis 35:22–26. It's very possible that other daughters were born, but were omitted from the Biblical listings, as was the custom. Dinah is included because she played a part in an event that will be discussed later. Children one through twelve were born in Padan-aram (Haran). Benjamin, however, was born later, in Canaan, but Rachel died while bringing him into mortality.

JACOB'S DEPARTURE FROM HARAN

After Joseph was born and Jacob's fourteen years of uncompensated service to Laban were completed, Jacob decided it was time to move away from Laban. Laban, however, proposed that Jacob stay on, agreeing that he would be paid wages. Jacob proposed that rather than being paid wages, Laban would give him all the speckled and spotted cattle, all the brown sheep, and all the spotted and speckled (ringstraked) goats, including animals born with those characteristics in the future. Laban agreed, and the animals given to Jacob were separated from those retained by Laban, with Jacob still responsible for feeding and caring for both of their herds, separately (Genesis 30:25–36).

Jacob then did some selective breeding, so the stronger animals that were born would be his, while the more-feeble animals would remain as Laban's property. So Jacob "increased exceedingly, and had much cattle, and maidservants, and menservants, and camels, and asses."

After a while, Laban's sons began to complain, and jealousy and mistrust began to turn Laban against Jacob (Genesis 30:37–43, 31:1–2).

When an angel came to Jacob and instructed him to return to Canaan, Jacob decided to leave—a decision with which both Leah and Rachel concurred (Genesis 31:3–16). Joseph (born at the end of Jacob's second seven-year period, see Genesis 30:22–25) was then about six years old (see Genesis 31:38, 41). When they left, with all their cattle and goods, they did it suddenly, without telling Laban they were going to depart. They were departing with considerable wealth, for Jacob "set his sons and his wives upon camels; And he carried away all his cattle, and all his goods which he had gotten, the cattle of his getting" (Genesis 31:17–18).

Angry, Laban and his men pursued them, but "God came to Laban the Syrian in a dream by night, and said unto him, Take heed that thou speak not to Jacob either good or bad" (Genesis 31:24), so Laban's wrath was diminished. Nevertheless, the hard feelings between Laban and Jacob remained so strong that they finally erected an altar, offered a sacrifice, and made a covenant that neither ever would pass beyond that heap of stones to do harm to the other. An all-night feast resulted following their agreement, and Laban finally bid his daughters and grandchildren farewell and returned to Haran (Genesis 31:25–55).

JACOB'S NAME CHANGED TO "ISRAEL"

Relieved of concerns about Laban's anger, Jacob and his family soon had to confront another long-standing concern. Jacob had fled from Canaan because his brother Esau had vowed to kill him. Though twenty years had passed, would Esau still seek to take his life? The southward route Jacob chose clearly shows that he intended to meet with Esau and, hopefully, be reconciled with him. Rather than come down on the western side of the Sea of Galilee and the Jordan River, he chose to come down on the eastern side of those bodies of water, through Gilead and, crossing the Jabbok, head not towards Canaan but towards Edom, down to the southeast of the Dead Sea.

Along the way, he sent messengers all the way down to Edom, where Esau lived, telling him that he and his family were returning to Canaan and saying, "I have sent to tell my lord, that I may find grace in thy sight." Unfortunately, the messengers quickly returned, reporting that Esau was coming out with four hundred men to meet them—a frightening prospect! (Genesis 32:3–6).

But as they continued their journey southward, Jacob had two "beyond the veil" experiences, which buoyed him up and gave him courage. First, as he was journeying, Jacob was allowed to see "the angels of God." And when he saw them, he said, "This is God's host" (Genesis 32:1–2).

The report that Esau was coming out to meet him with a large force still caused Jacob to divide his family and goods into groups, with the forward groups carrying lavish gifts for Esau to placate him.

That night, Jacob proceeded to offer up a prayer that showed his deep concern about the challenge that lay before him:

> O God of my father Abraham, and God of my father Isaac, the LORD which saidst unto me, Return unto thy country, and to thy kindred, and I will deal well with thee:
>
> I am not worthy of the least of all the mercies, and of all the truth, which thou hast shewed unto thy servant; for with my staff I passed over this Jordan; and now I am become two bands.
>
> Deliver me, I pray thee, from the hand of my brother, from the hand of Esau: for I fear him, lest he will come and smite me, and the mother with the children.
>
> And thou saidst, I will surely do thee good, and make thy seed as the sand of the sea, which cannot be numbered for multitude. (Genesis 32:9–12)

And then "he rose up that night, and took his two wives, and his two womenservants, and his eleven sons, and passed over the ford Jabbok. And he took them, and sent them over the brook, and sent over that he had" (Genesis 32:22–23).

Jacob remained behind—there, east of the River Jordan, just north of the brook Jabbok (the wadi Zerka). Suddenly, he found himself engaged in a strange contest—a hard-fought wrestling match, which continued until dawn:

> Jacob was left alone; and there wrestled a man with him until the breaking of the day.
>
> And when he saw that he prevailed not against him, he touched the hollow of his thigh; and the hollow of Jacob's thigh was out of joint, as he wrestled with him.
>
> And he said, Let me go, for the day breaketh. And he said, I will not let thee go, except thou bless me. (Genesis 32:24–26)

1. Jehovah changed Jacob's name to Israel (meaning "he perseveres with God") (32:27–28).
2. Why the name change? Because Jacob has power with God and men (32:28).
3. Jacob asked for the heavenly being's name (32:29).
4. Jacob had seen God face to face and lived (Genesis 32:30).

JACOB'S RECONCILIATION WITH ESAU

Jacob's long-dreaded day of confrontation with Esau then arrived. Would Jacob's company be attacked? Slaughtered? Taken as slaves? Fortunately, Jacob's meeting with Esau turned out to be a sweet time of reconciliation. No longer filled with their youthful animosities for one another, the two would be able to abide peacefully. Their meeting proved to be a tender moment:

> And Jacob lifted up his eyes, and looked, and, behold, Esau came, and with him four hundred men. And he divided the children unto Leah, and unto Rachel, and unto the two handmaids.
>
> And he put the handmaids and their children foremost, and Leah and her children after, and Rachel and Joseph hindermost.
>
> *And he passed over before them, and bowed himself to the ground seven times, until he came near to his brother.*
>
> *And Esau ran to meet him, and embraced him, and fell on his neck, and kissed him: and they wept.*
>
> And he lifted up his eyes, and saw the women and the children; and said, Who are those with thee? And he said, *The children which God hath graciously given thy servant.*
>
> Then the handmaidens came near, they and their children, and they bowed themselves.
>
> And *Leah* also with her children came near, and bowed themselves: and after came *Joseph* near and *Rachel,* and they bowed themselves.
>
> And he said, What meanest thou by all this drove which I met? And he said, These are to find grace in the sight of my lord.
>
> And Esau said, I have enough, my brother; keep that thou hast unto thyself.
>
> And Jacob said, *Nay, I pray thee, if now I have found grace in thy sight, then receive my present at my hand: for therefore I have seen thy face, as though I had seen the face of God, and thou wast pleased with me.*
>
> Take, I pray thee, my blessing that is brought to thee; because *God hath dealt graciously with me, and because I have enough. And he urged him, and he took it.*
>
> And he said, Let us take our journey, and let us go, and I will go before thee.
>
> And he said unto him, My lord knoweth that the children are tender, and the flocks and herds with young are with me: and if men should overdrive them one day, all the flock will die.
>
> Let my lord, I pray thee, pass over before his servant: and I will lead on softly, according as the cattle that goeth before me and the children be able to endure, until I come unto my lord unto Seir.
>
> And Esau said, Let me now leave with thee some of the folk that are

with me. And he said, What needeth it? let me find grace in the sight of my lord.

> So Esau returned that day on his way unto Seir. (Genesis 33:1–16)

Though the brothers discussed Jacob and his family coming to Edom, where Esau dwelled, Jacob instead crossed over the River Jordan and came west until he came to Shechem—a valley area between Mt. Ebal and Mt. Gerizim (west of the Jordan River, in central Israel). There he purchased a parcel of land and erected an altar (Genesis 33:17–20). Obviously, the people of the area recognized that the family was wealthy and had large herds and flocks. They wanted to integrate them into their community.

THE DINAH AND SHECHEM EPISODE

As Jacob was settling his family into the area, Leah's daughter, Dinah, went out exploring. Shechem, the son of Hamor who was the king of the area, saw her, desired her, and raped her.

Learning what his son had done, Hamor came to Jacob seeking reconciliation. Note the repeated indications that Jacob and his sons had several daughters.

> The soul of my son Shechem longeth for your daughter: I pray you give her him to wife.
>
> And make ye marriages with us, and *give your daughters unto us,* and take our daughters unto you.
>
> And ye shall dwell with us: and the land shall be before you; dwell and trade ye therein, and get you possessions therein. (Genesis 34:8–10)

All Dinah's brothers were incensed that their sister had been defiled, but they restrained their feelings for the moment. When Shechem asked what kind of a dowry Jacob and his family would require,

> the sons of Jacob answered Shechem and Hamor his father deceitfully, and said, . . . We cannot do this thing, to give our sister to one that is uncircumcised; for that were a reproach unto us:
>
> But in this will we consent unto you: If ye will be as we be, that every male of you be circumcised;
>
> *Then will we give our daughters unto you,* and we will take your daughters to us, and we will dwell with you, and we will become one people.
>
> But if ye will not hearken unto us, to be circumcised; then will we take our daughter, and we will be gone. (Genesis 34:13–17)

Requiring circumcision obviously was going to present a major problem to the men of the area, but Hamor and Shechem tried to sell them on the idea, saying:

> These men are peaceable with us; therefore let them dwell in the land,

and trade therein; for the land, behold, it is large enough for them; let us *take their daughters to us for wives,* and let us give them our daughters.

Only herein will the men consent unto us for to dwell with us, to be one people, if every male among us be circumcised, as they are circumcised.

Shall not their cattle and their substance and every beast of theirs be ours? only let us consent unto them, and they will dwell with us.

And unto Hamor and unto Shechem his son hearkened all that went out of the gate of his city; and *every male was circumcised, all that went out of the gate of his city.* (Genesis 34:21–24)

Then, Simeon and Levi, Jacob's second- and third-oldest sons, acted rashly in their desire to avenge their sister's rape, which resulted in Jacob's other sons involving themselves as well:

And it came to pass on the third day, when they were sore, that two of the sons of Jacob, Simeon and Levi, Dinah's brethren, took each man his sword, and came upon the city boldly, and slew all the males.

And they slew Hamor and Shechem his son with the edge of the sword, and took Dinah out of Shechem's house, and went out.

The sons of Jacob came upon the slain, and spoiled the city, because they had defiled their sister.

They took their sheep, and their oxen, and their asses, and that which was in the city, and that which was in the field,

And all their wealth, and all their little ones, and their wives took they captive, and spoiled even all that was in the house. (Genesis 34:25–29)

Jacob recognized that his sons' rash actions had brought dishonor upon their family and that their actions would soon result in attacks on their family from other tribal groups living nearby:

And Jacob said to Simeon and Levi, *Ye have troubled me to make me to stink among the inhabitants of the land,* among the Canaanites and the Perizzites: and I being few in number, they shall gather themselves together against me, and slay me; and I shall be destroyed, I and my house. (Genesis 34:30)

So Jacob quickly moved his family about twenty-five miles to the south, to Beth-el, the place where God had first appeared to him when he was fleeing from his brother Esau (Genesis 35:1–8). And once again, Jehovah appeared to him there, reiterating the promises he had previously made to Jacob:

1. God appeared to Jacob and blessed him (35:9).
2. God repeated the change of Jacob's name to "Israel." (35:10).
3. Jehovah again identified himself as "God Almighty." (35:11).
4. A commandment: multiply (35:11).
5. A prophecy concerning Israel's descendants (35:11).
6. A renewed promise that Canaan would be given to Israel and his descendants (35:12).

7.   God was there in person, then went up (35:13).

Israel again set up a pillar of stone there in Beth-el; he poured a drink offering and oil upon it, and "called the name of the place where God spake with him, Beth-el" (Genesis 35:15). This was the third time that he named the place Beth-el. (See Genesis 28:18–19 and 35:7.)

THE BIRTH OF BENJAMIN AND THE DEATH OF RACHEL

Sometime thereafter, when Israel's wife Rachel was heavy with child, Jacob and Rachel journeyed about fifteen miles southward to Beth-lehem. There Rachel went into hard labor. She gave birth to her second son, whom Israel named Benjamin, but died in the process:

> And they journeyed from Beth-el; and there was but a little way to come to Ephrath: and Rachel travailed, and she had hard labour.
>
> And it came to pass, when she was in hard labour, that the midwife said unto her, Fear not; thou shalt have this son also.
>
> And it came to pass, as her soul was in departing, (for she died) that she called his name Ben-oni: but his father called him Benjamin.
>
> And Rachel died, and was buried in the way to Ephrath, which is Beth-lehem.
>
> And Jacob set a pillar upon her grave: that is the pillar of Rachel's grave unto this day. (Genesis 35:16–20)

The location of Rachel's tomb is still known today, in the outskirts of Bethlehem. The site frequently is pointed out as tour buses pass it in their six-mile trips to and from Jerusalem. A maternity hospital now stands at the site.

By this time, Israel's oldest sons had attained manhood. It was about this time that Reuben committed adultery by sleeping with Bilhah, Israel's concubine (Genesis 35:22). As will be seen, this wicked act cost Reuben his birthright.

And it was also in this interval that Israel's father, Isaac, finally succumbed, at the age of 180. His sons Esau and Israel together buried him (Genesis 35:27–29). They would each have been 120 years old at this time.

Also, at some unknown time, Israel's wife Leah passed away. The time of her passing is not recorded. All that is known of her death is that Israel, on his deathbed, commented that he had buried her in the family burial plot in the Cave of Macpelah (Genesis 49:31).

JOSEPH IS SOLD INTO EGYPT

The account of Joseph's being sold into Egypt and the details of his varied experiences there will be retold in detail in the next chapter, which deals with Joseph's life. This chapter will treat those events only in summary form, focusing on how they affected Israel in his elderly years.

More time passed, and Israel was living in Hebron. At this point, Israel was almost 140 years old. He doted upon his second-to-youngest son, Joseph, perhaps using him as a living conduit to his treasured memories of his beloved wife, Rachel (Genesis 37:2). The Genesis account reports that "Israel loved Joseph more than all his children, because he was the son of his old age: and he made him a coat of many colours" (Genesis 37:3). This special treatment, along with Joseph's naivete in reporting several prophetic dreams to his older brothers, caused them to despise and continually mistreat him.

Joseph was seventeen when he was sold into Egypt (Genesis 37:2), and thirty when he interpreted Pharaoh's dream and was elevated to a position of power, being placed as the second-highest ruler in Egypt (Genesis 41:28–46). Seven years of plenty passed, and the seven years of famine were in their first year when Israel initially sent his sons down to Egypt to buy food (Genesis 42:1–2). They returned to Canaan and reported to their father Israel that Simeon had been retained in Egypt, and that the Egyptian ruler (Joseph, whom they did not recognize) required them to return the next time they came with Benjamin (Genesis 42:29–35). Israel grieved at their ill tidings:

> And Jacob their father said unto them, Me have ye bereaved of my children: Joseph is not, and Simeon is not, and ye will take Benjamin away: all these things are against me.
>
> And Reuben spake unto his father, saying, Slay my two sons, if I bring him not to thee: deliver him into my hand, and I will bring him to thee again.
>
> And he said, My son shall not go down with you; for his brother is dead, and he is left alone: if mischief befall him by the way in the which ye go, then shall ye bring down my gray hairs with sorrow to the grave. (Genesis 42:36–38)

Months passed, perhaps almost a year, before the famine made it necessary for Israel's sons to return to Egypt for more food. The dwindling supply of food compelled Israel to relent and finally agree for Benjamin to go to Egypt with his brothers. After several interactions with his unwitting brothers, Joseph demanded that Benjamin stay with him while his brothers returned (Genesis 43:1–44:17). Judah interceded for his youngest brother, telling Joseph that the effect of Benjamin's not returning with them would probably be fatal to their father:

> Our father said, Go again, and buy us a little food.
>
> And we said, We cannot go down: if our youngest brother be with us, then will we go down: for we may not see the man's face, except our youngest brother be with us.
>
> And thy servant my father said unto us, Ye know that my wife bare me two sons:
>
> And the one went out from me, and I said, Surely he is torn in pieces; and I saw him not since:
>
> And if ye take this also from me, and mischief befall him, ye shall bring down my gray hairs with sorrow to the grave.
>
> Now therefore when I come to thy servant my father, and the lad be not with us; seeing that his life is bound up in the lad's life;
>
> It shall come to pass, when he seeth that the lad is not with us, that he will die: and thy servants shall bring down the gray hairs of thy servant our father with sorrow to the grave.
>
> For thy servant became surety for the lad unto my father, saying, If I bring him not unto thee, then I shall bear the blame to my father for ever.
>
> Now therefore, I pray thee, let thy servant abide instead of the lad a bondman to my lord; and let the lad go up with his brethren.
>
> For how shall I go up to my father, and the lad be not with me? lest peradventure I see the evil that shall come on my father. (Genesis 44:25–34)

Judah's plea moved Joseph to tears, and he (Joseph) at last revealed his true identity to his brothers. Word soon reached Pharaoh that all the men were Joseph's brothers, and Pharaoh treated them with kindness, providing wagons and provisions for them to bring their families down to Egypt.

The account of the sons telling their father, Israel, that Joseph was still alive must rank extremely high in the list of world-changing understatements:

> And they went up out of Egypt, and came into the land of Canaan unto Jacob their father,
>
> And told him, saying, *Joseph is yet alive, and he is governor over all the land of Egypt. And Jacob's heart fainted, for he believed them not.*
>
> And they told him all the words of Joseph, which he had said unto them: and when he saw the wagons which Joseph had sent to carry him, *the spirit of Jacob their father revived:*
>
> And Israel said, *It is enough; Joseph my son is yet alive: I will go and see him before I die.* (Genesis 45:25–28)

More of the details of Joseph's experiences in Egypt will be related in the next chapter.

THE LORD SPEAKS TO ISRAEL AT BEER-SHEBA

So "Israel took his journey with all that he had." (Genesis 46:1) The group moved slowly, but in a day or two they came to Beer-sheba, about twenty-five miles south of Hebron. There, "God spake unto Israel in the visions of the night, and said, Jacob, Jacob. And he said, Here am I. And he said,"

1. Jehovah identifies Himself as the God of Jacob's father, Isaac (46:3).
2. Don't fear going to Egypt (46:3).
3. God will make Jacob's descendants a great nation while in Egypt (46:3).
4. God will accompany Israel to Egypt (46:4).
5. God will bring Israel back again (46:4).
6. Joseph's own hand will close Israel's eyes (when he dies) (46:4; see 50:1).

ISRAEL'S EXTENDED FAMILY
JOURNEYS DOWN TO EGYPT

How did Israel's extended family make their southward journey?

> Jacob rose up from Beer-sheba: and the sons of Israel carried Jacob their father, and their little ones, and their wives, in the wagons which Pharaoh had sent to carry him.
>
> And they took their cattle, and their goods, which they had gotten in the land of Canaan, and came into Egypt, Jacob, and all his seed with him:
>
> His sons, and his sons' sons with him, his daughters, and his sons' daughters, and all his seed brought he with him into Egypt. (Genesis 46:5–7)

Genesis 46:8–27 lists the names of each of those in Israel's extended family, ending with the total: "All the souls of the house of Jacob, which came into Egypt, were threescore and ten." (Genesis 46:27)

Israel sent Judah ahead, to invite Joseph to come up to northern Egypt's land of Goshen.

> And Joseph made ready his chariot, and went up to meet Israel his father, to Goshen, and presented himself unto him; and he fell on his neck, and wept on his neck a good while.
>
> And Israel said unto Joseph, Now let me die, since I have seen thy face, because thou art yet alive. (Genesis 46:29–30)

When the family arrived in the capital city, Joseph took his father for an interview with the Pharaoh of Egypt:

> And Joseph brought in Jacob his father, and set him before Pharaoh: and *Jacob blessed Pharaoh.*
>
> And Pharaoh said unto Jacob, How old art thou?

> And Jacob said unto Pharaoh, *The days of the years of my pilgrimage are an hundred and thirty years:* few and evil have the days of the years of my life been, and have not attained unto the days of the years of the life of my fathers in the days of their pilgrimage.
>
> And *Jacob blessed Pharaoh,* and went out from before Pharaoh. (Genesis 47:7–10)

With Joseph's help, Israel and his extended family were given a comfortable place to live "in the best [area] of the land":

> And Joseph placed his father and his brethren, and gave them a possession in the land of Egypt, in the best of the land, in the land of Rameses, as Pharaoh had commanded.
>
> And Joseph nourished his father, and his brethren, and all his father's household, with bread, according to their families. (Genesis 47:7–12)

The seventeen years that followed were good years for Israel and his extended family. The scriptural record shows that *"Israel dwelt in the land of Egypt, in the country of Goshen; and they had possessions therein, and grew, and multiplied exceedingly. And Jacob lived in the land of Egypt seventeen years: so the whole age of Jacob was an hundred forty and seven years"* (Genesis 47:27–28).

But as the end of his life drew closer, Israel clung to the Lord's promise, made back in Beer-sheba, that "I will also surely bring thee up again." Israel asked his son Joseph to promise him that he wouldn't leave his father buried in Egypt, but rather, that his body would someday be carried home to Canaan and reburied there:

> And the time drew nigh that Israel must die: and he called his son Joseph, and said unto him, If now I have found grace in thy sight, put, I pray thee, thy hand under my thigh, and deal kindly and truly with me; bury me not, I pray thee, in Egypt:
>
> But I will lie with my fathers, and thou shalt carry me out of Egypt, and bury me in their buryingplace. And he said, I will do as thou hast said.
>
> And he said, Swear unto me. And he sware unto him. And Israel bowed himself upon the bed's head. (Genesis 47:27–31)

Israel Gives Patriarchal Blessings to His Descendants

Israel's Blessing to Joseph. Shortly after Jacob committed Joseph to see that his remains would someday be returned to Canaan for burial, Israel became ill. Joseph brought his two sons, Manasseh and Ephraim, with him to visit their grandfather. When they entered his room, Israel "strengthened himself, and sat upon the bed" (Genesis 48:1–2), and began talking to Joseph:

1. Israel retells the account of God's appearance to him at Beth-el, or Luz (48:3–4).

2. Israel will count Joseph's two sons as recipients of the patriarchal blessings he will bestow on his (Israel's) sons (48:5).

This meant, in effect, that Israel adopted Ephraim and Manasseh as his two sons, giving them privileges equal to his other sons' privileges. As history unfurled, this made the descendants of these two men distinct tribes.

By adopting his two sons, Israel gave to Joseph the position and blessings of the firstborn son, who according to their custom, would receive a double portion for his inheritance (see Deuteronomy 21:17). This was clearly justifiable, for Joseph was the firstborn son of Rachel, whom Israel regarded as his true first wife.

3. Any other children Joseph may have are to be included in inheritances through Ephraim and Manasseh (48:6).

4. Joseph's mother, Rachel, is buried in Beth-lehem (48:7).

5. God will be with Joseph (48:21).

6. God will bring Joseph's remains back to the land of his fathers (48:21). (Fulfilled: Exodus 13:19; Joshua 24:32.)

7. Israel gave Joseph a double inheritance portion (48:22).

Thus, the tribe of Ephraim represented Joseph's portion; the tribe of Manasseh was the double portion. Also, the patriarchal line of the Abrahamic covenant passed from Israel to Joseph.

Some commentators have equated the word "portion" with "mountain slope," (in Hebrew: *shechem*), asserting that the reference is to Shechem, located in the mountainous area that would be assigned to the territory of the tribe of Ephraim when the land of Canaan would be divided among the twelve tribes of Israel.

Israel's Blessings to Ephraim and Manasseh. Then Israel offered to bless Joseph's two. "Joseph brought them out from between his knees, and he bowed himself with his face to the earth . . . And Israel stretched out his right hand, and laid it upon Ephraim's head, who was the younger, and his left hand upon Manasseh's head, guiding his hands wittingly; for Manasseh was the firstborn." When Joseph saw that Israel's right hand was on Ephraim's head rather than Manasseh's, "he held up his father's hand, to remove it from Ephraim's head unto Manasseh's head. And Joseph said unto his father, Not so, my father: for this is the firstborn; put thy right hand upon his head" (Genesis 48:12–19). But his father refused, and told Joseph,

1. Manasseh shall become a great people (48:19).
2. Ephraim shall be greater than Manasseh and become a multitude of nations (48:19).
3. Israel addressed God and God's angel, asking that the boys be blessed (48:15–16).
4. Let the names of Abraham, Isaac, and Jacob be upon them (48:16).
5. Let them grow into a multitude (48:16).
6. Make their descendants like Ephraim and Manasseh (48:20).

Israel's Blessings upon His Other Sons. Chapter 49 of the book of Genesis records the patriarchal blessings Israel conferred upon his eleven other sons. While the chapter records what probably were some of the last utterances of a man who was approaching death, the chapter obviously has additions and embellishments added at a later date.[2] It begins with Israel gathering his sons and then addressing each one individually:

> And Jacob called unto his sons, and said, Gather yourselves together, that I may tell you that which shall befall you in the last days.

---

2. Note the following:

It is generally considered that in its present form, this [chapter] gives us indeed the last utterances of the dying patriarch respecting the future of his sons, but with additions and developments of a later date. As it stands we have not the broken utterances of a dying man, but an elaborate piece of work full of word-plays and metaphors (see on vv. 8, 13, 16), and of those parallelisms in the vv. which are the chief feature of Hebrew poetry (cp. vv. 11, 15, 22, 25). It is in fact a poem, in which the fortunes of the tribes, which are impersonated by their ancestors, are delineated as they were at one special period, viz. after the Conquest of Canaan, when their territories had been finally settled, and their political importance or weakness had become recognized. Judah and, perhaps, Joseph are alluded to as ruling tribes (vv. 10, 26). No reference is made to the times of the exodus or captivity, but only to the beginnings of the monarchy; and it was probably during this period that the original Blessing was developed in its present poetical form. This conclusion is strengthened when we find the word "Israel" used of the nation, not of the person, and also that facts happening after the Conquest of Canaan are alluded to as past events: cp. vv. 14, 15. It is also significant that many definite political and geographical details are given, in a way which is inconsistent with the general character of the predictions of the Hebrew prophets on such matters. With the Blessing of Jacob should be compared that of Moses in Dt33 and notes there. (Taken from J.R. Dummelow, ed. *A Commentary on The Holy Bible* (New York: The MacMillan Company, 1958), p. 44.)

> Gather yourselves together, and hear, ye sons of Jacob; and hearken unto Israel your father. (Genesis 49:1–2)

The blessings Israel pronounced seemed to deal principally with the settlement of the twelve tribes in the land of Canaan following the Israelite exodus from Egypt. Each blessing is briefly considered below, from that perspective.

Reuben. The firstborn by Leah, could have been Israel's "firstborn, my might, and the beginning of my strength, the excellency of dignity, and the excellency of power," but he defiled himself. Israel's assessment of his son: "*Unstable as water, thou shalt not excel;* because thou wentest up to thy father's bed; then defiledst thou it." When the tribes of Israel settled in the promised land, the tribe of Reuben asked for and received the rich pasture lands east of the Jordan River (Numbers 32:33–38; Joshua 13:15–23). They were strong militarily in the days of Saul, but nothing was heard of them after the Ten Tribes were deported by Assyrian king Tiglath-Pileser III in 732 BC (49:3–4).

Simeon and **Levi.** Israel rebuked them because of their murderous rampage among the men of Shechem (See Genesis 34:25–30). Their fate: "*I will divide them in Jacob, and scatter them in Israel*" (49:5–7). The tribe of Simeon was assigned land in the far-south area of Canaan, within the area assigned to Judah (Joshua 19:1–9; 1 Chronicles 4:24–33). The tribe of Levi, which held the Levitical Priesthood, didn't receive a large tract of land as did the other tribes when Canaan was settled. Instead, they were divided up and assigned to live in scattered cities among the areas occupied by the other tribes (49:5–7; see Numbers 35:1–8).

Judah. "Judah, thou art he whom thy brethren shall praise: thy hand shall be in the neck of thine enemies; thy father's children shall bow down before thee." Judah received the chief blessing which his elder brothers forfeited. He was assured leadership among the tribes and a fruitful territory. The tribe of Judah led out in the conquest of Canaan and was the first tribe to secure its territory. The leadership of Israel was centered in Judah's area during the time of David. Judah was the center of the southern kingdom when the ten tribes formed their own land. "The sceptre shall not depart from Judah, nor a lawgiver from between his feet, until Shiloh come; and unto him shall the gathering of the people be." This passage has long been regarded by both Jews and Christians as a prophecy of the coming of the Messiah. Verses 11 and 12 speak to the fertility of Judah's lands—his foal, vine, choice vine, wine, grapes, milk (49:8–12).

Zebulon. "Zebulun shall dwell at the haven of the sea; and he shall be for an haven of ships; and his border shall be unto Zidon." The tribal assignment of Zebulon was to the west of the Sea of Galilee, but it may have extended westward till it reached the Mediterranean Sea, allowing it to be involved in the maritime trades of its day (49:13; see Deuteronomy 33:18–19).

Issachar. "Issachar is a strong ass couching down between two burdens: And he saw that *rest was good, and the land that it was pleasant*; and bowed his shoulder to bear, and *became a servant unto tribute*." The tribe of Issachar received some of the best and most fertile land in Canaan: the plains of Esdraelon and the Valley of Jezreel, so life there truly was pleasant, but for hundreds of years it was controlled as a vassal state by Egypt, Assyria, the Babylonians, the Persians, the Romans, the Muslims, and others. The last-days Battle of Armageddon will be centered in this territory (49:14–15; see Ezekiel 38–39).

Dan. "Dan shall be a serpent by the way, an adder in the path, that biteth the horse heels, so that his rider shall fall backward." Dan's assigned tribal area was in the south of Canaan, along the Mediterranean coast, bounded by Judah, Ephraim and Benjamin (Joshua 19:40–48). This area was frequently oppressed by the warlike Philistines, to the point that many of the tribe of Dan emigrated to Laish in the northern-most part of the land of Canaan (Judges 18:1–29). Thus, the tribe was divided and never was a strong military force, though wars constantly harassed them in both areas (49:16–18).

Gad. "Gad, a troop shall overcome him: but he shall overcome at the last." The descendants of Gad were cattle herders. They asked for and received the rich pasture lands east of the River Jordan, the area later called Gilead (Numbers 32:1–5). The people of Gad were oppressed by the Ammonites until they were conquered in the days of the Judges (Judges 10–11).

Asher. "Out of Asher his bread shall be fat, and he shall yield royal dainties." The tribe of Asher settled along the Mediterranean seacoast between Mt. Carmel and Lebanon. The area was famous for its production of olive oil (49:20).

Naphtali. "Naphtali is a hind let loose: he giveth goodly words." The tribe of Naphtali settled adjoining the northern portion of the Sea of Galilee in a narrow strip running northward, parallel to the Jordan River. The cities it occupied are listed in Joshua 19:32–39. It was the first tribe west of the Jordan to be invaded by the Assyrians when they came and carried the Ten Tribes into captivity.

Joseph. Latter-day Saints see in Israel's blessing to Joseph a significant prophecy related to the Book of Mormon. The entire blessing will be quoted first, then interpretational suggestions will be made:

Joseph is a fruitful bough, even *a fruitful bough by a well;* whose *branches run over the wall:*

The archers have sorely grieved him, and shot at him, and hated him:

But his bow abode in strength, and the arms of his hands were made strong by the hands of the mighty God of Jacob; (from thence is the shepherd, the stone of Israel:)

Even by the God of thy father, who shall help thee; and by the Almighty, who shall bless thee with blessings of heaven above, blessings of the deep that lieth under, blessings of the breasts, and of the womb:

The blessings of thy father have prevailed above the blessings of my progenitors *unto the utmost bound of the everlasting hills:* they shall be on the head of Joseph, and *on the crown of the head of him that was separate from his brethren.* (49:22–26)

1. Joseph is a fruitful bough. He would have many descendants (49:22).
2. A fruitful bough by a well, whose branches run over the wall. Some of his descendants (branches) would cross over the ocean: the oceans were "walls" to the land-based peoples. Lehi and his family, descendants of Joseph through Manasseh (Alma 10:3), crossed the oceans to the Americas (49:22; see Doctrine and Covenants 10:59–60. 27:9–10).
3. "The blessings of thy father have prevailed . . . unto the utmost bound of the everlasting hills." The chain of mountain ranges that extend north to south through North, Central, and South America is the world's longest mountain range—they are "everlasting" (49:26).
4. They shall be on the head of Joseph, and on the crown of the head of him that was separate from his brethren. Israel's blessings were upon the tribes of Ephraim and Manasseh, and especially upon Lehi's family and the Book of Mormon peoples in the Americas who were separate from their relatives in the Middle East (49:26). Lehi was a descendant of Manasseh (Alma 10:3).

So, there are very specific elements of prophetic fulfillment related to Israel's blessing given to Joseph. If there are those who don't agree with this interpretation, which has been used and preached by Latter-day Saint missionaries for more than a century, they should be prepared to offer a different interpretation with more specific validity.

Concerning the tribes that settled in Canaan following the Israelite exodus: The tribe of **Ephraim** received the fertile valleys and hill country to the west of the Jordan River valley, extending to the Mediterranean Sea. Ephraim played a major roll in the days of Israel's judges and kings. After the kingdom was divided and Ephraim was counted as one of the ten tribes, the name "Ephraim" often was used as a synonym for Israel—the name of the northern kingdom.

The tribe of **Manasseh** received lands on both sides of the Jordan River, just south of the Sea of Galilee. Their eastern portion was the northernmost Israelite settlement region on that side of the river. The western portion was the north-central hilly region up to where Issachar's territories began in the Jezreel Valley.

Benjamin. "Benjamin shall ravin as a wolf: in the morning he shall devour the prey, and at night he shall divide the spoil." This tribe occupied the mountainous region between Jerusalem and Bethel, between the inheritances of Ephraim and Judah. Joshua 18:11–28 lists the cities that were originally found in the area. The tribe was almost wiped out by the other tribes as punishment for a crime some Benjaminite men committed that offended the other tribes (49:27; see Judges 19–21).

Israel's Death and Burial

After concluding the patriarchal blessings that he pronounced upon the heads of all his sons, Israel charged them with the responsibility that after he died, he was to be buried with his fathers, back near Hebron.

And then, "when Jacob had made an end of commanding his sons, he gathered up his feet into the bed, and yielded up the ghost, and was gathered unto his people" (Genesis 49:29–33).

Just after he died, "Joseph fell upon his father's face, and wept upon him, and kissed him" (Genesis 50:1). Then it was time for the mortuary-type arrangements, a forty-day period of family mourning, and then a nation-wide mourning in Egypt for an additional seventy days:

> And Joseph commanded his servants the physicians to embalm his father: and the physicians embalmed Israel.
>
> And forty days were fulfilled for him; for so are fulfilled the days of those which are embalmed: and the Egyptians mourned for him threescore and ten days. (Genesis 50:2–3)

At that point, Joseph made arrangements with the Pharaoh for Joseph and his family to carry the coffin back to Canaan and bury his father there. It should be recalled that this was still in a period of dire famine when the journey northward was made.

The group constituted a sizeable company:

> And Joseph went up to bury his father: and with him went up all the servants of Pharaoh, the elders of his house, and all the elders of the land of Egypt,

And all the house of Joseph, and his brethren, and his father's house: only their little ones, and their flocks, and their herds, they left in the land of Goshen.

And there went up with him both chariots and horsemen: and it was a very great company. (Genesis 50:7–9)

In Canaan the group paused and held a seven-day-long mourning (Genesis 50:10–11), and then

His sons did unto him according as he commanded them:

For his sons carried him into the land of Canaan, and buried him in the cave of the field of Machpelah, which Abraham bought with the field for a possession of a buryingplace of Ephron the Hittite, before Mamre.

And Joseph returned into Egypt, he, and his brethren, and all that went up with him to bury his father, after he had buried his father. (Genesis 50:12–14)

Thus ends the account of Jacob's long and eventful stay in mortality.

ISRAEL BEYOND THE VEIL

One of the greatest attestations granted unto Latter-day Saints concerning the eternal significance of the labors performed by Israel in ancient times is that he (Jacob), along with Isaac his father and Abraham his grandfather, have now achieved their exaltation and godhood:

Isaac also and Jacob did none other things than that which they were commanded; and because they did none other things than that which they were commanded, *they have entered into their exaltation, according to the promises, and sit upon thrones, and are not angels but are gods.* (D&C 132:37)

OTHER SIGNIFICANT SCRIPTURAL ALLUSIONS TO JACOB/ISRAEL

A word search for the name Jacob in the four standard works brings up 474 passages—far too many to be commented on in this context. But what follows are some of the more notable passages concerning him from the LDS scriptures. They are presented in abbreviated form.

FROM THE OLD TESTAMENT

Exodus 3:14–15: "I AM THAT I AM: . . . the God of Jacob, hath sent me unto you."

Exodus 6:2–4: "I am the LORD: And I appeared unto . . . Jacob, by the name of God Almighty."

Hosea 12:3–6, 12: "Jacob fled into the country of Syria, and Israel served for a wife."

Malachi 1:2–3: "Saith the LORD: yet I loved Jacob, And I hated Esau." (See also Romans 9:13.)

From the New Testament

Matthew 8:10–11: "Many shall come . . . and shall sit down with . . . Jacob, in . . . heaven."

Matthew 22:31–32: "I am the God of . . . Jacob? God is not the God of the dead, but of the living."

Hebrews 11:8–10, 13: "Abraham, . . . Isaac and Jacob, the heirs with him of the same promise."

Hebrews 11:20–21: "By faith Jacob, when he was a dying, blessed both the sons of Joseph."

From the Book of Mormon

1 Nephi 5:14: "Joseph was preserved . . . [to] preserve his father, Jacob and all his household."

1 Nephi 17:40: "He covenanted with them, yea, even Abraham, Isaac, and Jacob."

1 Nephi 21:26: "I, the Lord, am thy Savior and thy Redeemer, the Mighty One of Jacob."

Alma 5:24: "To sit down in the kingdom of God, with Abraham, with Isaac, and . . . Jacob."

From the Doctrine and Covenants

D&C 27:5, 10: "I will drink . . . with Joseph and Jacob, and Isaac, and Abraham, your fathers."

D&C 52:2: "The land which I will consecrate unto my people, which are a remnant of Jacob."

D&C 98:32–33: "This is the law I gave unto . . . Joseph, and Jacob, and Isaac, and Abraham."

D&C 109:57–58: "Thy servants, the sons of Jacob, may gather out the righteous."

D&C 109:61–62: "We therefore ask thee to have mercy upon the children of Jacob, . . ."

D&C 109:68: "He has . . . vowed to thee, O Mighty God of Jacob."

D&C 132:1, 37: "I, the Lord, justified my servants Abraham, Isaac, and Jacob."

D&C 133:54–56: "Abraham, Isaac, and Jacob, shall be in the presence of the Lamb."

D&C 138:29–30, 38, 41: "Abraham, the father of the faithful; Isaac, Jacob, and Moses."

FROM THE PEARL OF GREAT PRICE

JS–History, Note 4: "The account given of the Savior's ministry to the remnant . . . of Jacob."

CHAPTER 9
JOSEPH

"JOSEPH WAS A GOODLY PERSON AND WELL FAVOURED, A MAN IN WHOM THE SPIRIT OF GOD IS"

Joseph and Daniel—two remarkable interpreters of revealed dreams. The Biblical account of Joseph's life shows how God positions His servants and uses them in His own due time, sometimes turning their misfortunes into rich blessings. He rewards them for their faithfulness in enduring the trials and calamities by which they have been tested and proven.

The history of Joseph also illustrates how God sometimes works to preserve His covenant peoples. Though much is known about Joseph and his prophetic gifts, many of the details of his life have been lost from the scriptural records.

THE ENVIRONMENT IN WHICH JOSEPH WAS RAISED

The Genesis chronological account of Joseph's life begins in chapter 37 when he was in his late teenage years. But many clues are available concerning his earlier years that answer such questions as: what are the events which shaped his childhood? and, who were the most influential people that were close to him in the early years of his life?

His mother, Rachel, was his father's chosen bride. However, through the caprice of Laban, Jacob's father-in-law, Rachel actually was Jacob's second bride, though he always regarded her as his first wife.

By agreement, Jacob worked for Laban for seven years, in effect laboring to pay the price of a dowry so he could marry Rachel. When the time came, his father-in-law, Laban, delivered the bride-to-be to Jacob late at night, following a lively wedding feast, in the darkness of his tent. They celebrated their wedding night together, but the next morning Jacob discovered that his unexpected lover was Rachel's older sister, Leah. He angrily challenged Laban's treachery, shouting "What is this thou hast done unto me? did not I serve with thee for Rachel? wherefore then hast thou beguiled me?" Laban's soothing reply was, "It must not be so done in our country, to give the younger before the firstborn." Then Laban said he would give Rachel to Jacob if Jacob would first honeymoon with Leah for a week and then work another seven years to earn a second wife. So, a week later, Jacob had two wives instead of one and an unplanned seven-more-years work commitment (Genesis 29:15–28). Maybe that wasn't too bad a situation: "Rachel was beautiful and well favoured," but Leah was "tender eyed."

Jacob was forty or more when he fled from Canaan and came to northern Mesopotamia. He'd spent seven years or so working to gain Rachel's hand in marriage; when he suddenly had two brides instead of one, he was nearly fifty years of age.

From the beginning there were rivalries in the family. Leah was fertile while Rachel was childless for decades. As the years passed and both sisters had difficulty having children, both followed the custom of the times and gave Jacob their handmaids to bear children for them vicariously. Thus it came to pass that Jacob sired six sons and a daughter with Leah, two sons with her handmaid Zilpah, two sons with Rachel's handmaid Bilhah, and finally—two sons with Rachel, though she died in childbirth as she brought Benjamin into the world[1] (Genesis 29:31–30:25;35:16–19).

These inter-family rivalries apparently festered, and the Genesis account certainly does not depict the various sons as a loving, homogenous family unit. It's clear that Jacob valued his children from Rachel and Leah more than his children from the handmaids, as evidenced by the way he sent them out to meet Esau, who apparently was advancing against him with 400 men. Jacob put the handmaids and their children first, then Leah and her children, then Rachel and her six-year-old son, Joseph. The first groups would be the first to be encountered by Esau's men and run the greater risk of being smitten by them (Genesis 33:1–2).

Joseph was raised by his mother, Rachel, in his younger years, but that relationship was lost when Rachel died giving birth to his younger brother, Benjamin. There can be no doubt that Jacob played favorites with his children, loving especially Joseph and Benjamin, the two sons born to him by Rachel. Concerning Joseph, specifically, the Genesis account says,

> Now Israel loved Joseph more than all his children, because he was the son of his old age: and he made him a coat of many colours.
>
> And when his brethren saw that their father loved him more than all his brethren, they hated him, and could not speak peaceably unto him. (Genesis 37:3–4)

---

1. For more information on the birth order of Joseph's brothers and sister, see "The Children of Jacob and His Wives" in chapter 8, pp. 171–72. The twelve sons are all listed in Genesis 35:23–26 and 1 Chronicles 2:1–2.

JOSEPH'S PROPHETIC DREAMS

The running scriptural account of Joseph's life doesn't begin with any substantial details until he was seventeen. Translating that age into today's terms, he was the age of a high school junior or senior. He'd outlived some of the early turmoils of becoming a teenager, and he was old enough to be trusted with responsibilities in the family business. But still, as the next-to-youngest child, he was almost the family's "caboose"—and that influenced his relationships with his much-older brothers.

Genesis chapter 37 begins with an account of Joseph reporting to his father some unnamed type of misconduct:

> And Jacob dwelt in the land wherein his father was a stranger, in the land of Canaan.
>
> These are the generations of Jacob. *Joseph, being seventeen years old, was feeding the flock with his brethren; and the lad was with the sons of Bilhah [Dan and Naphtali], and with the sons of Zilpah [Gad and Asher], his father's wives: and Joseph brought unto his father their evil report.* (Genesis 37:1–2)

To Joseph and Jacob, this reporting apparently was appropriate conduct, but in the eyes of Joseph's brothers, Joseph was tattling on them. They didn't just dislike their little brother; they hated him. And they spoke nothing but cross words to him. Apparently trying to gain his older brothers' acceptance and respect, Joseph naively shared with them two prophetic dreams that he had received through revelation. The first was an allegorical view of his brothers' sheaves, which bowed down in obeisance to Joseph's sheaf:

> And Joseph dreamed a dream, and he told it his brethren: and *they hated him yet the more.*
>
> And he said unto them, Hear, I pray you, this dream which I have dreamed:
>
> For, behold, we were binding sheaves in the field, and, lo, *my sheaf arose, and also stood upright; and, behold, your sheaves stood round about, and made obeisance to my sheaf.*
>
> And his brethren said to him, Shalt thou indeed reign over us? or shalt thou indeed have dominion over us? *And they hated him yet the more for his dreams, and for his words.* (Genesis 37:5–8)

The second prophetic dream Joseph shared with his brothers had the same theme: that they would someday bow down to him. This conversation was in a different setting, for in this instance, his father was present when he shared the dream, and even his father rebuked him for telling it. The dream was of the sun, moon, and eleven stars giving obeisance to Joseph:

And he dreamed yet another dream, and told it his brethren, and said, Behold, I have dreamed a dream more; and, behold, *the sun and the moon and the eleven stars made obeisance to me.*

And he told it to his father, and to his brethren: and his father rebuked him, and said unto him, What is this dream that thou hast dreamed? Shall I and thy mother and thy brethren indeed come to bow down ourselves to thee to the earth?

And *his brethren envied him;* but his father observed the saying. (Genesis 37:9–11)

Those who are acquainted with Joseph's life story know that these two dreams truly were prophetic. More than twenty years later, when Joseph was a ruler in Egypt, his family actually did give obeisance to him—they were dependent upon him for their very lives!

Sold into Egypt as a Slave

The next section of the Genesis account is interesting because it shows that Jacobs' huge flocks had to be cared for in areas a good distance from where their tents were pitched. Jacob sent Joseph north more than forty miles, from Hebron to Shechem, to see how his older brothers were faring with the flocks. When Joseph arrived in Shechem he found that his brothers had moved the flocks another 15 miles northward, to Dothan (Genesis 37:12–17). It was in that area that Joseph's life suddenly changed from the role of favored son to the status of a slave. Notice, in the account, that it is two of Leah's older sons, Reuben and Judah (Jacob's first and fourth sons), who manage to prevent Joseph from being murdered. They, at least, were able to deflect the other sons from the crime of murder to the slightly more humane crime of selling Joseph into slavery:

And Joseph went after his brethren, and found them in Dothan.

And when they saw him afar off, even before he came near unto them, they conspired against him to slay him.

And they said one to another, Behold, this dreamer cometh.

Come now therefore, and let us slay him, and cast him into some pit, and we will say, Some evil beast hath devoured him: and we shall see what will become of his dreams.

And *Reuben heard it, and he delivered him out of their hands; and said, Let us not kill him.*

And *Reuben said unto them, Shed no blood, but cast him into this pit that is in the wilderness, and lay no hand upon him;* that he might rid him out of their hands, to deliver him to his father again.

And it came to pass, when Joseph was come unto his brethren, that they stript Joseph out of his coat, his coat of many colours that was on him;

And they took him, and cast him into a pit: and the pit was empty, there was no water in it.

And they sat down to eat bread: and they lifted up their eyes and looked, and, *behold, a company of Ishmeelites came from Gilead with their camels bearing spicery and balm and myrrh, going to carry it down to Egypt.*

And Judah said unto his brethren, What profit is it if we slay our brother, and conceal his blood?

Come, and let us sell him to the Ishmeelites, and let not our hand be upon him; for he is our brother and our flesh. And his brethren were content.

Then there passed by *Midianites merchantmen;* and they drew and lifted up Joseph out of the pit, and sold Joseph to the Ishmeelites for twenty pieces of silver: and *they brought Joseph into Egypt....*

And the Midianites sold him into Egypt unto Potiphar, an officer of Pharaoh's, and captain of the guard. (Genesis 37:17–28, 36)

There are truly tragic elements to the account. One who experienced the tragedy was Reuben, the oldest son. He had talked his brothers into throwing Joseph into a hole instead of killing him, "that he might rid him out of their hands, to deliver him to his father again." Reuben apparently was away from the others when the Midianite traders passed by. When he came back and sought for his brother, "behold, Joseph was not in the pit; and he rent his clothes. And he returned unto his brethren, and said, The child is not; and I, whither shall I go?" (Genesis 37:22, 29–30).

Imagine the guilt that was settling into the minds and hearts of the other brothers as they tried to cover their sin: "they took Joseph's coat, and killed a kid of the goats, and dipped the coat in the blood" (Genesis 37:31). And what a challenge it must have been for so many of them to share the lie as they brought the tale of Joseph's "disappearance" to their father, Jacob, and allowed him to draw the false conclusion that Joseph was dead:

And they sent the coat of many colours, and they brought it to their father; and said, This have we found: know now whether it be thy son's coat or no.

And he knew it, and said, It is my son's coat; an evil beast hath devoured him; Joseph is without doubt rent in pieces. (Genesis 37:32–33)

What tremendous sorrow they inflicted upon their father. He'd already lost his beloved Rachel, now the favored son he'd sired of her was also gone! It's difficult to contemplate how deeply and how long this huge new burden of sorrow rested upon him:

And Jacob rent his clothes, and put sackcloth upon his loins, and mourned for his son many days.

And all his sons and all his daughters rose up to comfort him; but he refused to be comforted; and he said, For I will go down into the grave unto my son mourning. Thus his father wept for him. (Genesis 37:34–35)

Notice, too, the sorrow felt by others. Did the wayward sons tell their sisters or their spouses about their wicked dead? Probably not (By the way, this is one of the few verses which indicate that there were sisters in addition to Dinah.)

Now another aside before leaving this passage. Notice the flow of commerce shown in this account: merchants from Gilead (who were descendants of Ishmael) were moving spices down through Canaan to Egypt: using camels to carry spices and balm and myrrh. Trade already was flourishing—eighteen hundred years before the meridian of time! Note, also, that trading in slaves was a common business practice: a sturdy young man like Joseph could be purchased for twenty pieces of silver—they probably were able to double, triple, perhaps even quadruple that price after they transported their slave for hundreds of miles (Genesis 37:25, 28).

Experiences with Potiphar: Pharaoh's Captain of the Guard

The tale of Joseph is interrupted by Genesis chapter 38, which deals with Judah's activities. The chapter is interesting but not germane in this setting.

Chapter 39 reveals Joseph as being purchased and used as a house slave—one who worked diligently and was obedient, causing his master to benefit from his efforts. This soon leads to promotions and further responsibilities—heady experiences for a teenager.

And Joseph was brought down to Egypt; and Potiphar, an officer of Pharaoh, captain of the guard, an Egyptian, bought him of the hands of the Ishmeelites, which had brought him down thither.

And *the LORD was with Joseph,* and he was a prosperous man; and he was in the house of his master the Egyptian.

And his master saw that the LORD was with him, and that the LORD made all that he did to prosper in his hand.

And Joseph found grace in his sight, and he served him: and he made him overseer over his house, and all that he had he put into his hand.

And it came to pass from the time that he had made him overseer in his house, and over all that he had, that *the LORD blessed the Egyptian's house for Joseph's sake; and the blessing of the LORD was upon all that he had in the house, and in the field.*

And *he left all that he had in Joseph's hand;* and he knew not ought he had, save the bread which he did eat. *And Joseph was a goodly person, and well favoured.* (Genesis 39:1–6)

This must have been a good experience for Joseph. Not only did the Lord bless and prosper him in his work endeavors, it must have been an excellent learning opportunity for him too. Most likely he became proficient in speaking Egyptian. He was employed in an upper-class situation where, most likely, he observed the workings and niceties of Egyptian social life. He gained management and leadership skills and learned how to interact with people on various social levels. He learned how to receive delegated responsibilities and how to delegate assignments to others.

But that situation came to a crashing halt when Potiphar's wife's roving eye fell upon him, and she attempted to seduce him. Joseph's resistance to her advances, however, thwarted her improper actions. His firm refusals and his oft-quoted words: "How then can I do this great wickedness, and sin against God?" have been the basis for chastity lessons by the millions down through time.

> And it came to pass after these things, that his master's wife cast her eyes upon Joseph; and she said, Lie with me.
>
> But he refused, and said unto his master's wife, Behold, my master wotteth not what is with me in the house, and he hath committed all that he hath to my hand;
>
> There is none greater in this house than I; neither hath he kept back any thing from me but thee, because thou art his wife: *how then can I do this great wickedness, and sin against God?*
>
> And it came to pass, as she spake to Joseph day by day, that he hearkened not unto her, to lie by her, or to be with her.
>
> And it came to pass about this time, that Joseph went into the house to do his business; and there was none of the men of the house there within.
>
> And she caught him by his garment, saying, Lie with me: and he left his garment in her hand, and fled, and got him out. (Genesis 39:7–12)

It has been said that there is no wrath so great as that of a spurned woman. Perhaps Potiphar's wife's vindictive actions were the source of that observation. She sought for revenge against Joseph's because of his refusal of her advances. With Joseph's garment in her hand, she quickly decided to "frame him," making it appear that Joseph had tried to seduce her rather than the reverse:

> And it came to pass, when she saw that he had left his garment in her hand, and was fled forth,
>
> That she called unto the men of her house, and spake unto them, saying, See, he hath brought in an Hebrew unto us to mock us; he came in unto me to lie with me, and I cried with a loud voice:
>
> And it came to pass, when he heard that I lifted up my voice and cried, that he left his garment with me, and fled, and got him out.

And she laid up his garment by her, until his lord came home.

And she spake unto him according to these words, saying, The Hebrew servant, which thou hast brought unto us, came in unto me to mock me:

And it came to pass, as I lifted up my voice and cried, that he left his garment with me, and fled out. (Genesis 39:13–18)

There's a memorable passage in the book of Isaiah that speaks of such situations, saying, "*Woe unto them that call evil good, and good evil; that put darkness for light, and light for darkness; that put bitter for sweet, and sweet for bitter!*" (Isaiah 5:20). The scriptures don't say when and how Potiphar's wife reaped her "woe," but they do tell us that God sometimes uses "bad things" to prepare his children to receive "good things." What was the "bad thing" Joseph reaped in this experience? The false accusations against him landed Joseph in the king's prison:

And it came to pass, when his master heard the words of his wife, which she spake unto him, saying, After this manner did thy servant to me; that his wrath was kindled.

And Joseph's master took him, and put him into the prison, a place where the king's prisoners were bound: and he was there in the prison. (Genesis 39:19–20)

What were the "good things" that resulted from his imprisonment? People of faith learn that God has a way of positioning individuals so they will be able and available to accomplish His unique tasks when the proper time arrives.

LEARNING LEADERSHIP SKILLS IN PRISON

Certainly, the Lord positioned Joseph so he could accomplish His eternal purposes. Look at the positioning pattern that transpired. When Joseph was hauled to Egypt as a slave, he wasn't sold into the mines or onto the ships—he was purchased by a high government official who soon recognized Joseph's worth as a person and made him his overlord. Joseph learned important skills there. When his master's wife falsely accused Joseph and had him cast into prison, Joseph was lifted by the Lord to be favored by the prison keeper, who placed him in a position of importance right there in the prison:

But the LORD was with Joseph, and shewed him mercy, and gave him favour in the sight of the keeper of the prison.

And the keeper of the prison committed to Joseph's hand all the prisoners that were in the prison; and whatsoever they did there, he was the doer of it.

The keeper of the prison looked not to any thing that was under his hand; *because the LORD was with him, and that which he did, the LORD made it to prosper.* (Genesis 39:21–23)

The trust placed in Joseph, and his faithful fulfillment of his responsibilities so as to merit that trust, again positioned Joseph for his next step upward.

INTERPRETING THE DREAMS OF THE PHARAOH'S CHIEF BUTLER AND BAKER

Though Joseph probably didn't know it at the time, the admittance of two new prisoners into the King's prison was about to change his life's course:

> And it came to pass after these things, that the butler of the king of Egypt and his baker had offended their lord the king of Egypt.
>
> And Pharaoh was wroth against two of his officers, against the chief of the butlers, and against the chief of the bakers.
>
> And he put them in ward in the house of the captain of the guard, *into the prison, the place where Joseph was bound.*
>
> *And the captain of the guard charged Joseph with them, and he served them: and they continued a season in ward.* (Genesis 40:1–4)

Joseph, as the prisoners' supervisor, treated these men with care, "and he served them." What a remarkable tribute to serving others this statement makes, especially considering the circumstances of both the two prisoners and Joseph himself. Joseph's service and concerned care for the men opened the doors for what happened next. The next few verses clearly depict the personal interest Joseph was demonstrating as he talked and worked with the two men:

> And they dreamed a dream both of them, each man his dream in one night, each man according to the interpretation of his dream, the butler and the baker of the king of Egypt, which were bound in the prison.
>
> And Joseph came in unto them in the morning, and looked upon them, and, behold, they were sad.
>
> *And he asked Pharaoh's officers that were with him in the ward of his lord's house, saying, Wherefore look ye so sadly to day?*
>
> And they said unto him, We have dreamed a dream, and there is no interpreter of it. And Joseph said unto them, *Do not interpretations belong to God? tell me them, I pray you.* (Genesis 40:5–8)

It is apparent that by this time, Joseph was clearly in touch with God. The years of being blessed and guided by the Lord had given him confidence that he had access to inspiration and to answers to prayer, and that he could rely on that access to help others. When he said "Do not interpretations belong to

God? tell me them, I pray you," he knew he was going to be told the dreams, and he knew he would have the inspiration to discern their meanings.

First, the butler related his dream to Joseph:

> In my dream, behold, a vine was before me;
>
> And in the vine were three branches: and it was as though it budded, and her blossoms shot forth; and *the clusters thereof brought forth ripe grapes:*
>
> *And Pharaoh's cup was in my hand: and I took the grapes, and pressed them into Pharaoh's cup, and I gave the cup into Pharaoh's hand.* (Genesis 40:9–11)

Joseph's inspired response was immediate and decisive: "This is the interpretation of it: The three branches are three days: Yet within three days shall Pharaoh lift up thine head, and restore thee unto thy place: and thou shalt deliver Pharaoh's cup into his hand, after the former manner when thou wast his butler" (Genesis 40:12–13).

Then Joseph followed his interpretation of the butler's dream with a personal request: "*But think on me when it shall be well with thee, and shew kindness, I pray thee, unto me, and make mention of me unto Pharaoh, and bring me out of this house:* For indeed I was stolen away out of the land of the Hebrews: and here also have I done nothing that they should put me into the dungeon" (Genesis 40:14–15).

The chief baker was there with them as the chief butler's dream was interpreted. He was so impressed with Joseph's favorable interpretation that he ventured to relate his dream too: " I also was in my dream, and, behold, *I had three white baskets on my head:* And in the uppermost basket there was of all manner of bakemeats for Pharaoh; *and the birds did eat them out of the basket upon my head*" (Genesis 40:16–17).

Again, Joseph's interpretation was quick and decisive, but it undoubtedly brought no joy to the baker's heart: "This is the interpretation thereof: The three baskets are three days: *Yet within three days shall Pharaoh lift up thy head from off thee, and shall hang thee on a tree; and the birds shall eat thy flesh from off thee*" (Genesis 40:18–19).

And true to Joseph's interpretations, the fulfillment of both dreams came just three days later:

> And it came to pass the third day, which was *Pharaoh's birthday, that he made a feast unto all his servants:* and he lifted up the head of the chief butler and of the chief baker among his servants.
>
> And *he restored the chief butler unto his butlership again;* and he gave the cup into Pharaoh's hand:
>
> But *he hanged the chief baker:* as Joseph had interpreted to them. (Genesis 40:20–22)

And what did the chief butler do in response to Joseph's request that he speak to the Pharaoh in his behalf? Nothing: "Yet did not the chief butler remember Joseph, but forgat him" (Genesis 40:23).

INTERPRETING PHARAOH'S DREAMS

Joseph continued with his responsibilities in the king's prison. Patience, patience. God is in control and arranges events so they will occur when all pertinent aspects are in place and ready. More than a dozen passages in the Book of Mormon, the Doctrine and Covenants, and the Pearl of Great Price speak of how things have happened or will happen in the Lord's "due time."[2]

Joseph, apparently, had to remain in place, growing and serving, until the Lord's due time arrived for the Pharaoh, and for him! Two years passed—a long time to be patient. And then, Pharaoh received the first of two prophetic dreams:

> And it came to pass at the end of two full years, that Pharaoh dreamed: and, behold, he stood by the river.
>
> And, behold, *there came up out of the river seven well favoured kine and fatfleshed; and they fed in a meadow.*
>
> And, behold, *seven other kine came up after them out of the river, ill favoured and leanfleshed; and stood by the other kine upon the brink of the river.*
>
> And the ill favoured and leanfleshed kine did eat up the seven well favoured and fat kine. So Pharaoh awoke. (Genesis 41:1–4)

When he fell asleep again, Pharaoh dreamed another dream:

> And he slept and dreamed the second time: and, behold, *seven ears of corn came up upon one stalk, rank and good.*
>
> And, behold, *seven thin ears and blasted with the east wind sprung up after them.*
>
> And the seven thin ears devoured the seven rank and full ears. And Pharaoh awoke, and, behold, it was a dream. (Genesis 41:5–7)

The Pharaoh was both curious and troubled—he really wanted answers, and he wanted them fast! The next morning "he sent and called for all the magicians of Egypt, and all the wise men thereof: and Pharaoh told them his dream; but there was none that could interpret them unto Pharaoh" (Genesis 41:8).

---

2. They're well worth reading: Book of Mormon Preface, Title page 1; 1 Nephi 10:3; 14:26; 2 Nephi 27:10; Mormon 5:12; Ether 3:27; D&C 56:3; 68:14; 76:38; 117:14; 117:16; 127:1; 138:56; Abraham Facsimile 2, Fig. 12.

And then the chief butler's conscience shifted into gear, and he finally spoke up to Pharaoh in behalf of Joseph. In a way, he "bore his testimony":

> I do remember my faults this day:
>
> Pharaoh was wroth with his servants, and put me in ward in the captain of the guard's house, both me and the chief baker:
>
> And *we dreamed a dream in one night, I and he; we dreamed each man according to the interpretation of his dream.*
>
> *And there was there with us a young man, an Hebrew, servant to the captain of the guard; and we told him, and he interpreted to us our dreams; to each man according to his dream he did interpret.*
>
> *And it came to pass, as he interpreted to us, so it was;* me he restored unto mine office, and him he hanged. (Genesis 41:9–13)

So "Pharaoh sent and called Joseph, and they brought him hastily out of the dungeon: and he shaved himself, and changed his raiment, and came in unto Pharaoh" (Genesis 41:14). And then ensued a conversation that changed the course of history. How it began?

> Pharaoh said unto Joseph, I have dreamed a dream, and there is none that can interpret it: and I have heard say of thee, that thou canst understand a dream to interpret it.
>
> And Joseph answered Pharaoh, saying, *It is not in me: God shall give Pharaoh an answer of peace.* (Genesis 41:15–16)

Joseph knew he was authorized to speak for the Lord; he had full confidence that he would be given the ability to interpret Pharaoh's dreams. He was beyond faith on the matter; he had knowledge of what he had power to do, and what he would need to say. Where did he get it? The scriptures don't say—they just make it abundantly clear that he had it!

Pharaoh then related the two dreams he'd received to Joseph, in just about the same words as they were reported earlier. (Compare Genesis 41:17–24 with Genesis 41:1–7.)

Joseph gave Pharaoh a short overview of the meaning of the two dreams:

> Joseph said unto Pharaoh, The dream of Pharaoh is one: *God hath shewed Pharaoh what he is about to do.*
>
> The seven good kine are seven years; and *the seven good ears are seven years:* the dream is one.
>
> And the seven thin and ill favoured kine that came up after them are seven years; and the seven empty ears blasted with the east wind *shall be seven years of famine.* (Genesis 41:25–27)

Then Joseph repeated his interpretation of Pharaoh's dreams in greater detail, spelling out the implications of their meanings, and emphasizing that God Himself was showing Pharaoh what was going to come to pass:

> This is the thing which I have spoken unto Pharaoh: *What God is about to do he sheweth* unto Pharaoh.
>
> Behold, *there come seven years of great plenty throughout all the land of Egypt*:
>
> And *there shall arise after them seven years of famine; and all the plenty shall be forgotten in the land of Egypt; and the famine shall consume the land;*
>
> And *the plenty shall not be known in the land by reason of that famine following; for it shall be very grievous.*
>
> And for that the dream was doubled unto Pharaoh twice; *it is because the thing is established by God, and God will shortly bring it to pass.* (Genesis 41:28–32)

So there it was: seven years of great plenty, followed by seven devastating years of grievous famine. Now Pharaoh knew, now Joseph knew. So, what to do?

The Spirit obviously moved upon Joseph, who promptly proposed an inspired organizational plan and specific activities to be undertaken to prepare the nation for the coming crisis:

> Now therefore *let Pharaoh look out a man discreet and wise, and set him over the land of Egypt.*
>
> Let Pharaoh do this, and *let him appoint officers over the land,* and *take up the fifth part of the land of Egypt in the seven plenteous years.*
>
> And let them *gather all the food of those good years that come,* and *lay up corn under the hand of Pharaoh,* and *let them keep food in the cities.*
>
> And *that food shall be for store to the land against the seven years of famine,* which shall be in the land of Egypt; that the land perish not through the famine. (Genesis 41:33–36)

If this were a movie, there would probably be a pregnant pause at this point. Who knows what happened at that moment in real life, as Pharaoh and those around him assimilated the amazing information which had been provided for them?

Was it true? Would God really reveal the future to the Pharaoh, a pagan despot?[3] Could Joseph really be speaking for God and foretelling the future as he interpreted the two dreams?

---

3.   The Egyptian Pharaoh wasn't the only king who received profound revelations concerning coming world events. Recall the visions granted to Nebuchadnezzar, a pagan Babylonian king, (see Daniel 2:1–49; 4:4–37) and to Nebuchadnezzar's son, Belshazzar (see Daniel 5:1–30).

And then, that Holy Spirit, that Godhead Being who was surely prompting and leading Joseph, must have reached out and warmed Pharaoh's mind and heart, for he said to his servants: "Can we find such a one as this is, a man in whom the Spirit of God is?" Pharaoh must have felt and recognized the Spirit's presence, for him to be able to recognize Joseph as "a man in whom the Spirit of God is" (Genesis 41:38). And he glanced around, and it was apparent that "the thing was good in the eyes of Pharaoh, and in the eyes of all his servants" (Genesis 41:37).

And then Pharaoh made a decision and said something marvelous— something miraculous! Imagine, he'd never heard of Joseph until earlier that day. He'd never known him before the beginning of their conversation, an hour previous. He didn't interview him; he didn't check to see if Joseph had good letters of recommendation; he knew only that Joseph had been hurriedly extracted from his prison, cleaned up, and hustled into the castle—all based on a brief "testimony" offered by the butler whom he had sent to prison two years ago for some brief indiscretion. But Pharaoh had felt the Spirit, and he somehow recognized the feeling of "rightness" that the Spirit, in some strange way, had conveyed to him. So he turned to Joseph and said,

> Forasmuch as God hath shewed thee all this, there is none so discreet and wise as thou art: Thou shalt be over my house, and according unto thy word shall all my people be ruled: only in the throne will I be greater than thou.
>
> And Pharaoh said unto Joseph, See, I have set thee over all the land of Egypt.
>
> And Pharaoh took off his ring from his hand, and put it upon Joseph's hand. (Genesis 41:39–42)

So this was the result of God's maneuvering: of His revealing to Joseph his youthful dreams of others bowing down to him, of Joseph's being sold into Egypt, of his being purchased by Potiphar, of his education in Potiphar's mansion, of Potiphar's wife's false accusation which caused him to be thrown into prison, of his years of leadership over prison convicts, of the King's butler and baker suddenly being thrust into that same prison, of the butler's forgetting Joseph's plight in prison for two years until the Lord's own due time arrived.

Pharaoh exalted Joseph's role over the Egyptians as he began his gargantuan task as Egypt's second in command.

> [He] arrayed him in vestures of fine linen, and put a gold chain about his neck;
>
> And he made him to ride in the second chariot which he had; and they

cried before him, Bow the knee: and he made him ruler over all the land of Egypt.

And Pharaoh said unto Joseph, I am Pharaoh, and without thee shall no man lift up his hand or foot in all the land of Egypt.

And Pharaoh called Joseph's name Zaphnath-paaneah. (Genesis 41:42–45)

But Pharaoh went even further: he gave Joseph a wife—the woman who would become the mother of Joseph's sons, Ephraim and Manasseh. Pharaoh "gave him to wife Asenath the daughter of Potipherah priest of On" (Genesis 41:45).

And how old was he when all these changes took place: "Joseph was thirty years old when he stood before Pharaoh king of Egypt" (Genesis 41:46). That means he had spent thirteen years in Egypt, making the amazing change from teenage slave to overseer to prisoner to ruler—the second in power and authority in the great kingdom of Egypt!

JOSEPH AS A RULER IN EGYPT

Then, Joseph went to work, and enjoyed much success:

Joseph went out from the presence of Pharaoh, and went throughout all the land of Egypt.

And in the seven plenteous years the earth brought forth by handfuls.

And he gathered up all the food of the seven years, which were in the land of Egypt, and laid up the food in the cities: the food of the field, which was round about every city, laid he up in the same.

And Joseph gathered corn as the sand of the sea, very much, until he left numbering; for it was without number. (Genesis 41:46–49)

During those seven years of plenty, Joseph found time for some family life too, for he fathered two children who later would become the forefathers of great peoples:

And unto Joseph were born two sons before the years of famine came, which Asenath the daughter of Potipherah priest of On bare unto him.

And *Joseph called the name of the firstborn Manasseh:* For God, said he, hath made me forget all my toil, and all my father's house.

And *the name of the second called he Ephraim:* For God hath caused me to be fruitful in the land of my affliction. (Genesis 41:50–52)

Then the first part of Pharaoh's prophetic dreams was completed: "the seven years of plenteousness, that was in the land of Egypt, were ended." The seven years of plenty truly had been plenteous. But true to God's prophetic warning, the weather changed, the droughts set in, and hunger started to creep across not only Egypt, but the surrounding nations as well:

And the seven years of dearth began to come, according as Joseph had said: and the dearth was in all lands; but in all the land of Egypt there was bread.

And when all the land of Egypt was famished, the people cried to Pharaoh for bread: and Pharaoh said unto all the Egyptians, Go unto Joseph; what he saith to you, do.

And the famine was over all the face of the earth: And Joseph opened all the storehouses, and sold unto the Egyptians; and the famine waxed sore in the land of Egypt.

And all countries came into Egypt to Joseph for to buy corn; because that the famine was so sore in all lands. (Genesis 41:54–57)

JACOB SENDS HIS SONS TO BUY CORN IN EGYPT

Chapters 42–45 of Genesis describe how the widespread famine was affecting Jacob's family in the land of Canaan so severely that Jacob repeatedly sent his sons down to Egypt to purchase foodstuffs sufficient to keep them alive. Their first trip originated in this manner:

Now when Jacob saw that there was corn in Egypt, Jacob said unto his sons, Why do ye look one upon another?

And he said, Behold, I have heard that there is corn in Egypt: get you down thither, and buy for us from thence; that we may live, and not die.

And Joseph's ten brethren went down to buy corn in Egypt.

But Benjamin, Joseph's brother, Jacob sent not with his brethren; for he said, Lest peradventure mischief befall him.

And the sons of Israel came to buy corn among those that came: for the famine was in the land of Canaan. (42:1–5)

Certainly Joseph did not serve as the order-taker and fulfillment clerk for every person who came from all across Egypt, and from foreign countries, to purchase food from the great warehouses that had been erected. Those responsibilities undoubtedly had been delegated to others. Yet somehow Joseph was present when his brothers came to make their purchases. Perhaps that was another of those God-managed "putting him in the right place at the right time" experiences that had previously shaped his life. At any rate, Joseph saw his brothers approaching and decided to let his youthful "bow down to me" dreams begin to have their fulfillment:

And Joseph was the governor over the land, and he it was that sold to all the people of the land: and Joseph's brethren came, and bowed down themselves before him with their faces to the earth.

And Joseph saw his brethren, and he knew them, but made himself strange unto them, and spake roughly unto them; and he said unto them, Whence come ye? And they said, From the land of Canaan to buy food.

And Joseph knew his brethren, but they knew not him. (Genesis 42:6–8)

Then Joseph decided to play with his brothers, making them defend themselves and, in the process, tell him more about his family. In the course of his questioning, he learned that his younger brother, Benjamin, was alive. Joseph longed to see him:

And *Joseph remembered the dreams which he dreamed of them,* and said unto them, Ye are spies; to see the nakedness of the land ye are come.

And they said unto him, Nay, my lord, but to buy food are thy servants come.

We are all one man's sons; we are true men, thy servants are no spies.

And he said unto them, Nay, but to see the nakedness of the land ye are come.

And they said, *Thy servants are twelve brethren, the sons of one man in the land of Canaan; and, behold, the youngest is this day with our father, and one is not.*

And Joseph said unto them, That is it that I spake unto you, saying, Ye are spies:

Hereby ye shall be proved: By the life of Pharaoh ye shall not go forth hence, except your youngest brother come hither.

Send one of you, and let him fetch your brother, and ye shall be kept in prison, that your words may be proved, whether there be any truth in you: or else by the life of Pharaoh surely ye are spies.

And he put them all together into ward three days. (Genesis 42:9–17)

At the end of three days Joseph returned to his brothers and lessened his requirement he had made of them. In the course of his visit with them, he learned details of how he was sold into Egypt and how they felt about their wicked treatment of him those many years ago:

And Joseph said unto them the third day, *This do, and live; for I fear God:*

If ye be true men, *let one of your brethren be bound in the house of your prison:* go ye, carry corn for the famine of your houses:

But bring your youngest brother unto me; so shall your words be verified, and ye shall not die. And they did so.

And they said one to another, *We are verily guilty concerning our brother, in that we saw the anguish of his soul, when he besought us, and we would not hear; therefore is this distress come upon us.*

And *Reuben* answered them, saying, *Spake I not unto you, saying, Do not sin against the child; and ye would not hear? therefore, behold, also his blood is required.*

And they knew not that Joseph understood them; for he spake unto them by an interpreter.

> And he turned himself about from them, and wept; and returned to
> them again, and communed with them, and *took from them Simeon, and
> bound him before their eyes.*
>
> Then Joseph commanded to fill their sacks with corn, and to restore
> every man's money into his sack, and to give them provision for the way: and
> thus did he unto them.
>
> And they laded their asses with the corn, and departed thence. (Genesis 42:18–26)

Obviously, the brothers had decided that the harsh requirements that
were being made of them were the results of their mistreatment of Joseph
more than two decades previous. That thought was reinforced when they
found their money in their sacks on the way home:

> And as one of them opened his sack to give his ass provender in the inn,
> he espied his money; for, behold, it was in his sack's mouth.
>
> And he said unto his brethren, My money is restored; and, lo, it is even
> in my sack: and *their heart failed them, and they were afraid,* saying one to
> another, *What is this that God hath done unto us?* (Genesis 42:27–28)

The trip back to Hebron must have been about three hundred
miles—the returning leg of a six-hundred-mile journey. With camels
and donkeys laden with foodstuffs, it would have been a slow, miserable,
dust-blown journey as they passed through desert terrains and barren,
sun-bleached hills and vales: thirty days if they averaged only ten miles
per day. They had plenty of time to remember and ponder what they perceived to be the cause of their misfortunes—their mistreatment of their
younger brother.

How would they explain to their father that Simeon had been retained
as a hostage? That their money was still in their sacks? And that the Egyptian
had demanded that Benjamin be brought with them when they returned to
purchase more food? That's what they had to deal with when they finally
arrived:

> And it came to pass as they emptied their sacks, that, behold, every
> man's bundle of money was in his sack: and when both they and their father
> saw the bundles of money, *they were afraid.*
>
> And Jacob their father said unto them, *Me have ye bereaved of my chil-
> dren: Joseph is not, and Simeon is not, and ye will take Benjamin away: all these
> things are against me.*
>
> And Reuben spake unto his father, saying, Slay my two sons, if I bring
> him not to thee: deliver him into my hand, and I will bring him to thee
> again.
>
> And he said, *My son shall not go down with you; for his brother is dead,
> and he is left alone: if mischief befall him by the way in the which ye go,*

then shall ye bring down my gray hairs with sorrow to the grave. (Genesis 42:35–38)

Time passed. The famine was in its second or third year. The corn they had purchased in Egypt was nearly gone. Though Jacob had been resolute that he wouldn't allow Benjamin to go down to Egypt with them as the Egyptian overlord had demanded, the family had to face reality: no Benjamin would mean no food! They were growing desperate. Finally, Jacob relented and said:

> If it must be so now, do this; take of the best fruits of the land in your vessels, and carry down the man a present, a little balm, and a little honey, spices, and myrrh, nuts, and almonds:
>
> And take double money in your hand; and the money that was brought again in the mouth of your sacks, carry it again in your hand; peradventure it was an oversight:
>
> Take also your brother, and arise, go again unto the man:
>
> And God Almighty give you mercy before the man, that he may send away your other brother, and Benjamin. If I be bereaved of my children, I am bereaved.
>
> And the men took that present, and they took double money in their hand, and Benjamin; and rose up, and went down to Egypt, and stood before Joseph. (Genesis 43:11–15)

Joseph was aware of their arrival, and that they had brought Benjamin with them. Upon seeing them, Joseph told his steward to prepare a noon meal for them; Joseph would eat with them.

How old was Benjamin at this time? He was born sometime between when Joseph left Haran at age six (compare Genesis 30:22–25 and 31:38, 41) and when Joseph was sold into Egypt at age seventeen. Joseph was about forty when his father's family came to Egypt, so a reasonable guess would be that Benjamin was about thiry-five. Note that he was a full-grown married man with ten children when he came to Egypt! The record of those who moved included "the sons of Benjamin [who] were *Belah,* and *Becher,* and *Ashbel, Gera,* and *Naaman, Ehi,* and *Rosh, Muppim,* and *Huppim,* and *Ard"* (Genesis 46:21).

Joseph's brothers were extremely worried at this time, and fearful of how the Egyptian overlord (whom they still did not recognize as being their brother, Joseph) might treat them. They hastened to try to return the money that had been slipped back into their sacks on their previous trip:

> The man [Joseph's steward] brought the men [Joseph's brothers] into Joseph's house.
>
> And the men were afraid, because they were brought into Joseph's

house; and they said, *Because of the money that was returned in our sacks at the first time are we brought in; that he may seek occasion against us, and fall upon us, and take us for bondmen, and our asses.*

And they came near to the steward of Joseph's house, and they communed with him at the door of the house,

And said, O sir, we came indeed down at the first time to buy food:

And it came to pass, when we came to the inn, that we opened our sacks, and, behold, every man's money was in the mouth of his sack, our money in full weight: and we have brought it again in our hand.

And other money have we brought down in our hands to buy food: we cannot tell who put our money in our sacks.

And he said, *Peace be to you, fear not: your God, and the God of your father, hath given you treasure in your sacks: I had your money.* And he brought Simeon out unto them.

And the man brought the men into Joseph's house, and gave them water, and they washed their feet; and he gave their asses provender.

And they made ready the present against Joseph came at noon: for they heard that they should eat bread there. (Genesis 43:17–25)

The before-luncheon conversation that took place reveals how strong Joseph's emotions were at seeing his brother, Benjamin, for the first time in almost twenty-five years:

And when Joseph came home, they brought him the present which was in their hand into the house, and *bowed themselves to him to the earth.*

And he asked them of their welfare, and said, *Is your father well, the old man of whom ye spake? Is he yet alive?*

And they answered, *Thy servant our father is in good health, he is yet alive. And they bowed down their heads, and made obeisance.*

And he lifted up his eyes, and saw his brother Benjamin, his mother's son, and said, *Is this your younger brother, of whom ye spake unto me?* And he said, *God be gracious unto thee, my son.*

And Joseph made haste; for his bowels did yearn upon his brother: and he sought where to weep; and he entered into his chamber, and wept there.

And he washed his face, and went out, and refrained himself, and said, Set on bread. (Genesis 43:26–31)

They ate together, and lodging was provided for the brothers. The brothers were up the next morning, and ready to leave for home. But Joseph wasn't ready to reveal his identity to his brothers, and he wanted time to visit with Benjamin, so he hatched a plan which would make them have to return to Egypt:

And he commanded the steward of his house, saying, Fill the men's sacks with food, as much as they can carry, and *put every man's money in his sack's mouth.*

And *put my cup, the silver cup, in the sack's mouth of the youngest, and his corn money.* And he did according to the word that Joseph had spoken.

As soon as the morning was light, the men were sent away, they and their asses. (Genesis 44:1–3)

When they'd barely had time to leave the city, Joseph said to his steward, "Up, follow after the men; and when thou dost overtake them, say unto them, *Wherefore have ye rewarded evil for good? Is not this it in which my lord drinketh, and whereby indeed he divineth? ye have done evil in so doing*" (Genesis 44:4–5). The scene when the steward overtook the brothers and accused them must have been an extremely tense moment—one that caused them to wrestle with emotions of extreme anguish and intense fear for themselves:

And he overtook them, and he spake unto them these same words.

And they said unto him, Wherefore saith my lord these words? God forbid that thy servants should do according to this thing:

Behold, the money, which we found in our sacks' mouths, we brought again unto thee out of the land of Canaan: how then should we steal out of thy lord's house silver or gold?

With whomsoever of thy servants it be found, both let him die, and we also will be my lord's bondmen.

And he said, Now also let it be according unto your words: *he with whom it is found shall be my servant; and ye shall be blameless.*

Then they speedily took down every man his sack to the ground, and opened every man his sack.

And he searched, and began at the eldest, and left at the youngest: and *the cup was found in Benjamin's sack.*

Then they rent their clothes, and laded every man his ass, and returned to the city. (Genesis 44:6–13)

Another confrontation! Joseph wasn't above putting his brothers through an emotional wringer. Perhaps he wanted them to taste some of the feelings which plagued him while he was being carried down to Egypt as a slave. And it probably felt good having them bow in obeisance to him as his youthful dreams had indicated that they would:

Judah and his brethren came to Joseph's house; for he was yet there: and they fell before him on the ground.

And Joseph said unto them, *What deed is this that ye have done? wot ye not that such a man as I can certainly divine?*

And Judah said, What shall we say unto my lord? what shall we speak? or how shall we clear ourselves? *God hath found out the iniquity of thy servants: behold, we are my lord's servants, both we, and he also with whom the cup is found.*

And he said, God forbid that I should do so: *but the man in whose hand the cup is found, he shall be my servant; and as for you, get you up in peace unto your father.* (Genesis 44:14–17)

What an emotional roller coaster! Judah finally stepped forward and acted as spokesman for his brothers. He told in detail of his long conversation with his father, convincing Jacob that Benjamin definitely had to be brought down to Egypt, and finally offering himself as a surety that Benjamin would return home safely. Then Judah offered himself to Joseph to be the one kept as a slave rather than Benjamin, knowing that were his brothers to return without Benjamin, it would probably bring his father to his grave:

> For thy servant became surety for the lad unto my father, saying, If I bring him not unto thee, then I shall bear the blame to my father for ever.
>
> Now therefore, I pray thee, let thy servant abide instead of the lad a bondman to my lord; and let the lad go up with his brethren.
>
> For how shall I go up to my father, and the lad be not with me? lest peradventure I see the evil that shall come on my father. (Genesis 44:32–34)

That took courage! And it revealed Judah's love for both his father and for his brother. It was enough—Joseph knew it was time for him to reveal his identity to his brothers:

> Then Joseph could not refrain himself before all them that stood by him; and he cried,
>
> Cause every man to go out from me. And there stood no man with him, while Joseph made himself known unto his brethren.
>
> And he wept aloud: and the Egyptians and the house of Pharaoh heard.
>
> And Joseph said unto his brethren, *I am Joseph; doth my father yet live?* And his brethren could not answer him; for they were troubled at his presence.
>
> And Joseph said unto his brethren, *Come near to me, I pray you. And they came near. And he said, I am Joseph your brother, whom ye sold into Egypt.*
>
> *Now therefore be not grieved, nor angry with yourselves, that ye sold me hither: for God did send me before you to preserve life.* (Genesis 45:1–5)

So Joseph knew full well the reason he'd been guided by the Lord down to Egypt: "God did send me before you to preserve life." As a tool in the hands of the Lord, Joseph had saved, and would continue to save, literally millions of lives! And he soon personalized his mission statement by adding that "God sent me before you to preserve you a posterity in the earth, and to save your lives by a great deliverance."

Then he went on to warn them that the famine would continue for another five years, and that it would be essential for the entire family to move to Egypt to be able to save their own lives:

For these two years hath the famine been in the land: and *yet there are five years, in which there shall neither be earing nor harvest.*

And *God sent me before you to preserve you a posterity in the earth, and to save your lives by a great deliverance.*

So now it was not you that sent me hither, but God: and he hath made me a father to Pharaoh, and lord of all his house, and a ruler throughout all the land of Egypt.

Haste ye, and go up to my father, and say unto him, *Thus saith thy son Joseph, God hath made me lord of all Egypt: come down unto me, tarry not:*

And thou shalt dwell in the land of Goshen, and thou shalt be near unto me, thou, and thy children, and thy children's children, and thy flocks, and thy herds, and all that thou hast:

And there will I nourish thee; for *yet there are five years of famine;* lest thou, and thy household, and all that thou hast, come to poverty.

And, behold, your eyes see, and the eyes of my brother Benjamin, that it is my mouth that speaketh unto you.

And ye shall tell my father of all my glory in Egypt, and of all that ye have seen: and ye shall haste and bring down my father hither.

And he fell upon his brother Benjamin's neck, and wept; and Benjamin wept upon his neck.

Moreover *he kissed all his brethren, and wept upon them:* and after that his brethren talked with him. (Genesis 45:6–15)

The Move to Egypt

As related in the last chapter, about Jacob, the Pharaoh was generous to Joseph and to all his family. He sent wagons and helpers to implement the family's move down to Egypt, and the move was accomplished (Genesis 45:16–47:12).

Jacob was blessed with a revelation confirming that he should make the move: "God spake unto Israel in the visions of the night, and said, Jacob, Jacob. And he said, Here am I. And he said, I am God, the God of thy father: fear not to go down into Egypt; for *I will there make of thee a great nation*" (Genesis 46:2–3). So God once again was moving people into position so they could accomplish His eternal purposes. It was in Egypt that the house of Israel was to grow and prosper till it numbered in the millions. And who did he move to Egypt? The Bible gives a comprehensive listing:

They took their cattle, and their goods, which they had gotten in the land of Canaan, and came into Egypt, Jacob, and all his seed with him:

His sons, and his sons' sons with him, *his daughters,* and his sons' daughters, and *all his seed* brought he with him into Egypt.

And these are the names of the children of Israel, which came into Egypt, **Jacob** and his sons: **Reuben,** Jacob's firstborn.

And the sons of Reuben; Hanoch, and Phallu, and Hezron, and Carmi.

And the sons of *Simeon;* Jemuel, and Jamin, and Ohad, and Jachin, and Zohar, and Shaul the son of a Canaanitish woman.

And the sons of *Levi;* Gershon, Kohath, and Merari.

And the sons of *Judah;* Er, and Onan, and Shelah, and Pharez, and Zerah: but Er and Onan died in the land of Canaan. And the sons of Pharez were Hezron and Hamul.

And the sons of *Issachar;* Tola, and Phuvah, and Job, and Shimron.

And the sons of *Zebulun;* Sered, and Elon, and Jahleel.

These be the sons of Leah, which she bare unto Jacob in Padan-aram, with his daughter *Dinah: all the souls of his sons and his daughters were thirty and three.*

And the sons of *Gad;* Ziphion, and Haggi, Shuni, and Ezbon, Eri, and Arodi, and Areli.

And the sons of *Asher;* Jimnah, and Ishuah, and Isui, and Beriah, and Serah their sister: and the sons of Beriah; Heber, and Malchiel.

These are the sons of Zilpah, whom Laban gave to Leah his daughter, and these she bare unto Jacob, *even sixteen souls.*

The sons of Rachel Jacob's wife; *Joseph,* and Benjamin.

And unto Joseph in the land of Egypt were born *Manasseh* and *Ephraim,* which Asenath the daughter of Poti-pherah priest of On bare unto him.

And the sons of *Benjamin* were Belah, and Becher, and Ashbel, Gera, and Naaman, Ehi, and Rosh, Muppim, and Huppim, and Ard.

These are the sons of Rachel, which were born to Jacob: *all the souls were fourteen.*

And the sons of *Dan;* Hushim.

And the sons of *Naphtali;* Jahzeel, and Guni, and Jezer, and Shillem.

These are the sons of Bilhah, which Laban gave unto Rachel his daughter, and she bare these unto Jacob: *all the souls were seven.*

All the souls that came with Jacob into Egypt, which came out of his loins, besides Jacob's sons' wives, *all the souls were threescore and six;*

And the sons of Joseph, which were born him in Egypt, were two souls: *all the souls of the house of Jacob, which came into Egypt, were threescore and ten.* (Genesis 46:6–27)

Where did they settle? The Pharaoh gave them choice lands in Ramses, (which became Tanis), in the Nile Delta Land of Goshen: "And Joseph placed his father and his brethren, and gave them a possession in the land of Egypt, in the best of the land, in the land of Rameses, as Pharaoh had commanded" (Genesis 47:11).

There Jacob lived the rest of his life, finally pronouncing patriarchal blessings upon his sons, and adopting Ephraim and Manasseh on a level with his other sons, thus giving to Joseph (the firstborn son of Jacob's first wife, Rachel) the birthright blessings through his two sons. These blessings he bestowed while upon his deathbed (Genesis 48–49).

JOSEPH'S ONGOING LEADERSHIP IN EGYPT

There were still almost five years of famine which had to be endured in the land of Egypt and the surrounding countries. What happened in these years was a unique composite of socio-economic events that could happen in other countries undergoing severe crises. This period will be discussed in stages.

Stage 1: Extreme famine; food was scarce and expensive.

There was no bread in all the land; for *the famine was very sore,* so that the land of Egypt and all the land of Canaan fainted by reason of the famine.

And *Joseph gathered up all the money that was found in the land of Egypt, and in the land of Canaan,* for the corn which they bought: and *Joseph brought the money into Pharaoh's house.* (Genesis 47:13–14)

Stage 2: The monetary system collapsed; bartering goods became the norm.

And when money failed in the land of Egypt, and in the land of Canaan, all the Egyptians came unto Joseph, and said, Give us bread: for why should we die in thy presence? for the money faileth.

And Joseph said, *Give your cattle; and I will give you for your cattle, if money fail.*

And they brought their cattle unto Joseph: and *Joseph gave them bread in exchange for horses, and for the flocks, and for the cattle of the herds, and for the asses:* and he fed them with bread for all their cattle for that year. (Genesis 47:15–17)

Stage 3: The government acquired real estate; people obligated themselves in exchange for essential supplies.

When that year was ended, they came unto him the second year, and said unto him, We will not hide it from my lord, how that *our money is spent; my lord also hath our herds of cattle;* there is not ought left in the sight of my lord, but our bodies, and our lands:

Wherefore shall we die before thine eyes, both we and our land? *buy us and our land for bread, and we and our land will be servants unto Pharaoh:* and *give us seed, that we may live, and not die, that the land be not desolate.*

And *Joseph bought all the land of Egypt for Pharaoh; for the Egyptians sold every man his field,* because the famine prevailed over them: so *the land became Pharaoh's.* (Genesis 47:18–20)

Stage 4: People were moved off properties, assembled in cities.

And as for the people, he removed them to cities from one end of the borders of Egypt even to the other end thereof.

Only the land of the priests bought he not; for the priests had a portion assigned them of Pharaoh, and did eat their portion which Pharaoh gave them: wherefore they sold not their lands. (Genesis 47:21–22)

Stage 5: People were indentured on government-owned lands.

Then Joseph said unto the people, Behold, *I have bought you this day and your land for Pharaoh:* lo, here is seed for you, and ye shall sow the land.

And it shall come to pass in the increase, that *ye shall give the fifth part unto Pharaoh, and four parts shall be your own,* for seed of the field, and for your food, and for them of your households, and for food for your little ones. (Genesis 47:23–24)

Stage 6: Permanent taxation began: a 20 percent property-use tax payable to the government.

And they said, Thou hast saved our lives: let us find grace in the sight of my lord, and *we will be Pharaoh's servants.*

And *Joseph made it a law over the land of Egypt unto this day, that Pharaoh should have the fifth part;* except the land of the priests only, which became not Pharaoh's. (Genesis 47:25–26)

THE PROPHET LEHI EXPLAINS JOSEPH'S PROPHECY CONCERNING THE RESTORATION OF THE GOSPEL AND THE HOUSE OF ISRAEL

It is interesting that the most extensive knowledge concerning Joseph's prophetic utterances is found today, not in the Bible, but in the Book of Mormon. The information below was related by the Prophet Lehi, very near the end of his life, to his son Joseph. Where did he get it? Apparently it was recorded on the brass plates of Laban, making this a prime example of the "plain and precious things" that have been removed from the Biblical record.

1. The prophet Lehi was a descendant of Joseph, son of Israel (2 Nephi 3:4).
2. The Lord made great covenants with Joseph (3:4, 5).
3. Joseph saw Lehi's day (3:5).
4. The Lord's promise to Joseph: He would raise up a righteous branch (the Book of Mormon peoples) out of Israel (3:5).
5. The Messiah will be manifested to this branch in the latter days (3:5).
6. The message of the Messiah will come to these peoples with power (3:5).
7. Knowledge of the Messiah will bring these peoples out of darkness and captivity to freedom (3:5).

8. God will raise up a choice seer (Joseph Smith, Jr.) to the descendants of Joseph (3:6).

9. Joseph Smith will be highly esteemed by Joseph's descendants (3:7).

10. Joseph Smith's work will bring Joseph's descendants to a knowledge of God's covenants (3:7).

11. Joseph Smith will be great in God's eyes (3:8).

12. Joseph Smith will be like Moses (3:9–10).

13. Joseph Smith will be given power to bring God's word to Joseph's descendants (3:11).

14. Joseph Smith will convince Joseph's descendants of God's word (3:11).

15. The Book of Mormon and the Bible will grow together to confound false doctrines (3:12).

16. The Book of Mormon and the Bible will bring peace and knowledge (3:12).

17. Joseph Smith will be made strong in the day when the Lord's work will commence among His people (3:13).

18. The Lord will bless this choice seer and confound his enemies (3:14).

19. Three Josephs: Joseph sold into Egypt, Joseph Smith, Jr., and Joseph Smith, Sr. (3:15).

20. Joseph Smith's works will bring descendants of Joseph unto salvation (3:15).

21. God's promise to Joseph: to preserve his seed forever (3:16).

22. God would raise up a prophet like Moses and a spokesman who would write his words (3:17–18).

23. The prophet's words will go forth to Joseph's descendants (3:19).

24. The words of the Book of Mormon shall cry from the dust (3:20).

25. The Lord will strengthen their faith so they will remember His covenants (3:21).

26. These things were prophesied by Joseph of old (3:22).

27. Joseph's seed will accept the words of the Book of Mormon (3:23).

28. Someone will do much good in bringing to pass the restoration of Israel (3:24).

After the Book of Mormon records Lehi's reciting of Joseph's prophecies, Lehi's son, Nephi, commented on them, beginning with these informative words:

> And now, I, Nephi, speak concerning the prophecies of which my father hath spoken, concerning Joseph, who was carried into Egypt.
>
> *For behold, he truly prophesied concerning all his seed. And the prophecies which he wrote, there are not many greater. And he prophesied concerning us,*

and our future generations; and *they are written upon the plates of brass.* (2 Nephi 4:1–2)

Obviously, there are other prophecies made by Joseph which were on the brass plates in addition to those cited by Lehi, but at present they are lost. (Compare the above with the Joseph Smith Translation of Genesis 50:24, quoted later in this chapter.)

Israel's Patriarchal Blessing to Joseph

The blessings Jacob gave to his son Joseph and to Manasseh and Ephraim (Genesis 48:1–22; 49:22–26) were discussed in the previous chapter, but there are additional insights to be treated in this context. First, a comment by the Apostle Paul in his famous roll call of faith:

> By faith Jacob, when he was a dying, blessed both the sons of Joseph; and worshipped, leaning upon the top of his staff.
>
> By faith Joseph, when he died, made mention of the departing of the children of Israel; and gave commandment concerning his bones. (Hebrews 11:21–22)

Second, the Joseph Smith Translation of Genesis 48:5–6, which in the JST is Genesis 48:5–11, adds significant insights concerning both Joseph and his posterity, revealing that the tribes that sprang from Joseph's loins would be leaders in the gathering of Israel in the last days (The JST additions are in italics in the following passage):

> And now, of thy two sons, Ephraim and Manasseh, which were born unto thee in the land of Egypt, before I came unto thee into Egypt; *behold, they are mine, and the God of my fathers shall bless them; even* as Reuben and Simeon they *shall be blessed, for they are mine; wherefore they shall be called after my name (Therefore they were called Israel.)*
>
> And thy issue which thou begettest after them, shall be thine, and shall be called after the name of their brethren in their inheritance, *in the tribes; therefore they were called the tribes of Manasseh and of Ephraim.*
>
> *And Jacob said unto Joseph when the God of my fathers appeared unto me in Luz, in the land of Canaan; he sware unto me, that he would give unto me, and unto my seed, the land for an everlasting possession.*
>
> *Therefore, O my son, he hath blessed me in raising thee up to be a servant unto me, in saving my house from death;*
>
> *In delivering my people, thy brethren, from famine which was sore in the land; wherefore the God of thy fathers shall bless thee, and the fruit of thy loins, that they shall be blessed above thy brethren, and above thy father's house;*
>
> *For thou hast prevailed, and thy father's house hath bowed down unto thee, even as it was shown unto thee, before thou wast sold into Egypt by the hands of*

thy brethren; wherefore thy brethren shall bow down unto thee, from generation to generation, unto the fruit of thy loins for ever;

For thou shalt be a light unto my people, to deliver them in the days of their captivity, from bondage; and to bring salvation unto them, when they are altogether bowed down under sin. (Joseph Smith Translation–Genesis 48:5–11)

And third, when Moses pronounced his blessings upon the tribes of Israel, he repeated the blessings Jacob gave them, but with significant differences. Concerning Jacob's Genesis 49:22–26 blessing to Joseph, Moses said:

Blessed of the LORD be his land, for the precious things of heaven, for the dew, and for the deep that coucheth beneath,

And for the precious fruits brought forth by the sun, and for the precious things put forth by the moon,

And for the chief things of *the ancient mountains, and for the precious things of the lasting hills,*

And for the precious things of the earth and fulness thereof, and for the good will of him that dwelt in the bush: *let the blessing come upon the head of Joseph, and upon the top of the head of him that was separated from his brethren.*

His glory is like the firstling of his bullock, and his horns are like the horns of unicorns: with them *he shall push the people together to the ends of the earth: and they are the ten thousands of Ephraim, and they are the thousands of Manasseh.* (Deuteronomy 33:13–17)

JOSEPH'S DEATH AND LONG-DELAYED BURIAL

Joseph's long and significant life finally came to its end. Of his one hundred ten long years, all but the first seventeen were spent in Egypt: ninety-three amazing years! The Genesis account relates that he became a grandfather, and then a great-grandfather. Two of his final acts were the prophesying that God would bring his posterity back out of Egypt and into Canaan once again, and the extracting of an oath from his loved ones that his remains eventually would be interred in Canaan:

And Joseph dwelt in Egypt, he, and his father's house: and Joseph lived an hundred and ten years.

And Joseph saw Ephraim's children of the third generation: *the children also of Machir the son of Manasseh were brought up upon Joseph's knees.*

And Joseph said unto his brethren, I die: and God will surely visit you, and bring you out of this land unto the land which he sware to Abraham, to Isaac, and to Jacob.

And Joseph took an oath of the children of Israel, saying, God will surely visit you, and ye shall carry up my bones from hence.

> *So Joseph died, being an hundred and ten years old: and they embalmed him, and he was put in a coffin in Egypt.* (Genesis 50:22–26)

The Joseph Smith Translation of the Bible includes significant additions and changes to the history recorded in Genesis chapter 50, beginning with verse 24. Those added verses include Joseph's glorious prophecies of future and last-days events (Those items are shown here with the translation additions printed in italics):

> And Joseph said unto his brethren, I die, *and go unto my fathers; and I go down to my grave with joy. The God of my father Jacob be with you, to deliver you out of affliction in the days of your bondage; for the Lord hath visited me, and I have obtained a promise of the Lord, that out of the fruit of my loins, the Lord God will raise up a righteous branch out of my loins; and unto thee, whom my father Jacob hath named Israel, a prophet; (not the Messiah who is called Shilo;) and this prophet shall deliver my people out of Egypt in the days of thy bondage.*
>
> *And it shall come to pass that they shall be scattered again; and a branch shall be broken off, and shall be carried into a far country; nevertheless they shall be remembered in the covenants of the Lord, when the Messiah cometh; for he shall be made manifest unto them in the latter days, in the Spirit of power; and shall bring them out of darkness into light; out of hidden darkness, and out of captivity unto freedom.*
>
> *A seer shall the Lord my God raise up, who shall be a choice seer unto the fruit of my loins.*
>
> *Thus saith the Lord God of my fathers unto me, A choice seer will I raise up out of the fruit of thy loins, and he shall be esteemed highly among the fruit of thy loins; and unto him will I give commandment that he shall do a work for the fruit of thy loins, his brethren.*
>
> *And he shall bring them to the knowledge of the covenants which I have made with thy fathers; and he shall do whatsoever work I shall command him.*
>
> *And I will make him great in mine eyes, for he shall do my work; and he shall be great like unto him whom I have said I would raise up unto you, to deliver my people, O house of Israel, out of the land of Egypt; for a seer will I raise up to deliver my people out of the land of Egypt; and he shall be called Moses. And by this name he shall know that he is of thy house; for he shall be nursed by the king's daughter, and shall be called her son.*
>
> *And again, a seer will I raise up out of the fruit of thy loins, and unto him will I give power to bring forth my word unto the seed of thy loins; and not to the bringing forth of my word only, saith the Lord, but to the convincing them of my word, which shall have already gone forth among them in the last days;*
>
> *Wherefore the fruit of thy loins shall write; and the fruit of the loins of Judah shall write; and that which shall be written by the fruit of thy loins, and also that which shall be written by the fruit of the loins of Judah, shall grow together unto the confounding of false doctrines, and laying down of contentions, and establishing*

peace among the fruit of thy loins, and bringing them to a knowledge of their fathers in the latter days; and also to the knowledge of my covenants, saith the Lord.

And out of weakness shall he be made strong, in that day when my work shall go forth among all my people, which shall restore them, who are of the house of Israel, in the last days.

And that seer will I bless, and they that seek to destroy him shall be confounded; for this promise I give unto you; for I will remember you from generation to generation; and his name shall be called Joseph, and it shall be after the name of his father; and he shall be like unto you; for the thing which the Lord shall bring forth by his hand shall bring my people unto salvation.

And the Lord sware unto Joseph that he would preserve his seed forever, saying, I will raise up Moses, and a rod shall be in his hand, and he shall gather together my people, and he shall lead them as a flock, and he shall smite the waters of the Red Sea with his rod.

And he shall have judgment, and shall write the word of the Lord. And he shall not speak many words, for I will write unto him my law by the finger of mine own hand. And I will make a spokesman for him, and his name shall be called Aaron.

And it shall be done unto thee in the last days also, even as I have sworn. Therefore, Joseph said unto his brethren, God will surely visit you, and bring you out of this land, unto the land which he sware unto Abraham, and unto Isaac, and to Jacob.

And Joseph *confirmed many other things unto his brethren,* and took an oath of the children of Israel, saying unto them, God will surely visit you, and ye shall carry up my bones from hence.

So Joseph died *when he was* an hundred and ten years old; and they embalmed him, and *they* put him in a coffin in Egypt; *and he was kept from burial by the children of Israel, that he might be carried up and laid in the sepulchre with his father. And thus they remembered the oath which they sware unto him.* (Joseph Smith Translation–Genesis 50:24–38)

More than four hundred years passed while the descendants of Israel and Joseph dwelt in Egypt—first in honor, then as slaves. Then God spoke to the house of Israel through his prophet Moses, who eventually led them out of Egypt. Prominent in the exiting caravan was the transporting of the coffin holding Joseph's remains: "Moses took the bones of Joseph with him: for he had straitly sworn the children of Israel, saying, God will surely visit you; and ye shall carry up my bones away hence with you" (Exodus 13:19). How remarkable that this promise should be remembered and fulfilled after so many years had passed.

Moses and his Israelite followers transported the coffin, but it was under Joshua that the actual interrment took place: "And the bones of Joseph, which the children of Israel brought up out of Egypt, buried they in Shechem, in a parcel of ground which Jacob bought of the sons of Hamor the father of Shechem for an hundred pieces of silver: and it became the inheritance of the children of Joseph" (Joshua 24:32; see Genesis 33:18–20).

OTHER SCRIPTURAL INSIGHTS CONCERNING JOSEPH

FROM THE OLD TESTAMENT

Exodus 1:6–14: "And Joseph died, and all his brethren, . . . And they made their lives bitter."

1 Chronicles 5:1–2: "Judah prevailed above his brethren, . . . but the birthright was Joseph's."

Psalms 81:1, 5: "This he ordained in Joseph for a testimony, when he went through . . . Egypt."

Psalm 105:16–22: "The king made [Joseph] lord of his house, and ruler of all his substance."

Ezekiel 37:16–17: "Take another stick, and write upon it, For Joseph, the stick of Ephraim."

Ezekiel 47:13: "Ye shall inherit the land . . . Joseph shall have two portions."

Amos 5:15: "It may be that the LORD God of hosts will be gracious unto the remnant of Joseph."

FROM THE NEW TESTAMENT

John 4:5–6: "Sychar, near to the parcel of ground that Jacob gave to his son Joseph."

Acts 7:8–10: "The patriarchs, moved with envy, sold Joseph into Egypt: but God was with him."

FROM THE BOOK OF MORMON

1 Nephi 5:14–17: "Joseph . . . was preserved . . . by the Lord, that he might preserve his father."

2 Nephi 25:21: "That the promise may be fulfilled unto Joseph, that his seed should never perish."

Jacob 2:25: "That I might raise up unto me a righteous branch from . . . the loins of Joseph."

Alma 10:3: "Manasseh, who was the son of Joseph who was sold into Egypt by . . . his brethren."

Alma 46:23: "We are a remnant of the seed of Joseph, whose coat was rent by his brethren."

Alma 46:24: "Jacob, . . . saw that a part of the remnant of the coat of Joseph was preserved."

3 Nephi 10:17: "Our father Jacob also testified concerning a remnant of the seed of Joseph."

Ether 13:6–8: "The Lord brought a remnant of the seed of Joseph out of the land of Jerusalem."

Ether 13:10: "They are they who are numbered among the remnant of the seed of Joseph."

FROM THE DOCTRINE AND COVENANTS

D&C 96:7: "He is a descendant of Joseph and a partaker of the blessings of the promise."

D&C 98:31–32: "This is the law I gave unto my servant Nephi, and thy fathers, Joseph, and Jacob."

INDEX

& personality, 151; sold his
birthright, 152–54; marries 3
wives, moves to Edom, 157–58;
receives blessing from Isaac,
159–62; threatens to kill Jacob,
162; buries Isaac, 164; allegories
concerning, 164–66; reconciled
with Jacob, 175–76.

Eve—what's known about, 8–9.

F

Facsimiles in Book of Abraham—
Fac. # 1, being offered as a
sacrifice, ; Fac. # 2, key-words
revealed, 14, 39; Fac. # 3: Egypt,
110–11.

Fall of Adam & Eve—10–12; results
of, 10–11; forgiven while still
in Eden, 13–14, 50; A of F 2 &
3, 14; brought mortality, death,
49–50; Christ atoned for original
sin, 50.

Famine—causes Jacob to send to
Egypt for food, 179–80; seven
years of begin in Egypt, 208.

Flood—Enoch saw flood would
come in Noah's day, 54–55, 66;
God's covenant: flood not to be
repeated, 55; floods would come
unless people accepted Christ,
66–67; general, not local, 75–76;
all flesh died, 76.

G

Gabriel—an archangel, 30; Noah is,
69; next to Adam in priesthood
authority, 69; wept in heaven, 75.

Garden of Eden—created after
Adam, 2, 3, 8; events in,
9–12; fall forgiven in, 13–14;
priesthood keys revealed in,
14–15; Adam given priesthood

in, 21; events in, 21–22; agency
given in, 66.

Genealogy, records—Adam's kept,
18–19.

Gerar—Abraham's stay in, 124–25;
Isaac in, 155–56.

Giants—in Noah's day, 66–67; in
Enoch's day, 66.

God the Father—identified himself
as Man of Holiness, 54; Christ
pleads for mankind before him, 55.

Godhead—all three involved in
creation, 4; earth created by
"Gods," 5.

Goshen, Land of—Joseph's family in
Egypt settled in, 181–82, 215–17.

Gospel—preached from beginning, 33.

H

Hagar—Abraham commanded to
mate with, 115–17; promises to,
117; separation from Abraham,
125–27; cast out by Sarah, 141.

Ham—born, 64; entered ark, 74;
where his descendants settled,
84–85; father of Egyptus,
grandfather of first Egyptian
Pharaoh, 87.

Haran—person: Abram's youngest
brother, 89; father of Lot, 144;
place: Abram moved to, 106;
described, 106–107; events in, 107;
Jacob's departure from, 172–73.

Hell—prepared for wicked, 47.

Hebron—Abram settled in, 112;
information concerning, 126–27;
burial places in, 130–31, 132; 300
miles from to Egypt, 210.

Holy Ghost—fell upon Adam, 14;
Spirit of the Lord caught Adam
away, 16; Adam born of the
Spirit, 16; all men called upon

ABOUT THE AUTHOR

Duane S. Crowther is well-known and highly qualified as an author, theologian, teacher, and lecturer. He graduated with high honors from Brigham Young University with a BA in music education. He also holds a Master's Degree from Brigham Young University in Old and New Testament, an MBA from the University of Phoenix, and he has completed course work for a Ph.D. in music education at the University of Utah.

A creative and prolific author, Mr. Crowther has written more than fifty books, including such well-known favorites as *Prophecy—Key to the Future*, *Life Everlasting*, *The Prophecies of Joseph Smith*, *Inspired Prophetic Warnings*, *Gifts of the Spirit*, *Prophets and Prophecies of the Old Testament*, *The Godhead*, *Jesus of Nazareth: Savior and King*, *How to Understand the Book of Mormon*, *How to Write Your Personal History*, *Key Choral Concepts*, and *You Can Read Music*. He also is the author and narrator of more than three dozen cassette talk tapes, in addition to numerous magazine articles and music compositions.

In his professional life, he has served as a Latter-day Saint Seminary instructor and principal; taught university classes for Brigham Young University, the University of Utah, and the University of Phoenix; and still teaches music, Old and New Testament history, and writing-skills classes in public school adult-education programs. For more than three decades he has been President and Senior Editor of Horizon Publishers and Distributors, Inc. in Bountiful, Utah.

Mr. Crowther has written and produced national-award-winning patriotic pageants. He has lectured at numerous business and writer's seminars, BYU Education Week, youth conferences, and other Church gatherings. He also has hosted and escorted tours to Israel, Mexico, Central America, Hawaii, and other locales.

His has been a life of continued and varied service within the Church. He has served two full-time and three stake missions. He has been a district president, branch president, high priests group leader, stake mission president, seventy's quorum president, and elders quorum president. He also has served as a sunday school and YMMIA superintendent and president; ward music chairman; stake music and drama director; a member of several stake boards; a director of numerous regional, stake, and ward choirs; and a teacher and teacher-trainer. A gifted and knowledgeable teacher, he has served as a gospel doctrine instructor for more than twenty-five years. Other Church assignments have included callings as a temple worker and as a guide on Temple Square. He and his wife presently serve as temple workers in the Bountiful Utah Temple; he also is serving currently as a high priests instructor, boy scout troop committee chairman, stake employment specialist, and ward chorister. He is a Master M-Man and an Eagle Scout.

Mr. Crowther is married to Jean Decker, who also is an author, editor, teacher, and musician. The parents of eight children and grandparents of twenty-eight grandchildren, the Crowthers reside in Bountiful, Utah.